The Damned
and other essays

Robert Mercer-Nairne

GRITPOUL INC * WASHINGTON * USA

First edition 2017

ISBN-13: 978-0-9748141-6-2
Library of Congress Control Number: 2017901547

Published in the United States of America by Gritpoul, Inc.,
2025 First Avenue, Penthouse A
Seattle, WA 98121-3125
www.gritpoul.com

Interior Design and Typesetting: Danscot Ltd, Scotland
Cover Design: Larry Rostant, England
Front cover sculpture: Sina Farrugia, Malta
Author Photograph: Jill Furmanovsky, London

Printed by Friesens Corporation, Canada.

10 9 8 7 6 5 4 3 2 1

The paper used in this publication meets the minimum requirements of the American National Standard for Information Sciences – Permanence of paper for Printed Library Materials ANSI Z39.48-1948

BY ROBERT MERCER-NAIRNE

POETRY

Mercer-Nairne in Malta
    illustrated by Marisa Attard
On Fire
    illustrated by Marisa Attard

PLAY

The Arrow

NOVELS

The Letter Writer
Like No Other
Warlord
The Storytellers

NON-FICTION

Notes On The Dynamics Of Man
A Paper (illustrated monograph)
The Damned and other essays

We walk.....

.....from the past.....

For

My wife, Jane
My Children, Emily, Sam and Joe
And my grandchildren,
Aramay, Skyla, Pearl
Violet, George, Harold
Fergus, Florence and Angus

What you make of all this, time will tell!

.....to the future......

Table of Contents

.....in the present.

Introduction

F O R as long as I can remember I have been interested in how the world worked. Plato's *Republic* was my first port of call, read somewhat guiltily in the intellectual backwater I grew up in, a backwater made worse by dyslexia which consigned me to scholastic oblivion. This, however, instilled in me a certain stubbornness. If I was going to find out anything I would have to do it alone. The great benefit fate bestowed upon me was that I have always had the means to do so. Now in my seventy-first year I want to set down what I have learnt.

We are all the product of many things. For me, being an outsider was – on balance - a blessing. It could have gone horribly wrong and ended in wanton dissipation and on occasion, it nearly did, but a little voice always pulled me back. Life was just too interesting to squander! One consequence of my circumstances has been a deep desire never to become wholly dependent upon any institution. This has been both liberating and limiting.

Doing your own thing might sound good, but that is not how social systems work: things get done collaboratively which means through existing structures and these possess their own point of view. To get on within them you have to embrace that point of view. This is one reason why reform is often slow: by the time anyone is in a position to alter things they are so imbued with the mores of the system they are part of that they not only see no need for adjustment but actively resist it. Another reason is that institutions tend to attract those who already admire what they do. Staying aloof liberates one from this, but it also denies one a platform from which to initiate change.

* * *

I think my parents must have been attracted to one another for polar-opposite reasons: she from the New World was fascinated by the old, he from the Old World wished to absorb the new. In any event, I owe what I am to their chance encounter. This is just one example of the randomness that pervades our universe. Growing up aware of my parents' different worlds made me appreciate the power one's background has over one. Wholly invisible, it affects one's outlook and so one's actions in countless ways. Unsurprisingly, perhaps, this stimulated an interest in history: where had they, and so I, come from?

My mother's family had two distinct strands. On her father's side were Baptists, hardy New England Puritans who had braved a perilous journey across the Atlantic to live a godly life in a land unsullied by European corruption. On her mother's was a French family I know little about. They pitched up near Toronto and worked a dirt farm to make a living. This was not a life that appealed to my great-grandfather. With an aptitude for things mechanical he scoured the continent in search of opportunity (there were no border controls then), finally ending up in Detroit where he and the company he had formed rode America's industrial ascent.

These two families came together in California. The New Englanders headed west in search of opportunity after the family shoe business failed (a matter of shame rarely discussed). My grandmother, whose brother would be killed on the Altoona Speedway shortly after winning the Indianapolis 500, also came west, two children in tow, but in her case to escape a bad marriage. These two failures turned to success when my grandparents consummated what became a very happy union and my mother was born.

My father's family was so steeped in history that one almost had to hide under the bed covers to escape from it. In his case there were four strands: Scottish, Irish, English and French. My Scots forebears seem to have come to Scotland's then capital, Perth, in the 11th century as merchants from the Low Countries, part of what is now Holland. They must have been astute in business and along the way married into a landed family who fought against the English twice, eventually losing everything in the process. My Irish family also rebelled against the English, but eventually saw the light and married one whose father just happened to be a rather remarkable man.

William Petty came from humble beginnings but was obviously smart and secured the contract to map Ireland for Oliver Cromwell who wanted to know what he had conquered so that he could hand out parcels of it to his soldiers. Naturally a great many soldiers did not want the fractional interests they were allocated and were happy to sell them to Petty who then set about consolidating and improving what he had bought. On the side he developed social statistics, invented a double-bottomed boat to speed up trade (which sank in the Irish Sea) and became a fellow of England's emerging scientific establishment, the Royal Society.

Petty's heirs included one English Prime Minister (who also happened to be a friend of Benjamin Franklin), a chancellor of Britain's exchequer who amassed a superb collection of art (some of it now in J Paul Getty's Malibu Museum) and a man who served as Britain's Governor General in Canada, Viceroy in India and as his country's Foreign Secretary for five years at the start of the 20th century. One of this man's two sons, my grandfather, was killed in the opening stages of the First World War.

In another of those random happenings, the Foreign Secretary's grandfather had been an aide-de-camp to Napoleon as well as the illegitimate son of Talleyrand, France's wily foreign minister who, along with Lord Castlereagh (Britain), Count Nesselrode (Russia), Prince Hardenberg (Prussia) and Prince Metternich (Austria) had helped stabilize Europe at the Congress of Vienna (1814-15) after the French revolutionary wars. Following Napoleon's final defeat, the still-young Frenchman had fled to Britain, of all places, where he married into the merchant side of my Scots family. It was the daughter of this union who married one of William Petty's descendants, the father of the Foreign Secretary, Lord Lansdowne. Now you can see why one might wish to hide under a blanket.

* * *

In spite of a poor start academically, I did make it to university and read economics, squeaking out with an indifferent degree – *Eros* proved more absorbing than theories about Supply and Demand. There then followed over twenty years in business with a master's degree (in business) and doctorate (in organization theory) along the way: one has to knuckle down at some point or go off the rails entirely. But the urge to think more about the whys and wherefores of the human condition grew ever stronger. So when the opportunity arose I took myself off and published two collections of poetry, four novels and an exploratory work, *Notes on The Dynamics of Man* later summarized in *A Paper* which was richly illustrated – people seem to respond better to images than to text. For better or worse, this present collection of essays pretty much sets out what my experience of life has driven me to conclude.

* * *

Gradually I came to realize that one could not think about the human journey without putting it into the context of the universe as a whole. This prompted me to take an interest in physics as well as biology (and in fact in most areas of study because all have something useful to say). My wife (an Anglo-Scot with Portuguese-Hungarian roots) tells me that the first essay, *The order we are subject to*, is not an easy read so I would urge you to persevere. That said I <u>am</u> trying to change the way you see the world, so a certain amount of pain is unavoidable – no pain, no gain, as the saying goes.

You will also notice that I do not include references. This is not supposed to be an academic tract and I could see no point in them. Little of what I use as a basis for the arguments I put forward is contentious. It is only the way I have arranged what we believe we know that might be, and that is down to me and me alone. The thirty three essays are arranged in a rough order from the universal to the specific and the framework is essentially evolutionary. We all have our favourite examples from history, I dare say, and some of mine are used several times to illustrate different points. So take it or leave it, although I hope you at least will be stimulated to think further for yourself.

Of one thing I am certain, however. If we are to survive we are going to have to change the way we function and the way the systems that guide us are put together. To do this we have to understand what drives us and how these systems work. Expanding that understanding is what these essays are about.

1

The order we are subject to

IN THE beginning God created heaven and earth and the earth was without form and void: so begins Genesis, The First Book of Moses. The book goes on to set out the steps God takes to create the world as it was known, its days and nights, its plants, its insects, its fish, its animals and finally, before resting on the seventh day, he creates man in his own image – 'male and female created he them.' There has scarcely been a better start to any book or a more accessible description of how our universe began. Sixty short paragraphs later human awareness is born together with the capacity to choose. Defying God's edict and incurring His wrath Adam and Eve choose to eat from the tree that will furnish them with an understanding of good and evil, rather than remain passive creatures in Eden. With this, mankind's lonely journey into the moral unknown begins.

How does this 5th or 6th century BCE ordering of the universe compare with our understanding of it today? Physicists wrestle with in the beginning and the jury is still out as to what is the best way of thinking about this period. For now we start almost 14 billion years ago with a singularity, a hypothetical starting point in which three-dimensional space and time are one and infinite. While this starting point may be problematic (mathematics loses its way when predicted values become infinite) what followed has been modelled remarkably well.

From its infinitely dense, hot, energy state (as hypothesized anyway), our universe reversed course and started to expand, cooling as it did, triggering a phase transition - what happens when one thing becomes another thing in response to some external change (water to ice at a certain temperature, for example) - into a brief period of rapid exponential inflation (during which the homogeneous nature of the universe was determined) followed again by expansion. What the composition of the universe was at the time of the hypothesized singularity defies easy description, save only that it was extremely hot and extremely dense, a sort of raw energy, if you will. Milliseconds after the Big Bang (an expansion not an explosion) what has been called quark-gluon plasma predominated, an early precursor of what we think of as matter.

Four fundamental forces have been identified as coming out of the initial hot dense state: electromagnetism (which regulates the relationship between electrically charged particles), gravity (the way space-time distortion pulls large energy-laden objects towards one another), together with what has been called the strong force (the force that binds protons and neutrons together to form the nucleus of atoms) and weak force (which leads to absorption or transmission between particles but does not serve to bind, such as in radioactive decay).

That the order we know can be described by these elements (or by the interaction between them) means that the potential for this order existed within the initial hot dense state, just as the egg of a hen contains the potential for a fully formed chicken. The childhood conundrum as to which came first (chicken or egg) has had its parallel in countless debates about the nature of the universe and won't be touched here, save to say that the order which describes the universe clearly describes us, so we need to have a feel for how that order evolved and is evolving.

* * *

Some minutes after the Big Bang, nucleosynthesis caused atoms to form out of protons and neutrons, mostly helium and hydrogen. This essentially gaseous universe continued for some 150 to 800 million years (a period known as the Cosmic Dark Ages). Gradually, however, these gaseous particles were pulled into clouds by gravity with clusters compressing further into stars, fusing hydrogen into helium under intense gravitational pressure, attaining stability when the outward thrust from nuclear fusion at the core offset the inward pressure from gravity. Clusters of stars formed galaxies like our own Milky Way.

When a star has burned up its fuel, the collapse of its core can send the material in its crust back out into space to be collected by other stars. Larger stars can fuse heavier materials, such as iron, and when these elements are expelled they can end up in planets, objects large enough to be pulled into a more or less round shape by gravity, but not so large that gravity causes fusion to occur at their core. A solar system comes into being when aspirant planets have eliminated any competition and find an orbital home around a star.

Some planets, like Jupiter and Saturn, consist primarily of hydrogen and helium atoms (the large gaseous planets), while others like our Earth and Mars consist mostly of the heavier elements and so are terrestrial. There also are planets made up largely of ice like Uranus and Neptune. The life of a solar system is governed by the life of its star and so is finite. When a particularly large star collapses the gravitational pull at its core can be so great that even light particles cannot escape, causing it to appear as a black hole. But these gobbling monsters may emit radiation and so in time die too. There is a lot going on in a galaxy.

* * *

One cannot pretend that the trajectory of our universe, as we understand it, points relentlessly toward us. Life is thought to have first appeared on Earth nearly 4 billion years ago, although it is still not exactly clear how this came about. The chemical elements generated by stars and prior evolution metabolized into single cell organisms, an organism being defined as a structure capable of some degree of response to stimuli, reproduction, growth, development and homeostasis. Clearly the start was a chemical reaction of the kind any schoolboy or girl might observe between atoms joined together by chemical bonds we call molecules (CO_2, H2O). One of the most stable elements is carbon and the simplest organic molecule is hydrocarbon (consisting of hydrogen and carbon) which can bond to form more complex molecules.

A polymer is a large molecule consisting of many repeated subunits. One such is Ribonucleic acid (RNA) which, along with proteins (polymer chains of amino acids which serve as building blocks for human tissue and as a fuel source) and carbohydrates (molecules consisting of carbon, hydrogen and oxygen which serve as a store of energy, are the backbone of the genetic molecule RNA and play a role in the immune system and in fertilization), constitute the three major macromolecules essential for life as we know it. The evolution of the simple single cell organism - a structure enclosed within a membrane and able to process energy from the sun (photosynthesis) to produce glucose from CO_2 and H2O (a sugar which powers metabolism within a cell, the process by which it maintains itself), while giving off oxygen as a byproduct - was undoubtedly crucial.

Early life on earth was likely to have been tentative. An important first step must have been the creation of a boundary or membrane within which certain chemical activities took place, moderated by what could pass through the membrane. Prokaryotes, amongst the earliest single cell organisms, hold a nucleoid containing the cell's genetic material (that which determines how the proteins inside a cell will develop), have a little tail for locomotion and sensing (flagellum) and ribosomes (molecules which work as protein synthesizers). Reproduction is by cell division (the cell splits in two with each – subject to mutation - mirroring the other, and attaining the size of the original).

Prokaryotes probably lived in large clusters but variations in the environment of these clusters will have impacted their development and two different types emerged: Bacteria and Archaea. Bacteria have developed into a large number of types and are ubiquitous (it is estimated that there can be as many as 40 million bacteria cells in a gram of soil and a great many more in the human body). They are similar to Prokaryotes in structure and can multiply rapidly by cell division in the right environment. Archaea developed more metabolic pathways and the ability to use more energy sources and can be found in a wide variety of environments (from hydrothermal vents to the human gut and the ocean's plankton).

The next class of organisms to develop were what have been called the Eukaryotes which differed from both Bacteria and Archaea in that they possessed a membrane-protected nucleus and other membrane-protected organelles (sub-units within cells that embody certain functions). This added complexity (and its attendant flexibility) gave rise, over time, to the development of plants, fungi and animals, although getting to where we are now has been far from a smooth ride.

For much of the early organic period the oxygen produced by photosynthesis was absorbed by dissolved iron ore and biological matter, but some 2.3 billion years ago this absorption capacity seems to have been overwhelmed and the free oxygen in the atmosphere increased rapidly, killing off the large number of organisms which found high concentrations of oxygen toxic. It also triggered the onset of a 300 million year glacial period known as the Huronian: the increased oxygen, it seems, decreased the greenhouse gas methane, thereby lowering the earth's surface temperature. This may have been the first of thirteen named extinctions which have challenged and rearranged organic life on earth (the last being the ongoing one human activity is largely responsible for).

The largest extinction event that we have hard evidence for, the Permian-Triassic, occurred about 250 million years ago killing off around 96% of all marine species and 70% of all terrestrial vertebrate ones. The fact that a number of plausible causes have been advanced (meteor impact, volcanism, methane hydrate gasification, anoxia – the lowering of oceanic oxygen levels, hydrogen sulfide emissions, Pangea – the super continent caused by continental drift, and even an explosion of methane-producing microbes) attests to the instability organic life on earth has had to contend with.

* * *

So what does all this say about the order we are subject to? The most obvious is that it is not static. Clearly this has profound implications for how we organize ourselves. The next is progression. This is often a difficult concept because it suggests movement from somewhere to somewhere, frequently with the inference that the somewhere we are moving to is in some sense 'better', than the somewhere we are moving from. It could simply mean movement along a line without any value inference, although even this presents a problem: what is this line and what is its nature? As everything that was in the universe in the past is still in the universe today, we might be better talking about transformation only.

That said, an objective progression is identifiable: one from simple to complex matter mediated by energy. Furthermore the nature of this progression exhibits changes in system state (such as the phase transition into the inflated universe mentioned earlier). Within a given state, the matter that can form does so, attaining a degree of stability and serving as a platform from which a new set of arrangements become possible: alpha (the singularity) – quantum (quark-gluon plasma) – atomic – galactic, chemical, planetary – biological.

An issue that has exercised and still exercises people who think about these things (philosophers, theologians, metaphysicians and scientists more generally) is the extent to which the universe we live in is deterministic, that is to say, is following a preset path. This bumps into the free will debate – do we or do we not have it and if we don't, how can we be held responsible for what we do? Statisticians use a concept called "degrees of freedom" to describe how many outcomes are consistent with a model. Clearly a universe in which matter not only differentiates, but the nature of matter itself can be transformed, has many degrees of freedom and so many possible outcomes. And if consciousness (as I will discuss later) entails a degree of agency, then we can influence the evolutionary process we are part of.

But as any creative artist will affirm, what is created cannot come out of thin air or break the rules governing paint, marble, music or representation. It has to deal with the order it finds and invent some fresh way of expressing it. There is a big difference between a system that supports many outcomes and a system that supports only one. If our universe is more the former than the latter – and everything we can observe suggests that it is – then it behooves us not only to understand its nature but also to have a life enhancing trajectory in mind.

* * *

The Genesis conception starts from a perfect place – Eden and then follows something more like Dante's descent into the inferno before finally making it through purgatory into heaven (*Divina Commedia*, 1320). Indeed all the major religions have struggled with the conflict between what man does do and what it is assumed man should do. St Augustine spoke in terms of Adam and Eve's disobedience passing through generations of mankind as original sin. The task of religion, as set out by St Paul, was to help man follow the redemptive pathway opened up by Jesus of Nazareth so as to find his way back to the perfection he had thrown away.

The conception I will develop in the next essay is a little different and is essentially this: man is subject to his evolved biological drivers and in the absence of consciousness would be governed by them. By their nature, these processes are retrospective; that is to say, they embody instinctive behaviours that have proved useful in the past. However, with the evolution of consciousness (the ability to model actions and their likely outcomes) man has developed an ability to override (or redirect) instinctive behaviours in order to attain specific goals. Adam and Eve are portrayed as giving in to lust (an instinctive reaction) and are then punished for not having made the choice to override it.

While acknowledging that the evolution of human society has been built by moderating our evolved instincts, I will contend throughout these essays that we need to develop a better grasp of the interaction between the social structures we build and those instincts without which we would be nothing. Adam and Eve were damned if they did and damned if they didn't: damned to being two of God's pretty creatures for all eternity or damned to a life of trial and error. Luckily for us they chose life.

However all Churches were surely right to zero in on the dynamic interplay between individual instinct and socially mandated objectives. Mankind's journey has been and continues to be driven by it. In the next essay we will look at the consciously constructed arrangements mankind is building which are taking us away from the biological world.

2

Cerebral Structure

I H A V E written about this elsewhere (*Notes on the dynamics of man*, 2010), but in this essay I want to cut to the chase and so ask you to humour me. My launch pad is simply this: I contend that evolution is a creative process that has produced layers of matter (from the Big Bang, which I call the alpha state, through the quantum, atomic, galactic, chemical and biological states) with each building on the one(s) before and that a new conscious system state is emerging whose matter I call cerebral structure. Here I want to explore what cerebral structure is.

* * *

In Gene Roddenberry's Star Trek there is a clever creation (amongst many) called the Borg, a collective of species melded together to function as one and seek perfection. The idea of a cyborg (**cyb**ernetic **org**anism) was developed by Nathan Kline and Manfred Clynes in 1960 to describe an organism whose abilities are enhanced by some added technology which feeds back into how it performs.

When the Borg first appear on the scene in Star Trek there is no central command structure, rather a system akin to distributed processing. But the Borg queen, who appears in *Star Trek: First Contact* to 'bring order out of chaos', becomes the focus of the collective conscience, referring to herself as both *I* and *We*. Of course this was not entirely novel: to denote the people they represented, English monarchs had traditionally referred to themselves as *We*, a usage which got Margaret Thatcher, as Britain's Prime Minister, into some light-hearted trouble after she told the world's press that *We have become a grandmother* when announcing the birth of a grandson.

Naturally, in Star Trek, our heroes do battle with the collective (which proclaims that *resistance is futile*) using individual initiative to baffle its logic. This theme is picked up again in George Lucas's Star Wars series when the film's heroes do battle with Darth Vader, personification of the Galactic Empire and a thinly disguised reincarnation of Satan, the fallen angel. As it was in Eden, the dynamic is individualism versus mechanistic perfection. Or, if one wants to go back an evolutionary step, it is the interaction between mercurial energy and matter which has driven evolution and underpins what we call life.

* * *

To get a handle on what I am calling cerebral structure it is helpful to consider what the biological system state we are undoubtedly still part of is. And to repeat, I am defining a system state as a set of arrangements, expressed through matter, which are distinct, as the early gaseous universe was distinct from the galactic agglomerations that evolved out of it.

The start of the biological system state can be characterized as the moment when, by chance, chemicals combined in such a way as to interact with their environment and replicate (absorbing energy from the sun and releasing waste matter such as oxygen and CO_2).

Unlike a star pulled inwards by gravity causing nuclear fusion to occur which converts hydrogen into helium and fuses atoms into metals, etc., releasing large amounts of energy (as sunlight) and the metals themselves when the star eventually uses up its energy and collapses, biological structures are short-lived, but have proved extraordinarily adaptable.

What is sometimes called the biosphere is the biological matter which we know exists on Earth within that narrow band between earth and sky. Of course one cannot think about the biosphere in isolation: it needs the earth just as much as it needs the sunlight which floods in across some 93 million miles of space from our sun. The universe is a coherent whole, but it appears to be layered with each layer exhibiting a unique set of characteristics; a set of arrangements able to elaborate, albeit only to the extent that its particular set of rules allows.

The maverick thinkers, James Lovelock (chemist) and Lynn Margulis (microbiologist) put forward their Gaia hypothesis in the 1970s which essentially described the Earth and its biosphere as one integrated system. They argued that the biosphere interacted with the earth's inorganic matter and its spatial environment to sustain itself in a synergistic way. Naturally this idea ruffled the feathers of many of those in other fields who hadn't authored it. To suggest that the biosphere possessed a 'purpose' – that of sustaining itself: oh no!

But in fact, such a purpose was not contentious at all. All systems, by definition, function to sustain themselves otherwise they would not exist. What was contentious about the Gaia hypothesis was to treat the biosphere as a coherent entity and, thereby, one which would seek to sustain itself. I am with Margulis and Lovelock on this, although my emphasis is slightly different. Their critics argue that there is nothing in natural selection (and specifically within the genes of living things) to suggest forethought, such that evolving life might as easily be detrimental to the biosphere as supportive of it.

This is right, but I believe incomplete.

Natural selection is certainly opportunistic and backward looking: the structures that can find a way of propagating themselves will do so based upon the environment which already exists without any appreciation of what their existence might do to that environment in the future. But you could say exactly the same about a planetary system, one of the components of the galactic layer of matter that evolved out of the gaseous universe.

Furthermore, one would need to be a very obtuse thinker not to recognize a progression in the universe as we know it and to classify that progression in terms of types of matter, or more precisely, in terms of types of energy-matter relationships. Obviously I am going a little further in suggesting that these 'types' can best be thought of as system states with coherent sets of characteristics, albeit ones which are part of and linked to the whole in dynamic layers. On this basis it is quite reasonable to think of the biosphere as a coherent whole and as such, one with a structure's propensity to sustain itself.

Now this is where cerebral structure comes into the frame. If there is no particular reason to think that evolution has stopped and if one accepts my broad premise that evolution is manifest as a progression through system states, each emerging creatively out of the state before, then the evolution of forethought – which Margulis and Lovelock's critics rightly say is not evident in biology - suggests the emergence of a new evolutionary system state.

* * *

In support of the Gaia hypothesis Earth's biosphere has proved to be remarkably tenacious, even when Gaia's arrangements have become unbalanced and worked against her. There have been times when there has been too little oxygen and others when there has been too much; times when continental drift has altered weather patterns and destabilized biological matter; and times when volcanism and meteor impact have rendered biological life extremely difficult. But after each of these challenges, biological life has managed to reassert itself. So even from a backward looking point of view the biological structures which have survived into the present possess some trace memory of the past which has a bearing on the future.

For all structures, existence is an end in itself – and it is surely not unreasonable to look upon the biosphere as a structure without imbuing it with a sense of purpose. But throw conscious awareness into the mix and a structure so endowed will search for ways to counter anticipated environmental change. However, as the environmental argument raging around the world at present attests, the tentative nature of foreknowledge has to do battle with the sure knowledge of what exists at present. So even if a group of people become convinced that the end of the world is nigh, they might have neither the means nor the knowledge to do anything about it. In such circumstances, partying until the end (as some members of the Third Reich are supposed to have done before its final demise) or resorting to prayer make perfect sense.

* * *

Societies are arrangements which have evolved to support those individuals who make them up, even at the expense of individuals who might be used as slaves, cannon fodder, or ritually killed in support of some aspect of the shared story that explains the nature of a society to its members. We call its customs, rules, technologies, art and buildings its culture. As an essentially functional arrangement, societies do much of a people's thinking for them and their culture is often clung to long after external changes undermine its functionality.

So is what people call culture the same as what I am calling cerebral structure? Yes and no. A culture is unique to and defines a particular group of people. It is, in a sense, equivalent to the characteristics which define the populations of dinosaur or chimpanzee. Both of these can be described as being animals and more generally, as being biological. What I mean by cerebral structure is a layer of arrangements beyond the biological (out of which it is evolving) which embraces cultures.

Because it is in the process of formation (at least as I am arguing) it is not possible to describe precisely, although its shape is coming into view. At its heart is the evolution of consciousness (the subject of the next essay) and by consciousness I mean the ability to imagine outcomes and the steps needed to bring them about. In Star Trek, the perfection the Borg seek is never made explicit, beyond being tightly bound to the collective, any more than Darth Vader's mission appears to be other than to subjugate all comers to the Galactic Empire's will – presumably his own.

We know that biological life on earth has a finite existence (our sun is already about half way through the stable part of its life). When our solar system reaches the end of its term it is hard to see how biological matter can be recycled into anything other than its base elements (chiefly carbon). However – and it is a very important 'however' – as self-directed structures with imagination, humans have developed a facility to probe the nature of their environment. It will be open to us as biology's most cerebral arrangement (here on earth, at least) to build an ark and escape the constraints of our solar system. The question is what will we have to become in order to do this?

The cerebral structure which is evolving is far more than just knowledge. To put it a little glibly, the universe already knows how it works. Even if we come to know everything there is to know we would still be faced with a far bigger challenge: what to do with that knowledge. However this is not just a question of wish fulfilment. The problem runs far deeper. Knowing how the universe works is akin to knowing how to paint or play the piano. A natural sound triggers some feeling within us; we discover that a dye can be used on a cave wall to represent a hand or an animal. Then we begin to rearrange those bits of knowledge, partly deliberately, to achieve something we have in mind and partly experimentally, just to see what happens.

But what we see is largely determined by what we are already part of (by how the bits of knowledge are currently arranged). If we are to see something different, a disruptor is needed.

* * *

As every creative marketing man will tell you, part of his art lies in knowing how to persuade people to want things they did not previously know they wanted. In the Garden of Eden, when Adam had been given his companion Eve, God believed he had provided the couple with all they could possibly want. But along comes the marketing man in the form of a serpent. He persuades the two innocents that there is a whole world of new experiences out there for the taking (all unspecified) and the young couple is hooked.

This hurts God greatly and makes him furious because he has lost control of his world to the MAD man Satan disguised as a snake. Naturally he takes it out on the errant pair, banishing them from the garden and cutting off their inheritance: they are on their own. Mankind's uncertain journey into the future has begun. But a hurt God is a vengeful God and for a long time Adam and Eve's descendants are not allowed to forget where they came from and the prospect of returning to Eden's heavenly garden is dangled before them if only they would atone for their ancestors' sin. However no amount of atoning seems to do the trick and in exasperation God sends down his Son to show the way. But this, too, ends badly.

Now doubly hurt, God washes His hands of His creation which infuriates Satan who is only interested in his contest with God, not in man. Freed from Divine guidance and malign intervention, men and women gradually come to realize that they are on their own and that it is the experience of life itself which matters. Meanwhile God and Satan bury the hatchet, order up a pizza and settle down to watch the whole thing on TV.

* * *

This irreverent summary of the Bible story is not intended to detract from the role of religion in human society, although there are those who blame religion for every ill mankind has suffered. Quite the contrary, religions have been attempts at creating cerebral structure.

Gutama Buddah (c 563BCE – c 480BCE), Jesus of Nazareth (c 4BCE – c 30CE), Saul of Tarsus or St Paul (c 5CE – c 67CE) and Muhammad (c 570CE – 623CE) were all teachers of a special kind. What they taught conscious man was that he could be more than he appeared to be – an entity driven by instinct that could disregard the sufferings of his own kind, fight wars and commit degrading acts. If God was a metaphor for the universe, there is, they told their followers, a truth to be found within it. A thousand years separate their teachings and, in light of the fact that over a further thousand years from the death of the last of these we are still disregarding the sufferings of our own kind, fighting wars and committing degrading acts suggests they were failures. Yet their popularity clearly shows that they were saying something our conscious minds were hungry for.

Individual forethought has turbo-charged our ability to adapt the way our collectives work so as to bend the environment to our needs. The tension between individual will and collective need (between Luke Skywalker and the Empire) has driven this process. The problem, of course, is that we are still biological entities, governed by instinctive drives and the cerebral structure we have so far constructed to organize ourselves is not yet fully effective. One example will suffice – there will be many more in the essays which follow.

After the official conclusion of the First World War in 1918, the American president, Woodrow Wilson, a man of high-minded ideals and with his countrymen's detestation of empire (having once been part of one), put forward his principle of self-determination as being the bedrock for the ensuing disposition between victors and vanquished. Across what had previously been the German, Austro-Hungarian and Ottoman Empires this was taken as a signal for ethnic groupings to claim nationhood.

With rights previously upheld by the defunct imperial structures now gone, individuals unlucky enough to find themselves amongst an ethnic minority within these new 'nations' became fair game for vengeful paramilitaries. Rape, murder, starvation and forced migrations became the norm as instinctive rearrangements transformed the map of Europe and morphed relentlessly into the horrors of the Second World War. The President's much vaunted League of Nations, intended as a bastion for peace, failed spectacularly and was not even supported by his own people.

Human history is replete with horrific progressions of this kind and it is small wonder that people crave a level of existence where such things do not occur. Like Adam and Eve, it seems as though we simply can't help ourselves. In the biological world, conflicts between groups would be quickly resolved and a balance restored. Our curse has been that, while our ability to act with intent has enabled us to sustain ever larger numbers, the social mechanisms we have developed to achieve this have proved unstable. But there is an irony here. It is this same instability that has driven the process forward.

* * *

All species have a propensity to increase their numbers. In 1798, the Reverend Thomas Malthus suggested that the human population would increase exponentially until food shortages and disease reined it back. In the absence of moral restraint, the good minister suggested, vice, misery and war would do the trick. What Malthus missed was what anyone living two hundred years ago would have missed: mankind's remarkable ability to reorganize the environment to suit himself. In spite of there having been tens of millions of premature deaths on account of war during these same two centuries, we have prospered. On the face of it, this hardly makes sense.

* * *

If our species evolved in Africa, as the evidence suggests, and gradually spread out from there, it is hard to escape the conclusion that the Mediterranean served as a crucible for the often disruptive cultural interactions which propelled Homo sapiens to where he now is. The South China Sea and Indian Oceans are also crucible candidates, both fomenting the technological development needed to master them and the trading systems which were required to use them, but the size, enclosed nature and relatively benign character of the Mediterranean made it unique in this regard.

The Phoenicians (c 1200-800BCE), Greeks (c 500-200BCE), Romans (c 100BC-400CE) and Venetians (c 700-1600CE) all built trading networks around the Mediterranean and the fertile valley of the Nile could hardly have been exploited as it was without the complex social arrangements of Ancient Egypt (c 3100BCE – 332BCE). The interplay between these social entities through trade and competitive warfare stimulated innovation and the development of new social structures. The Phoenicians, for example, perfected the use of standardized components in shipbuilding, a technology later copied by Rome whose leading citizens absorbed and admired much of Greek thinking.

If one could observe human evolution over the last five thousand years compressed into an hour or so, one would see interactions between polities with a shift over time between those leading the pack in terms of cohesion, projection, innovation, art and wealth;

and all the time our numbers would increase, sometimes slowly, sometimes after setbacks and sometimes in bursts. What this tells us is that underlying the competitive fermentation has been our ability to exploit, rearrange and dominate our environment. Egypt has a population today of some 92 million even though it has not led the world for over four thousand years: the achievements of civilizations outlast them.

One could say that individual aspiration has become the disruptor (perhaps amongst elites it always was). In any event, modern humans do not appear to be satisfied with mere self-sufficiency – as other animals generally are – but have a weakness for differentiating possessions. MAD men may have been preaching to the already converted. From princes (and now billionaires) building palaces to Olympian athletes striving for gold, from the biggest hamburger, most highly priced work of art, most popular songs to the fastest fighter jet, largest aircraft carrier and most exclusive universities, we strive for and are motivated by the exceptional. By putting 'conspicuous consumption' at the heart of his *The Theory of the Leisure Class* (1899), Thorstein Veblen was onto something. But now we are in a bind. Governments face rejection unless they can deliver economic growth and in the conventional sense, in the developed world at least, this may no longer be possible.

* * *

If cerebral structure is the social arrangements we consciously put in place to achieve specific ends, can we simply not say let there be growth? Well we can, until we are blue in the face and like a well-timed rain dance economic growth might ensue. Economists, like witch doctors and priests of old, are called upon to give advice but the truth is, human societies are like Russian dolls: complex things nested within complex things. A polity may be directed towards a specific end, such as in war, but this requires a people to share the objective and their government to control the levers of power so that all the activities of the polity can be directed to that end.

At the other end of the spectrum is social chaos of the kind that existed in many parts of defeated Europe after World Wars I & II. With respect for authority gone (with the promised victory that had held people together now dust), individuals turn fearfully to those closest and most like them in their struggle to survive, lashing out at anything different. This is raw biological instinct at work. Into such a maelstrom it is hard men like Lenin (and in a later period, Spain's Franco) who grasp the reins of power and instil order once more. But they too must have a story (be it fascism, communism, or whatever) capable of binding their followers together.

And this is the central characteristic of cerebral structure – it fuses biological instinct with intent. The reason is simple enough. For a group of conscious individuals capable of some degree of volition to function together they must share a view of the world (share a story about how the world they are in works at that point in time). The convict on a work detail might choose to make a run for it but decides not to because he calculates that the guard will shoot him. The power structure of society is threaded through with such checks and balances to make it work in a machine-like way, even though its components are far from being machines, which is precisely what has enabled human society to adapt as successfully as it has.

Although a society's power structure bestows benefits on those who hold power this merely reflects the fact that it is beyond anything else a functional arrangement. The power holders have a job to do that requires skill and effort which society must assess and they must be willing to deploy. If a power structure fails to meet the basic needs of a majority of those in it, it will fail. Strong-arm tactics and a strong story might keep it afloat for a while, but sooner or later, unless it can deliver, it will be abandoned.

The evolution of social structure has been more inductive

(progressing from what is observed) than deductive (the result of applying some grand theoretical principle). Utopias (the perfect social conception of a single mind) have had an abysmal record. This is hardly surprising because the universe we are part of is clearly dynamic and creative such that what might seem like a good arrangement today may seem a lot less good tomorrow and this is quite apart from the fact that a society of conscious individuals is unlikely to be something any one of them can successfully conceptualize. Even so, there are still some things that can be said about the design of cerebral structure.

The first is that it requires order: that's one for the Empire. The second is that individual volition is central to adaptation: that's one for Luke Skywalker. To function collectively, individuals need to operate within a coordinating framework consisting of both hard structures (buildings, roads, computer terminals, etc.) and soft structures (customs, laws, rules, etc.), which we might as well give to the Empire. That said, the ability to create structure in response to human need and retire it when it no longer serves any need (as happens when a corporation's products are no longer required and new corporations are formed to take its place) is crucial: another for Skywalker.

The tension between the Borg collective and the individuals aboard the Starship Enterprise are two sides of the cerebral coin and we had better get used to it. As conscious beings, the way we communicate with one another is crucial. We need a shared language about how our social systems work so that we avoid the temptation to place form above substance, a failing that belies good intentions and has been the undoing of religions and governments. We need systems of communication which empower individuals. We need power structures and the incentives that go with them which are transparent and effective, not ones whose opacity shields the self-serving or incompetent.

Above all, we need a shared story about what we are and where we are going which all of us regard as worthy and against which our individual and collective actions can be judged. This is the great challenge for education. In a dynamic universe which is creative, one characterized by its loose-tight properties, trial and error is inevitable and a willingness to learn essential.

In summary, cerebral structure is an evolving set of assumptions about the nature of human existence which draws on human emotion and is reflected in our customs, laws, technologies, social arrangements and buildings. Its function is to organize collective action for the purpose of survival and it does much of our day-to-day thinking for us. It both plays on and is influenced by individual consciousness. Polities have some of the characteristics of organisms in that they exist within permeable boundaries inside which are differentiated sub-structures similarly bound. Their loose-tight properties enable adaptation, although a tendency towards rigidity (often indistinguishable from the appearance of a reasonably contented equilibrium) can make them vulnerable to external change because they resist it until they are overwhelmed and then fall into disarray. We need to be on our guard, constantly. We have much to learn.

3

Consciousness

A G R E A T many trees have been sacrificed to consciousness. This is hardly surprising: we see consciousness as defining what we are. But what is it? At the cost of a few more branches, at least, let me suggest an answer.

Whatever consciousness is, it has evolved (and here I part company with those who see it as man's uniquely spiritual self – that which enables him to comprehend absolute right from absolute wrong). The evolutionary approach suggests three things. The first is that its components are likely to be evident in the evolutionary progression. The second is that it must have rendered some utility to those who possess it. The third thing, profoundly important for us as a species, is that the evolution of consciousness, as we know it, is hardly likely to be the end of it.

Our nearest ancestors are animals. What animals (and insects) have that plants do not is a degree of agency. Individual plants remain rooted, relying on various 'strategies' to propagate and 'find' environments that suit them. These strategies, however, are not forward-thinking plans designed to achieve specific ends like finding environments known to be suitable. And this can be said of evolution generally. Evolution does not possess foreknowledge. Evolution is dynamic and has a predisposition to create structure. The emergence on earth of organic arrangements (what we call 'life') some 4 billion years ago heralded a new type of organization (different from, say, chemical compounds) in that it was able to replicate itself. Malleable and with a short lifespan at the individual level it interacted with and adapted to its environment, which it came in part to generate, fragmenting, through random variations, into the interdependent biosphere we know.

Whatever organic configurations could form did form, feeding off one another in a symbiotic orgy of trial and error inventiveness. Although most compositions that have ever lived on earth have become extinct, the trend has been towards entities of increasing complexity. However, there is a limit to the complexity of particular structures (and we will return to this when we consider where evolution goes next) such that for evolution to progress, it has to come up with new arrangements. The important difference between animals and plants is that the former have more independent agency: they can move around under their own steam.

This necessitates 'memory' and interaction: memory to navigate the space they traverse and interaction to reproduce. Although asexual reproduction would seem more efficient (only one of a kind is required to produce the next generation rather than two), the mixing of genes, with 50% coming from each partner to create something new, probably enhances adaptation. Even more important, for the evolution of consciousness, the interaction between two independent agents leads to the creation of what I call (for want of a better word) cerebral structure: a reference outside each individual which both share.

When an albatross returns to one location after scouring hundreds of miles of ocean for food it is exercising memory. When it dances with its lifetime mate (divorce, apparently is rare) it is generating a pair bond both will recognize. The buzz of the colony (the remote location the birds find suitable for nesting) possesses a social dimension. What is shared is real and outwith each individual. Our closest evolutionary neighbour, the chimpanzee, with whom we share some 94% of our DNA (Deoxyribonucleic acid, the molecule carrying most of the genetic instructions that determine an organism's development) has evolved a more complex social dimension than the albatross. Life is lived communally necessitating continuous communication and so a more complex cerebral structure which each individual has to tap into.

Language is essentially sound that carries meaning, at least for those who share the cerebral structure those sounds are part of. Humans who study chimpanzees are able to identify which sounds are associated with aggression, anger, frustration, fear and submission, just as we and our pet dog (if we have one) can understand a good deal about each other's state of mind and, importantly, the actions this might portend. And sound is only part of what goes to make up this cerebral structure, that invisible entity that links the individuals who share it. There are visual cues, as well as cues which emanate from smell, touch and taste. And clearly the physical environment we are part of is reflected in these mind maps we share. The island colony the albatross returns to, year in, year out means something to it and to the others who use it.

Now this does raise an ontological question. Does this thing I am calling cerebral structure exist when it is merely a shared understanding which resides inside the brains of individual agents who act in concert? You can't see, hear, taste, smell or touch it. When a conductor conducts an orchestra you can see his arm movements, you can see the musicians blow, bow, strike and move their hands, you can see the music sheets and perhaps some notes, you can hear the sound which emanates from their endeavours but what you can't see, hear, taste, smell or touch is the mental map which guides all their actions in accordance with the composer's vision and conductor's interpretation. And yet without it, nothing would happen: clearly, it exists.

This also takes us into the realm of metaphysics – the fundamental nature of being. But as there are those who labour all their working lives in this area all I wish to do here is acknowledge the issue. It is thought that the structure of music, for example, taps into the fundamental rhythms (wave structures) of our cosmos and it seems likely that our own emotions are more deep-seated than we realize. So let me simply assert that cerebral structure exists and recognize that it, like everything else that has evolved, is part of the mystery of our universe.

* * *

The transition from what we class as animal to what we call human may have been less abrupt than we imagine. The crucial innovation, doubtless tentative at first, was a facility to imagine, to project aspects of the merely experienced onto a mental screen, if you will, which we could observe (as if we were outside ourselves looking in) and manipulate. The chimpanzee using a stick to crack open a nut placed on a rock might be an accidental discovery which, proving useful, is then transmitted sub-consciously, but when combined with group living and rudimentary communication could have been externalized (again by accident) as some simple awareness of cause and effect.

Most animals have evolved behaviours which entail manipulating material for their benefit (moss – nesting material – nest building – safe egg laying and incubation) with the most successful techniques being transmitted sub-consciously by natural selection (the techniques that work in that they most often produce the next generation are thereby carried forward). Anticipating what techniques might be successful, however, requires some conscious 'modelling' of possible outcomes - of cause and effect.

That there are still isolated tribes today (albeit a rapidly diminishing number of them) whose members communicate using sounds that carry meaning we can (with help) understand, and yet which have evolved no more than the simple techniques necessary to sustain themselves, suggests that the facility to imagine (to externalize shared feelings about cause and effect) offered – in itself – no great advantage. Like the curved beak of the hornbill (useful for plucking fruit from trees) or extended front claws of the brown bear (used for digging up food), the ability to engage in shared speculation was just another of evolution's mutations which proved helpful in differentiating and sustaining a particular structure – the one we have grandly called Homo sapiens.

Although not all 'primitive' tribes discovered have creation myths (the Pirahä of the Amazon, for example), most seem to. What utility this affords is hard to say beyond the bonding generated by being part of a shared story as well as the resolution it affords to the ultimate question arising out of a sense of cause and effect: who (or what) caused us? And we are still exercised by the question. From gravitational waves to black holes, the subject matter of astrophysics fascinates us. But the evolutionary utility of this speculative urge is less obvious. As far back as the book of Genesis, we were warned (by God, Man's alter-ego?) that our curiosity might damn us, and had we blown ourselves to smithereens in the 1960s, as seemed eminently possible, an outside observer would have concluded that our relentless pursuit of cause and effect had led only to an evolutionary dead end! So what gave rise to this obsession?

* * *

This line of enquiry threatens to lead away from consciousness, so let us return to it. If, as I have suggested, the onset of consciousness was an evolved facility to project awareness into a shared model of cause and effect and that this was as much a comforting (that is to say identity confirming) social exercise as one with practical use, what changed to make the pursuit of cause and effect so much more?

The ancient Egyptians had a well-developed and coherent explanation of how the universe worked which was reflected in and validated their social structure. As it has been in more recent societies, the person of the leader was held to possess divine qualities. The great fruitfulness of the Nile Delta supported craftsmen, engineers, a priesthood and the office of Pharaoh, together with the construction of monuments we still marvel at today. Had their agricultural arrangements been less productive none of this would have happened and, indeed, when altered weather patterns led to a succession of poor harvests, the effectiveness of Egyptian society was undermined (as was the Ancien Régime in France four-and-a-half thousand years later, compounded by excessive military spending and high taxation).

The stability of a society is not unlike that of a bank: so long as everyone believes in it, it works. Marble-clad banking halls, like massive Pharaonic monuments, convey a sense of strength, efficiency and permanence. But if individuals cannot feed their families (or depositors withdraw their funds) these symbols ring hollow and the social cohesion they serve is undermined. What this tells us is that consciousness is a story about, or model of the world an individual inhabits which he shares with his group (those people he must interact with in order to survive), supported by a whole raft of hard (such as pyramids) and soft (such as laws and customs) structures.

The fact that the ancient Egyptians' understanding of how the universe works was rather different from our own underscores that it is not the absolute rightness or wrongness of a society's story, but its believability that matters. Furthermore, believability rests more upon our immediate sense of wellbeing (or expectation of wellbeing) than upon rigorous analysis. On becoming Prime Minister on May 10th, 1940 Winston Churchill addressed the parliament of the English people with these words:

We have before us an ordeal of the most grievous
kind. We have before us many, many long months of
struggle and of suffering. You ask, what is our policy?
I can say: It is to wage war, by sea, land and air, with
all our might and with all the strength that God can
give us; to wage war against a monstrous tyranny,
never surpassed in the dark, lamentable catalogue of
human crime. That is our policy. You ask, what is our
aim? I can answer in one word: It is victory, victory at
all costs, victory in spite of all terror, victory, however
long and hard the road may be; for without victory,
there is no survival.

There were still those who preferred the message of his
predecessor, Neville Chamberlain who, following his return from
a meeting with the Nazi leader, Adolph Hitler in 1938, promised
peace in our time and was cheered to the rafters. But by 1940 most
shared Churchill's gloomy assessment of the Third Reich and were
prepared to accept his vision of reality. And that is the crucial thing
about consciousness: it is work in progress. Hitler and Churchill each
painted pictures of their country's future. That was their genius. They
crafted the consciousness of two nations, one to endure hardship the
other to forgo moral scruple, but both for the same end: victory.
In ancient Egypt, by comparison, the priesthood's drive to propel
their Pharaoh into the afterlife, and secure privileges in this life for
themselves, seems rather benign.

In all of this, cause and effect is almost a byproduct of the
process. It wasn't until the nineteenth century, with Friedrich
Engels and the followers of Karl Marx more generally, that the
idea of false consciousness – meaning socially-determined beliefs
that were not grounded in reality – emerged. That there was such
a thing as objective reality (in what we would call the scientific
sense) can certainly be traced to ancient Egypt and doubtless

beyond, but was generally restricted to concrete relationships such as π (the mathematical constant 3.14159 26535 89793....) used in monumental construction, π being the relationship between the circumference of a circle and its diameter.

That something caused, or led to, something else was integral to consciousness from the start for the obvious reason that observed life (and so discussed life) followed a pattern: the sun rose and set, the moon came and went, the stars in the heavens appeared to follow a complex dance and, of course, mortal life was sandwiched between birth and death. For the people of ancient Egypt the annual flooding of the River Nile, which infused the soil they farmed with richness, was an essential event. To try to intercede with the gods who orchestrated this event was sensible and widely applauded. Today, aware of how dependent we have become on the stability of our environment, we are inching towards a pact with those same gods: we have been advised by our own priesthood, that if we limit our CO_2 emissions, the stability we rely on will be maintained. It has to be hoped that our understanding of cause and effect is greater than that claimed by the priesthood of ancient Egypt, although one cannot deny that the story they wove underpinned a remarkably successful and long-lasting civilization.

Consciousness might reside within each of us as individuals, but it is a social construct. To talk about 'false consciousness' as if there is a consciousness out there ready to be grasped if only we had the sense to do so, is quite disingenuous. No such thing can exist. When Europeans descended upon Amerindians in the sixteenth century, two sets of consciousness collided. The consciousness of one was no more false than the other was true. One thing was clear, however: the social organization of the Europeans embraced more people, used more complex technologies and could command more resources. Consequently it came to overwhelm the indigenous societies in both North and South America.

Scientific determinism, the belief system which underpinned Marxism and upended countless societies based upon the idea of a God-ordered universe in which hereditary relationships were divinely ordained (even today there are many who regard aborting a foetus as interfering with God's will), was no more or less than an attempt to alter consciousness in the same way early Christians had been intent upon altering the consciousness which underpinned the Roman Empire.

By claiming that societies were doomed or destined (take your pick) to follow a predetermined path towards social enlightenment, Marxists were making a similar claim to that made by early Christians who held that God's will for mankind would ultimately prevail. That one came to be believed at one point in time and the other at another, with both grounding their appeal in absolute objectivity (what was outside the template of each was 'false'), shows that consciousness is situation-specific and embraces two key, mutually re-enforcing components: believability and functionality.

The Roman state was based upon organizational efficiency (legal, political, economic, mechanical and above all military) and the power those in control of its organization could wield. So long as it was able to expand its reach, thereby pulling ever more wealth towards the centre, its social structure and belief system were mutually reinforcing: Rome was great; ergo what the Roman Empire did was great. But for those who bridled under Roman control, the idea that there was a God whose rule was superior to that of a Roman emperor held increasing appeal, so much so that in the 4th century CE the emperor Constantine attached Christianity to the belief system of the empire itself.

When Rome's military power over its western empire collapsed in the middle of the 5th century CE, the belief system of the Roman Church, together with its ecclesiastical structures, survived, becoming the bedrock of the secular power structures which emerged to fill the gap left by Roman retreat. In 799 Pope Leo III (for reasons of realpolitik, it must be said) crowned the Frankish king, Charlemagne, *Imperator Romanorum*, sealing the division between what had become the eastern and western Roman Empires which had arisen out of Emperor Diocletian's administrative reforms instituted around 293 to hold the then sprawling (and almost ungovernable) empire together. When Marx suggested that religion was the opium of the masses he was implying that the people in any functioning polity need to believe in its legitimacy. Had he lived one hundred years later would he have recognized that belief in communism was serving the selfsame purpose?

So if, as I have suggested, consciousness was an evolved facility to project awareness into a shared model of cause and effect, how were individual agency and hierarchy reconciled? When an Inuit finds and kills a seal it would be inconceivable for him not to share his bounty with the members of his group. In his harsh arctic habitat food is hard to come by so there is utility in individual agency (where one hunter fails another might succeed). The group as a whole, however, benefits from sharing, not just food but information as well as the customs that make living as a group possible. The trade-off is between individual agency and collective functionality with a shared consciousness about the legitimacy of their arrangements reconciling the two.

As the longevity of isolated tribes attests, there seems to be nothing intrinsic to push a group in balance with its environment out of its arrangements and the belief system that underpins it. While the causes of things at a local level are likely to be accurate and frequently validated (hunting in this way, in those areas, at that time should bring success), the nature of the unknown (what happens after death, for example) is likely to be 'explained' by stories largely incapable of validation but which provide comfort and solidify group identity. The evolved belief system of the ancient Egyptians sustained a complex and multifaceted civilization even though the machinations of their priesthood had no direct influence on the behaviour of the Nile. In the same way the belief system developed by the Roman Catholic Church managed to bestow legitimacy on, nurture and sustain European civilization for over a thousand years even though some of its core articles of faith (the virgin birth, the existence of heaven and hell) could neither be observed nor proved. At the very least, it was a more effective opiate than communism.

What pushed human societies out of their comfort zones, stimulating further evolution, was conflict between them. On the whole, animals do not engage in this practice. The members of a species will mark out a territory and defend it against raids from their own kind, but such raids require a level of group organization which is not common. There are certainly examples of one species pushing aside another but this is not the same thing and seems to take place when a species pushes its way into the territory of another upsetting a prior balance (after rabbits found their way into Australia they caused mayhem).

When human society became sufficiently well organized to sustain a ruling class, the ambition of that class became significant. After organizing the resources of one's own group to best advantage the temptation to raid the resources of another group must have arisen. When productive groups started supporting armies (notionally for their defense) the temptation to raid can only have increased with this dynamic becoming embedded within group consciousness. This competitive activity will have stimulated the development of arms, tactics and gradually, social organization, with the entities commanding the most human and material resources taking a lead.

The reason no one group was ever able to sustain a dominant position, and so bring human evolution into passive balance, was presumably because consciousness and the identity it sustains is fluid. With individuals always reaching for some personal advantage, gradual changes in circumstance (the Roman imperium's administrative overreach, for example) would bring about organizational realignment. And although economic organization could quite easily slip backwards (conflict tends to be destructive in the short term), dispersed human ingenuity – stimulated by this competition - has so far outrun competition's negative effects.

That millions of men have been largely willing to sacrifice themselves in this competition is testament to the power of the consciousness we are part of. Notions of glory, honour, sacrifice and identity have all worked to frame this dynamic. Only gradually has cause and effect (or more precisely, the scientific method) moved from the periphery towards centre stage and away from the prerequisites of power towards human enhancement.

* * *

Any discussion of consciousness would be incomplete without mentioning the role of art, although even what we mean by art is not straightforward. Perhaps the best way of thinking about it is to recognize that art operates on the margins of consciousness: that is to say it must utilize some concrete medium and recognizable symbolism, but is one step removed from the existing constraints of day-to-day life. In this way it can 'surface' concerns about the status quo and even serve as a signpost toward things to come. However, in the way that dreams are often hard to fathom and transitory, art too is a reflection of our subconscious. It is consciousness in the making.

* * *

So consciousness is not really what we think it is – an awareness of the world around us independent of that world. Rather it is an interaction between us and it in the form of an operational model which means broadly the same to all of us who share it. This model encompasses a view about how we fit into the universe, how the human hierarchy we are part of works and what its purpose is. The structural elements of this model are anchored to real physical things, some soft, like laws and customs, some hard, like monuments, houses and roads. This cerebral structure (as I have taken to calling it) operates on us as individuals and makes many of our decisions for us. It is a coherent whole made up out of concrete interrelationships; of give and take expectations. In affording us essential stability it resists change, but the evolutionary dynamic of consciousness is that it can and does adapt and grow.

Only very gradually are we coming to appreciate the power this structure holds over us and to understand how to access it and alter it. Every day, our interaction with it as individuals serves to define us and is like life pulsing through a corpse. Take the unearthed city of Pompeii, for example. It displays the sinews of a past consciousness and there is much that we can relate to, but the living breathing thing has long gone.

4

When identity means opposition

WE GROW UP facing a choice. Do we accept the identity assigned to us by birth and circumstance or seek out a different one? The problem, of course, is that as we grow into adulthood we change, becoming more self-aware. Even if our family situation is supportive and the life of a craftsman under our father's guidance, for example, lies before us, our makeup might not suit us to that role. Then what? Or conversely, if we are unlucky and have abusive (or just absent) parents, how do we escape (if escape is necessary) and find our way? In both situations we are at the mercy of the society we inhabit and the opportunities it affords.

The feminist movement took issue with the traditional role allotted to females, but it was the intervention of science and effective birth control that enabled women to at least influence the role assigned to them by biology. And as for individuals whose orientation was not heterosexual, they have had to carve out lives on the margins of society, at least when it came to their sexuality.

As conscious beings, identity is central to our existence. This is because consciousness entails an evolved ability to visualize a context (a depiction of what we believe to be the real world) within which we, our actions and their consequences can be imagined. Necessarily, our point of reference is ourselves and this requires a sense of identity: an alter ego able to exist within our imagined world. Now it is important not to lose sight of the fact that this evolved facility (consciousness) only exists because of its utility to us as a species. So although consciousness resides within individuals, its value (in terms of species survival) has to be judged against its benefit to the whole.

Consequently, there exists an inbuilt conflict between an individual's drive to survive and the need for the group the individual is part of to survive. In nature, countless examples exist of individuals clustering as a survival strategy, the tactic requiring that some be exposed to danger so that the majority might be shielded from it. While the anchovy on the outside of a shoal being attacked by a porpoise might dart and dash, the clustering instinct predominates. Conscious beings, however, have to justify why they are being sacrificed (or exposed to heightened risk) for the good of the group they are part of. The promise of heavenly rewards or posthumous glory are well-used scripts as well as is an emphasis on protecting the next generation of one's own kind.

The great success of Homo sapiens rests upon how this conflict is resolved. A degree of individual volition whereby individuals seek out the best for themselves given the situations they encounter and within the constraints of the social organism they are part of, affords that organism a degree of flexibility unavailable to more 'hard wired' structures. This improves not only decision-making but also evolutionary adaptation. The fact that human societies have competed against one another for resources has spurred on technical as well as organizational innovation, a process accelerated (albeit at the cost of increased volatility) by competition between the leaders of societies (as well as between the leaders of the social entities that go to make them up) for power and prestige.

Why some individuals come to oppose the status quo - to view their identity in terms of opposition to it – is not always clear cut. We talk about sentiments such as a sense of injustice giving rise to opposition to the existing order, but opposition can as easily come from within the existing power structure as from the socially disadvantaged. And in any event, what does socially disadvantaged actually mean? The three slave revolts during the so-called Servile Wars which broke out towards the end of the Roman Republic (135BCE – 132BCE, 104BCE – 100BCE, and 73BCE – 71BCE, this last led by Spartacus) appear easy to understand – for most, slavery was an unpleasant state to be in, but slavery has a long history and revolts were comparatively rare. Life is full of hardships and our natural default seems to be to endure.

Opposition, beyond mere disgruntlement, requires a degree of organization which western democracies have sought to formalize on the grounds that inching our way towards the future is a process of trial and error over which no ruling elite can claim a monopoly of good ideas. When developments in optics allowed Galileo Galilei to study the night sky in more detail, causing him to suggest that far from being at the centre of the visible universe, the body on which we lived was not even at the centre of our solar system, the Catholic Church – whose vision this idea challenged – attempted to shut him up just as the Roman Republic had attempted to suppress opposition with the expedient of mass crucifixions. That the instrument of the latter became the symbol of the former and that both ultimately failed to arrest change speaks for itself. Evolution cannot be tethered.

So what leads people to slip their moorings and seek to forge an identity in opposition to the status quo? While disgruntlement must surely be a sine qua non for action – and slaves (not just Roman) had plenty to be disgruntled about – the Garden of Eden is portrayed as being in every way perfect, and still Adam and his Eve desired something more. Or was it something less? Did they simply want to escape God's velvet-clad grip?

At the time of writing, the Middle East is awash with turmoil. In part this is to do with that world's wish to escape the self-serving grip of foreigners. In part it is to do with a desire amongst some of the better-educated young for freer, more open societies unconstrained by the secret police that keep the autocratic governments they are subject to in power. Inside this power vacuum, aggravated by confused outside interference, the Sunni-Shia fracture within Islam and the rebelliousness of the autocratic elite's children (the beneficiaries of state education), a new identity is being forged.

Appealing to a feeling of impotence amongst the many young Islamic men, both in the West and Middle East, who see little prospect of advancement or adventure inside the status quo, as well as appealing to their lust for vengeance for slights, real or imagined, this new identity travels under a black flag, is extremely opposed to Western values and is dressed in religious clothes. It is a potent mix offering empowerment through violence to the dispossessed. There is a suggestion that the puppet masters behind the movement are some of those who were on the losing side of Iraq's invasion by America and her allies. If true, perhaps the West is being served up its just desserts for those weapons of mass destruction which existed only to justify the war.

It seems likely that individuals forging an identity in opposition to the status quo has a lot to do with a social entity's own evolved survival mechanism. Although each of us is primarily concerned with our immediate needs, be they at work or at home, we do have a sense about whether the social entity we are part of is meeting them. If we are its prisoner in the literal sense, as a slave would be, we are faced with limited options. We can try to escape and accept the high probability that we will be caught and subjected to vicious retribution. Or we can make the best of a lousy situation as 'trusties' do in almost all prison situations where the life of those in control is made somewhat easier by co-opting the help of some of those incarcerated. The Roman Empire was clever in this regard by offering the possibility of manumission.

Of course, and although we prefer to think otherwise, almost all of us are prisoners of the social structure we find ourselves part of and generally try to do whatever we think will afford us the best outcome. Most of the time this entails working within the system. As we grow into adulthood we shape our identity to match our circumstance. It has almost become a tradition for students to rebel against the status quo, before becoming its prime beneficiaries. There is almost certainly functionality in this. By probing their society's weak points, students force its hierarchy to confront them and perhaps make some necessary adjustments. But if, as is the case across much of the Middle East (and was the case in pre-revolutionary France, Russia and China), the power structure has become threadbare, the need for a new identity in opposition to the old becomes necessary if the society is to survive.

Although it has become customary to regard 'revolution' (and the identities that go with it) as a progressive force, it is far from clear this view is justified other than on the basis of winner's justice. More correctly, revolution (if by revolution we mean revitalizing a power structure by reformulating its identity) is as much a reactionary force as a progressive one. The progressive element rests on the claim made by the challenging identity that its 'vision' offers a better future. The reactionary element rests on the simple fact that, for order to be re-established in the chaotic situation threadbare power-structures induce, their raw sinews must be re-energized.

The Spanish civil war of 1936-39 was as brutal as the French, Russian and Chinese revolutions and like them had its roots in the transition of society from a rural to an urban oligarchy. In their use of power, all were reactionary. In Spain, however, the ruling elite retained its grip through the military, although even here the need to shift society from an agrarian economy to an industrial one was grudgingly accepted.

It is probably fair to say that at any given time a society projects an identity, burnished by a range of symbols supportive of its power structure. Citizens of North Korea are habitually treated to images of their great leader and to displays of marching soldiers and military hardware (nothing unusual about that, you might think), but what differentiates that country from many others is the extent to which ignorance is propagated and dissent crushed. This may hold the North Korean state together, but it severely restricts its transformative ability.

What will emerge out of the turmoil unfolding across the Middle East is unclear, but warring identities may be no better than repressive ones and they may even be worse. When China's communist government decided to embrace market capitalism, the impact on its people's wellbeing was dramatic and fast. At least North Korea has such an option. Because of the rampant anarchy across much of it, the Middle East does not.

In the main and to a greater or lesser extent, most of us accept the identity foisted on us by the societies we are part of. Indeed, for a society to function effectively the majority of those individuals who make it up must do so. How its people's grumblings and aspirations are channelled is the key to that happening. A mixture of carrot and stick, with the stick making even the most meagre carrot seem like a blessing from the gods: that is the political art.

From time to time, however, a polity proves inadequate to the task and this affords an opportunity for a new identity to be articulated. Christianity and Islam outlasted the Roman Empire; communism displaced hereditary autocracy in Russia and China; and, for a while, fascism displaced Germany's ill-fated experiment with liberal democracy after the First World War. Identity as opposition to the status quo is a society's evolved way of forestalling collapse.

This does not mean that it is always successful, only that it is successful more often than not. While everything is explainable, not everything is predictable.

5

The law

W E   H O L D   the law in great reverence. We regard it as our bastion against capricious government. Each of us is supposed to be equal before it. We like to think that its rulings are blind to all considerations save justice. But what exactly is the law?

Although the second paragraph of the United States Declaration of Independence makes this rousing assertion - *We hold these truths to be self-evident, that all men are created equal, that they are endowed by their Creator with certain unalienable Rights, that among these are Life, Liberty and the Pursuit of Happiness*, sentiments that infuse the American Constitution, it is palpably not the case that all men are created equal, other than in the rather bland sense that we are all equally part of the same universe – along with worms, stones, planets and raindrops. And yet these sentiments hold great emotional appeal. Why?

When Jesus of Nazareth was asked whether it was lawful for Jews to pay Roman taxes, he is reported (in the Synoptic Gospels) to have asked his challengers whose head was on the coins they used and when they said Caesar's, answered their question with the words: then give unto Caesar what is Caesar's and to God what is God's. The power of both Christianity and later Islam lay in that both placed God's law above men's law, however powerful those men might be. And yet in his reply Jesus recognized a simple truth: the evolved social entities we are part of (whatever their shortcomings) do provide us with things we need (in the example above, the stability of the Roman currency and the peace which went with it) and for that we must pay a price.

The rousing words Thomas Jefferson, a slave owner, composed when declaring independence from America's overlord, Britain, went along with a belief amongst the rebel colonists that they could get on perfectly well without the benefit of the English empire's tender embrace. But they had to fight for it. When one hundred and eighty-seven years later Martin Luther King declared on the steps of the Lincoln Memorial in America's capital that *I have a dream that one day this nation will rise up and live up to its creed, "We hold these truths to be self-evident: that all men are created equal." I have a dream...* he was trying to shame his countrymen into treating black and white equally. The disproportionate number of black Americans incarcerated within the United States penal system today makes it clear that King's (and Jefferson's) dream has yet to be realized.

So what is the law if it is neither even-handed, a bastion against the capricious power of government, nor a blind upholder of justice? When, on the 15th of June, 1215, the then Archbishop of Canterbury, Stephen Langton, in order to prevent a civil war, persuaded a faction of rebel barons and the unpopular King John to sign an agreement recognizing the limits of the king's power over them, this Magna Carta (Great Charter) as it was called, came to be seen as a cornerstone of individual rights, informing the drafting of the American Constitution five hundred and seventy-two years later.

The 1215 Magna Carta did not prevent civil war and further revisions under King John's son Henry III in 1216, 1217 and 1225 and the charter's reissue under his son Edward I in 1297 (to smooth the way toward securing much needed tax revenues) gradually brought the relationship between barons and monarch into some sort of balance.

There are two broad categories of law, that which has evolved by custom (common law) and that which owes its authority to government statute (civil law). Under common law, jurists search for cases similar to that which they are arguing in order to establish general principles which might be applied. With civil law, scholarly interpretation of how a statute should be interpreted plays a substantial role. There are many subtleties in both systems and some overlap between the two. But what is important here is to recognize that the law is primarily a mechanism for regulating behaviour and resolving disputes. As groups of people grew in size and the range of interaction increased, it became essential for consistency to be established. A free-for-all between disputants and a resort to vigilante justice would only undermine the smooth running of society and the prosperity it brought about.

It goes without saying, however, that rules will only be followed if individuals consider it in their interests to do so - and the resolution of conflict between individuals and between individuals and the state be accepted - if the process is considered reasonable by most people, and certainly by the state's most powerful people. When a combination of rural Protestants and social Progressives managed to push a prohibition bill through the American Congress in 1920 (as the eighteenth amendment to the Constitution), banning the sale, production, importation and transportation of alcoholic beverages across the nation, it remained on the statute books for thirteen years. It also served to corrupt the judicial system (police chiefs and judges were regularly paid off) and helped to make a number of influential people extremely rich. In parts of Latin America the illegal drugs trade is doing much the same today.

So again, why do Thomas Jefferson's words and Martin Luther King's for that matter, resonate so richly and do they have any substantive connection with the law? If the law is really only a functional machine, subject to endless revisions and improvements, designed to facilitate the smooth running of society, should we imbue it with emotional content? Perhaps not, but when you witness the joy and relief (and sometimes anger) on the faces of those made at least partially whole by a legal ruling, you have to wonder. And then you have to wonder where these feelings about what is and is not *just* come from. As Christ, the prophet Muhammad, Confucius and the Buddha all taught, do they draw from a deeper well than that which sustains much of our secular world?

Common law has evolved over time on the basis of what is deemed to be reasonable by those involved in its creation and interpretation. The largely Anglo-Saxon jury trial (as opposed to a judicial or magisterial ruling preferred under the civil law or statutory system) was based upon the assumption that one's peers were best able to judge whether one's behaviour was heinous or not. Occasionally popular villains escaped punishment on this basis (causing the authorities to move proceedings to another locale). The do-as-you-would-be-done-by concept has an ancient lineage and it was often hard for the powers that be to secure a conviction for 'crimes' jurors felt they might (and possibly did) perpetrate, such as smuggling.

If the law is an artefact constructed to protect a community, then the community it is designed to protect should surely have the final say. Jefferson's words, echoed by the civil rights campaigner King, were clearly a shared dream. But that's the point: they were aspirational. The community which formulated and interpreted the law in the Normanized Anglo-Saxon world was very narrow at first: the barons at the time of King John. It never occurred to the signatories of Magna Carta and its offspring that the charter should apply to the relationship between the common man and the barons. Magistrates could and frequently did, hang individuals for poaching game from the estates of landowners. It wasn't that one less rabbit would cause a baron much harm, but rather that if people did as they liked the social hierarchy everyone relied upon would be undermined.

When Christ challenged the group about to stone an adulterous woman to death - *He that is without sin among you, let him cast the first stone* – he was (as he almost always did) placing compassion above all other considerations. In the twenty-first century West, we have come to realize that adultery does not cause society to collapse (a view not shared in all parts of the world, however) so it is treated as a personal matter outside the law. But it was not so long ago that a book like Lady Chatterley's Lover was banned on account of its supposed detrimental effect on public morals (the publisher of the unexpurgated edition, Penguin, was found not guilty of obscenity in 1960 by twelve jurors).

That the book's sexual content would be considered remarkably tame today, or that depicting an upper class lady romping with a working class man (perhaps the book's most egregious error when it first came out) would nowadays raise little more than a yawn, illustrates not compassion but the primacy of social cohesion as being the law's foundation. We may laugh in disgust at the Communist Party's show trials in Moscow between 1936 and 1938 during which Stalin effectively eliminated opponents (real and imagined), but the way that states dress their actions (no matter how barbaric) in legal clothes demonstrates the law's central role. No state can exist without it and those in charge of the state must bend it to their will. Because the Soviet people feared social collapse more than they yearned for justice as an abstract concept, they applauded 'Uncle Joe' for his ruthlessness in keeping the ship of state afloat. Saddam Hussein exhibited the same qualities and following his forced retirement the Iraqi ship of state has descended into chaos.

Compassion is a feeling of generosity towards others, it is our do-as-you-would-be-done-by selves rising to the surface, but make no mistake: if we find ourselves in a tight corner and our own interests challenged, our circle of trust becomes ever more tightly drawn. In the 1930s the German people were desperate and the great majority (including most in the Catholic and Protestant churches) acquiesced as their government deliberately, methodically and legally destroyed a minority – an apocryphal cohort of evildoers, all six million of them – who they had persuaded themselves threatened their social existence. It was the Salem witch trials with a vengeance.

So let us not put the law, merely because it is the law, on a pedestal. The law does not have a separate existence excusing us of all thought, as convenient as that often is. The law encapsulates the rules we have agreed to follow in order to function collectively and we function collectively to serve our own interests. The great thinkers of the past were right. Morality sits above the law and is its judge.

6

Morality

WHEN WE think about morality we tend to think too much, although most of the time we don't think about it enough. The intellectual conceit is that morality can be articulated as a carefully crafted set of axioms which require a person of letters to lay out. In practice morality is one simple thing: compassion. The non-thinking person, the person engaged in the business of getting on with life without undue reflection, encounters compassion as a feeling, along with anger, love, fear, frustration, hatred – one spark among many that may, or may not kindle a longer-lasting fire.

In *The Pianist*, the World War II memoir by the Polish-Jewish pianist Wladyslaw Szpilman (turned into a film by Roman Polanski in 2002) a German officer, on hearing Szpilman play *Chopin's Ballade in G minor* on an old abandoned piano inside a building in war-ravaged Warsaw is moved to protect him. Did the music trigger this act of compassion by lifting the officer out of the moral quagmire he was in, or did the imminent arrival of the advancing Red Army cause this German to see beyond the Nazi hate-machine he was part of? Who knows? But in that place, at that moment, empathy struck a richer note for him than any other. The Officer, Wilm Hosenfeld, died in Soviet captivity in 1952 and it is thanks to Szpilman that his act of compassion has been remembered.

There will be those who think it outrageous to equate morality with no more than a feeling, let alone one on a par with fear, anger, hatred or any of the other primary feelings we humans can experience. Furthermore, they might also say that morality as no more than a feeling is meaningless unless it is translated into specific codes of behaviour. But the trouble with rules is that they become ends in themselves and allow people to imagine that abiding by a rule is the same as abiding by the sentiment that gave rise to the rule. It is not.

The rule Wilm Hosenfeld was subject to as an officer in the army of the Nazi state, demanded that a Jew should be turned in so that the body politic the soldier was part of could be purified of any non-Arian, no-German blood - for the good of the motherland. Follow the rule: good German. Flaunt the rule: bad German. Millions of Germans believed that they were being good Germans by following this rule. Now supposing Nazi Germany had won the war and all non-Arian individuals had been eradicated (and all witnesses to the 'cleansing' process eliminated), what sort of polity would Germany have been? Rather pleased with itself, I dare say!

And today Europe is faced with what is rapidly being perceived as a 'Muslim problem' causing governments to insist that Muslims in Europe behave like good Dutchmen, Frenchmen or Englishmen. The feeling is that Muslims identify with something outside their country of residence and that this undermines the solidarity of the state. As it was for the Americans after the attack on Pearl Harbour in 1941, following which Japanese Americans were treated as a potential fifth column and interned, the war of Isis against the West is persuading Europeans that all members of the Islamic faith might be part of a fifth column (as a tiny minority undoubtedly are).

The American example is as good as any of the moral difficulties states (or the people who run them) encounter. The forced relocation of Japanese Americans after the attack on Pearl Harbour (which was Japan's attempt to destroy America's Pacific fleet and prevent her from waging war in Asia – the United States had already attempted to restrict supplies of oil to Japan) was achieved by the simple expedient of an executive order. Signed by the then president, Franklin D Roosevelt, in February 1942, this allowed regional military commanders to designate "military areas" from which "any or all persons may be excluded".

Some 110,000 Japanese Americans (two thirds of whom lived on the west coast) were forcibly moved to camps in the interior. The loss and hardship they suffered as a result was finally recognized in 1988 when President Ronald Reagan signed the Civil Liberties Act granting reparations. A state that does not feel secure is a dangerous beast, and by 'state' one must mean its ruling elite, because it is they who purport to control the sinews that turn a collection of people into a state. During civil wars (often the most barbaric of wars) rival factions vie for that control. Be it the slaughter of Tutsi by Hutu in Rwanda (1994) or the elimination of Bosnian Muslims by Bosnian Serb Orthodox Christians in Bosnia (1995), when the genie that holds people together escapes the bottle, all hell breaks loose - and hell it invariably is.

And that is the point. Hell is ever-present, perhaps in our psyche even more than in reality, although human history gives us ample reason to fear. We are, frankly, terrified of things falling apart around us – and quite rightly so. Brothers turning against brothers, sisters against sisters and parents against each other and their offspring: this is the stuff of nightmares. When such a fracturing occurs we thrash around grasping at any stability we can find, clinging to those who seem to be like us and recoiling in horror from those who do not. This is primitive, primal, violent stuff, the way the debris from exploding stars clusters to form planets, or how organic matter struggles to regroup in some way after an environmental disruption shatters its previous balance.

So if one asks what the moral responsibility of those who run a state is, it is hard to escape the answer: to preserve it. That was the basis upon which King Charles I confronted the Parliamentarians under Oliver Cromwell (the man who, for nine years, would become England's effective dictator after masterminding the king's execution). That was the basis upon which Saddam Hussein, with a rod of iron, ruled the fractious Iraqi state for twenty-four years (and who is to say that for Iraqis those twenty-four years were less bad then the twelve years since his deposition). For Niccolò Machiavelli, the sixteenth century Florentine and political thinker, a prince had only one moral responsibility: to hold the ring.

But of course this is where it becomes difficult. Machiavelli was no supporter of incompetent rulers. Holding the ring meant guiding the ship of state through the shoals of intrigue (internal as well as external) towards continued prosperity. England's protestant republicans simply did not believe that the country would flourish under a monarchy (especially one with Catholic leanings). They were proved partly right (no king since has seriously challenged the authority of Parliament) even though after Cromwell's death the country greeted the return of Charles II to the throne with a sigh of relief. Those external powers who toppled Saddam Hussein, arguing that it would lead to a better future for Iraqis, have so far been proved spectacularly wrong. Whatever the dictator's failings (and they were many, he lost control of his country after all), destroying a nation without putting a working alternative in its place, could hardly be described as a moral act, whatever the motives.

And this is, perhaps the thing: moral motives may be well and good, but it is moral outcomes that count. When Adolph Hitler marginalized German Jews and Franklin D Roosevelt marginalized Japanese Americans, both men were seeking to protect their states from a fifth column (the Jews as perceived financial manipulators responsible for the economic depression that had savagely afflicted

German lives, Japanese Americans as the ethnic relatives of those who had decimated America's fleet in Pearl Harbour). The fact that German Jews had nothing to do with the causes of the depression and that Japanese Americans were as ignorant of the Japanese high command's intentions as everyone else, was neither here nor there.

Circling the wagons in order to protect their nations may have been the motive of both men, and their actions probably made the majority of their citizenry feel more secure, but it was at the cost of marginalizing a minority of their citizens along racial lines. How Machiavelli would have viewed such a moral calculus is hard to say, but he would probably have said that a leader should do enough to be effective (including doing enough to galvanize a majority of his people into action), but not so much as to be self-destructive. Roosevelt's actions fell well short of the latter whereas Hitler's quite clearly did not.

Having experienced humiliation (for the Americans being attacked by another power, for the Germans suffering defeat in World War I and having to endure the economic collapse that eventually followed) being able to lash out was undoubtedly therapeutic. Shared schadenfreude (deriving pleasure from the misfortune of others) is undoubtedly a bonding experience, in the way that being exposed to the ritual of human sacrifice and capital punishment was: women jostling for the best vantage when the guillotine was being used to decapitate France's aristocracy is no fiction. But however understandable and even justified such emotions are, they are a long way from compassion. Can the needs of a state ever be reconciled with morality?

At one level this is a hard, perhaps even impossible question to address. States are hugely complex entities and are always work in progress. In addition, the arrangements that work well at one point in time and in one location (think of Ancient Egypt, for example, at the height of the Old Kingdom – 2686-2181BCE, when improved administration, increased agricultural productivity, advances in art, architecture and technology, all came successfully together) can never be, or have never been, sustained. This is because states (or societies, if you prefer) are working wholes whose component parts are human individuals, their evolved belief systems which enable them to function together, the physical structures they create, their technologies, the physical (or environmental) structures they have to work with, the other social entities they have to butt up against - and all are dynamic. In such a maelstrom compassion seems to belong to a different universe.

But this may be the point. Individual survival and so social survival have to be our starting point, even though no individual and no society survives forever. So the question then becomes, how well do we survive? This is not just a quantitative issue, but a qualitative one. Is what we are part of – that which our forebears have bequeathed to us and we will pass on to our descendants – life-enhancing? Conscious life, after all, is the sum total of what we are. For it to be miserable and degrading would hardly be worth surviving for. So of course it is right for African Americans to put up a fight for their rights, just as it was right for Rome's slaves to rebel, Russia's masses to revolt and the Jewish people to point an accusing finger, but to imagine that states are not hardwired to defend themselves is utter folly.

That this interaction can have devastating consequences if handled badly by rulers and ruled alike should be compulsory learning. Because rulers have less power than they imagine and the ruled are more dependent upon the social entities they are part of than they realize, change, especially fundamental change – Rome no less than America's pre-civil war southern states was dependent upon slavery – is invariably combative and destructive. For this to be otherwise continuous small adjustments must surely be preferable to periodic earthquakes measuring 8 on the Richter scale, or its social equivalent.

To build change into our social systems is essential and largely lacking. As a rule of thumb – and the state-level version of do-as-you-would-be-done-by mantra – one might say this: those in charge of a state should enable people to improve their lives as much as possible and those requiring change should demand no more than can be delivered. Naturally this requires judgement on both sides. It also requires a sound knowledge of how social systems work (a subject sorely lacking in our schools). A successful politician is one who can say *I changed this specific thing for the better*, not one whose claim to fame rests on longevity. Morality in the public sphere (as much as in the private) is best exercised one step at a time and with a good heart.

7

Change

FOR change to occur within social systems, various things have to take place. Let us turn to a rugby football analogy (union or league) and consider the rule that no player can pass the ball forward, a rule which does not apply in American football.

The first thing to ask is where does this rule come from? What is its legitimacy? Almost immediately a myriad of factors have entered the picture. But before we delve into these let's look at the change from the standpoint of the individual player. Firstly, the rule change must be communicated to him. Secondly, he must understand it. Thirdly, he must accept it. Fourthly, he must internalize it and build it into his game. Fifthly, he, his fellow players and manager must amend their strategies to take account of it. Sixth and lastly, he must play the game in front of his supporters, opponents, referee, linesmen and media commentators with the new rule in place and experience their reaction: and all this for the impact of one rule change on one individual. Now imagine how change affects a government department or large corporation - and make it a multinational one for good measure.

That human systems do change, and change remarkably quickly

in comparison to biological change, is the reason Homo sapiens has come to dominate the planet, notwithstanding the profligate loss of life which has frequently accompanied it. And this is in spite of the fact that individual humans have changed far less. Put a New Yorker or Londoner on a deserted island with an aboriginal whose customs had not altered for several thousand years and once the language barrier had been overcome, you would probably be more surprised by the similarities than the differences.

What has changed is the invisible mental map both are attached to. Initially, the aboriginal might have the advantage, especially if the island had characteristics he was familiar with. But the 'Yondoner' (let's call him that) would certainly have a pool of knowledge to draw on. If he could apply any of it to food production and the provision of shelter as well as to the construction of transport, he might have been able to keep his end up. Although invisible to both of them would be their bacterial defenses. The 'plague' killed off swathes of Europeans in the fourteenth century, just as diseases European colonizers had developed some immunity against killed off legions of indigenous Americans in the sixteenth. What our two islanders carried that might prove fatal to the other would not be known.

Outside this, the interplay between the aboriginal and Yondoner's mind maps and their physical surroundings would define their immediate future, and on this score their new shared world would remain closer to the former's experience than that of the latter. All this emphasizes is that Yondoner's world is an evolved collective technological construct as real as the geological-biological makeup of an island. But as the ghostly remains of once-thriving cities attest, unlike islands, depopulated cities cease to function.

A further consideration would be the 'character' of aboriginal and Yondoner. Would one try to dominate the other? Would they interact constructively or destructively? Would one or other, or both, fall apart? Human variability, like biological mutations, drives the change process over time, but as with mutations, human variability is not forward looking. A mutation might flourish into a new biological approach but that is not why it happens and most wither. Human variations are different in that they are driven to express themselves and it is the interaction between human differences that energizes a society. How much weight these differences are given is a function of the perceived needs of a society as expressed through its structure and the resolution of these needs tends to be backward looking: we favour what has worked in the past.

What differentiates humans from other forms of biological life is that we can learn from experience abstractly and, using analysis, apply that 'knowledge' to how we organize ourselves and resolve, as well as utilize, individual differences. This is a trial and error process because in a dynamic creative universe, analysis can only ever be hypothetical. Our aboriginal and Yondoner are stuck with what they are, and unless they can start a family, no matter how constructive their interaction, nothing long lasting will come of it. So this two person stuck-on-an-island story has taken us as far as it can.

* * *

The initial presumption must always be against change simply because humans are born into a working system (unless enslaved into one) with all its hard and soft structures. Our struggle at first is to understand what we are part of when we are not yet in a position to consider alternatives. Certainly we might rail against the strictures we come up against (the times we must go to bed, the food we must eat), but we have no critical ability to question them. Gradually, however, we encounter borders to our freedom of behaviour and consequences if we breach them. This allows us to develop a critical faculty and to insert into our mental map of how the world works things we might like to change. Perhaps gingerly at first, we sidle up to others with similar concerns about the status quo. This might lead to a modest change or no change, all the way to the establishment of a new tribe, or even a new country whose inhabitants evolve a new language, in the same way as biology can produce a new species.

All social groups are defined by rules they follow, beliefs about how the world works that they share, a common space and whatever physical structures and technologies they have evolved. Returning to the football analogy a team consists of individuals (both behind the scene and on the pitch) operating within a defined space and governed by a common set of rules, with a clear objective: to get a ball more times over the goal line of their opponents, similarly constituted. Technological innovation (such as performance-enhancing drugs) is discouraged and the only variables that can be manipulated are player fitness and skill, team cohesion, game strategy, money-making and how that money is spent. The wild card, as always, is luck.

In the wider world where, in theory (although not in practice) anything goes, the variables appear limitless although in fact are not so very different from what they are in football. What is different, however, is that decision-making power is competed for more widely. Although the turnover in football managers is hardly a passive activity, it is circumscribed. The difference lies in the fluidity of real-life's rule book where the interpretation of rules becomes part of the game and securing resources the objective.

What constrains decision-making power is the power structure itself (how decisions at all levels are made) and the success of that structure in providing the individuals who make it up with the resources they have come to expect. A well-led, well-trained, well-rewarded, well-fed army will be more effective than one which is less organized, and any individual who controls such an army is likely to possess great power, a fact not lost on Julius Caesar. But without territories to conquer plunder will dry up, opportunities will dwindle and soldiers become flighty. How power is fashioned is contingent on circumstances as the same Julius Caesar discovered when members of the Roman elite took exception to his imperial ways.

All power structures allocate resources and administer sanctions with a view to maintaining themselves and it is entirely reasonable to talk about these things as entities in their own right, but like the depopulated ghost cities mentioned earlier, their force comes from their ability to coordinate and direct individuals. At any given moment in time, the individual members of a power structure have a vested interest in it. Even the slave has a vested interest in avoiding the slave master's whip. He may dream of better times, but his reality is the here and now. Politics, in large measure, is the art of persuading people that things will be better tomorrow if they but hang in there and worse if they don't. For those seeking change, politics is about persuading people otherwise.

* * *

Does this mean that politics is a con game in which one group of rogues tries to outdo another group of rogues in fooling a gullible citizenry? It certainly sometimes seems so. But let's start this line of enquiry on an optimistic note with a happy polity, in which a king sits benignly in his castle, his officials administer justice fairly and efficiently, his nobles run their estates intelligently, the taxes he levies are reasonable and well spent and the populous is usefully employed, well housed and well fed. Such periods have existed (in modern times, the United States in the 1950s came close) but they have never lasted. Why not? Well, let's look at 1950s America. There was the Korean War, the Cold War, the Suez crisis, the Cuban revolution, the McCarthy hearings and the civil rights movement. No period is perfect. But the middle class expanded rapidly, wealth increased greatly, consumer goods proliferated and popular culture flowered with dizzying profusion. For the majority of Americans it was a splendid time to be alive.

Uniquely, human consciousness enables individuals to imagine alternatives. As far as we know, the livestock a good farmer cares for have no inkling that at some point in the future most are destined for the knacker's yard. Were they human they might start to wonder where the transports which took their kind away from time to time were destined. Humans spend a great deal of time thinking about death and have developed elaborate scenarios about what it might entail. Instead of accepting things as they are, consciousness has allowed humans to imagine alternatives, both better and worse. This has fostered analysis, the working out of alternative scenarios and the steps necessary to bring them about.

Analysis need not be rigorous to be effective. The invention of heaven and hell as states beyond death, were powerful mechanisms whereby priestly elites could maintain order. Exercise these behaviours and go to heaven; exercise those and go to hell. People probably saw the merit in acting in socially responsible ways in spite of the temptation to do otherwise, but the imagined reward of heaven (and imagined sanction of hell) helped tie their instinctive emotions – the draw towards the pleasurable and away from the painful, into an evolved social structure with collective functionality which relies upon a certain level of individual loss. Stand in front of any war memorial and you will understand what I mean. In battle, men may die in solidarity with those around them. But the call to war is accepted on account of feelings of honour and in solidarity with an abstract notion called nationhood. Those who did not sign up to fight in the murderous First World War were sometime handed white feathers (a symbol of cowardice) by patriotic females.

That the hard and soft structures which make it possible for a large number of individuals to function as a coherent whole are imbued with subtle (and not so subtle) emotional hooks, is another factor making change difficult. No army could function if every soldier questioned the order he was given. But then again, some of the most effective military leaders have been those able to bend a strategy in an innovative way given the unique circumstances of the situation. The old saw that generals are forever fighting the last battle could be applied to many types of leader.

* * *

In spite of all impediments, change does occur, but how? Before considering how it takes place in the human world, let's look at how change happens in the biological one. What we know of the past suggests that change tends to follow a wave-like pattern. When a type of structure becomes possible and comes into existence it then expresses itself in as many ways as it can. This is a pattern evident in the evolution of all structure. There has been much debate in biology about the speed of these expressions – were they rapid or gradual, and did types narrow over time as circumstances favoured some over others. But a few things are clear enough.

In the earth's early history there was no free oxygen. This only came about as a result of photosynthetic prokaryotes expelling O2 as a waste product over 3.5 billion years ago. However, when oxygen in the earth's atmosphere reached 15-35%, countless other life forms began their evolutionary journey. The Cambrian period (beginning around 540 million years ago) saw a large number of life forms emerge (principally soft-shelled creatures). Dinosaurs ruled the roost for 135 million years (from around 230 million years ago) and when conditions turned against them, mammals came into their own. Homo sapiens has not been around long at all (perhaps 200,000 to 1.8 million years) but in that time we have transformed life on earth, substantially over the last 5,000 years and increasingly so recently.

This suggests several things about change. The first is that it does not occur until it can. The second is that it seems to take place in bursts. These two observations can be reconciled by throwing in the notion of balance. Because structure must hold itself together, evolving structures will tend to butt up against one another until they achieve symbiotic stability. While such interdependent ecosystems are tenacious and resistant to change, they become vulnerable to alterations in external conditions. Like generals, they are products of the last war (the last wave of change) and can collapse rather quickly (as did Tsarist Russia) when conditions (such as people's wellbeing and attitudes) vary substantially. Change begets change.

* * *

There is an expression that the more things change the more they stay the same which has some wisdom in it. Imagine a structure made of loosely fitting bricks, with the position of each brick dependent on the bricks around it and some bricks – the foundation bricks – larger than the others. Now subject the structure to cannon fire. To start with not much seems to happen. A few bricks are dislodged, but the structure seems intact. However, after a time the steady bombardment so weakens it that the ramparts collapse onto the foundations. When Tsarist Russia collapsed, the Tsarist autocracy had lost legitimacy under a bombardment of bad news (military and economic setbacks) and negative propaganda (which recast the obvious point that power emanates from the people into a new religion which upended the concept of divine right).

But Russia's foundations, autocracy itself, did not collapse. Attempts were made (as they were in revolutionary France between 1889 and 1899, and after the overthrow of the Kaiser in Germany in 1919) to construct a parliamentary democracy, but the participants argued incessantly (the bricks could not be made to fit) and their attempt at structure building was overwhelmed by events. Stability only came when the Bolshevik leadership, first under Lenin and then under Stalin, re-energized the autocracy (as Napoleon did in France and Hitler did in Germany). Even in China, probably the world's oldest continuous state, which experienced the collapse of the imperial structure in 1912 and its eventual replacement by the Communist one in 1949 (with an attempt at republicanism in between), what is as striking as the upheavals the Chinese people passed through is the Chinese state's structural continuity.

When a pine forest burns down it is generally a pine forest that replaces it. When an oak forest burns down it is generally an oak forest that replaces it. In part this is because the trees in a forest lay down their genetic character (as seeds) and in part because the conditions which gave rise to the type of forest in the first place may not have changed much. Social structures are no different. Unless the people are eliminated by conflict (as native North Americans largely were) those of them who remain will tend to reach for what sustained them before. So even if what is offered is dressed in fresh clothes, its nature is likely to be the same, something post-revolutionary leaders need to appreciate if they are to succeed. Over and above this, the geography a people inhabit – its scale, its climate, its topography - will all have served to mould their character. Like wind through trees, a poet's words may carry more meaning than we realize.

* * *

Empires wash over peoples and on the surface appear to change everything. But when the tide turns, as it always does, and empires ebb, the character of those once submerged re-emerges. There is a reason for this. Structure forms from the bottom up. Think of the bricks again. What constitutes an 'original brick' is hard to say. Is it the biological unit of mother, father and children or the immediate group they are part of? Communism tried to abolish the family because the architects of that ideology recognized its tenacity and hold over people. Fascism, too, attempted to implant a greater loyalty – loyalty to the führer – above that of the family. Monarchy was also based upon the notion that the monarch was the ultimate father to his people, with fatherhood being part of the natural order and so mandated by God.

The great monotheistic religions attempted to bind often disparate groups of people together within a common framework of rules on the basis that there was only one God (one ultimate father) and that His writ was absolute, not relative. In both Christianity and Islam the role of the earthly father is given prominence as head of the primary building block of social life, casting mother as the indispensable soft centre and father as the essential hard carapace. With the emergence of rationalism and its offspring liberalism, attempts have been made to replace God with a set of ideas. But this is running into a problem.

Having raised rationalism and its instrument science to a great height – both Marxism and liberalism assume the scientifically inevitable outcomes of the processes they favour – it is dawning on people that science is no more (and no less) than a way of interrogating the universe we find ourselves in, and that it has absolutely nothing to say about how we should use that knowledge. Value creation is down to us. But when values conflict, whose and which do we follow? Once again we find ourselves in need of the certainties Moses brought down from Mount Sinai on God's tablets of stone. And once again we are tossed into questions of identity. Are we exclusively Jewish or more widely Christian and if not these, followers of Islam or some other faith? And if those points of reference appear inadequate, are we German, Chinese, American or citizens of the world and if the latter, who should promulgate and enforce the rules we follow and pass judgement on disputes?

* * *

In the history of the human world the United States is unusual. The people who populated it came predominantly from Europe in the first instance and the indigenous population of North America was insufficiently large or strong to influence the structures Europeans brought with them and subsequently developed. As a social entity it emerged out of ideas rather than organically out of its history. There was little existing structure, only ideas about what its structure should be and why. Certainly these ideas emanated from the experience of European individuals, both through writing and felt directly, but with the exception of black Americans locked inside an institution called slavery, they were remarkably unencumbered.

The principles which predominated and produced the structure that came to characterize the United States were essentially of four main types. They were Protestant in the sense of religion being focused on the individual; legal in the sense of placing a body of law above familial, religious or political obligations; commercial in recognizing that economic wealth was the product of contractual exchange; and republican in the sense that government was to be an instrument of the people, not of elites. It took a war of independence for the new state to break free from the British Empire. It took a civil war to overthrow the institution of slavery. A constitution was drafted detailing the relationship between the law courts, the legislature, the executive and the states which made up the union. This has been amended twenty-seven times as issues have arisen. And while human turpitude has not been abolished, over 300 million disparate individuals live reasonably constructively under its umbrella and as a polity it has amassed substantial wealth and projected great power.

It would be nice to think that when a happy state is achieved – or even a reasonably happy state - things could be frozen save for a little tinkering round the edges to make everything better still. But that is not how it works. One of the few certainties about the universe we live in is that change is ubiquitous. This is because of what I call *the space between*. Essentially structure forms locally against an unfolding background and although it aspires to stability, interactions are stretched by this unfolding, quite literally, to breaking point. This then prompts a rearrangement and it is the space between structures which allows this creative process to occur. As to what will be created, all one can say is that it must build upon what remains of prior structures, so the possibility of a progression exists although not the attainment of permanent stability. Eden was always an illusion.

As the United States is finding, the movement towards an ideal is more rewarding than the realization it may have been, in part at least, a mirage. It is not that achievements were lacking. Ancient Egypt, the Roman Empire, Imperial China, the British Empire were all, like the United States, remarkable political achievements, but what made them work was not just internal (that is of their own making) but contingent upon the environment they occupied. The fertility the River Nile offered within a region bathed in sunlight and surrounded by desert, justified the Egyptians' reverence for their gods. The Mediterranean Sea gave Roman military organization leverage neither the Greeks nor Phoenicians had chosen to use for much more than trade. Imperial China was the product of a centralized, largely meritocratic bureaucracy and three great rivers, the Yellow and Yangtze (joined by the one thousand mile long Grand Canal, completed under the Sui dynasty in 581-618CE) and the Xi River to the south. Britain's island status allowed her not only to develop politically and economically without repeated invasion, but spurred on what was for a time her unbeatable maritime and financial expertise, both a consequence of trade.

The success of a political structure depends upon its ability to gather resources and direct them towards the sustenance of its people and benefit of its elites. This generates a reinforcing momentum and a belief in the efficacy of the polity's social arrangements. Success does indeed breed success. But when the members of a polity start to worship form over substance, the polity's ability to adapt to shifts in its environment (difficult in any event) is compromised. When the earth changed 66 million years ago, dinosaurs could do no more than stick to being dinosaurs and what had worked superbly for 135 million years worked no more (although it seems a few did manage to develop feathers and survive as birds into the present day).

* * *

The one thing my rugby football analogy did not address head on, and which in many respects is the hardest notion to describe, is power. Perhaps this is because it is ubiquitous and something we feel we understand. Genghis Khan possessed power, as did Ivan the Terrible, Hitler, Stalin and Mao Zedong. The United States is a powerful nation. These are things we just know. At one level, power is a simple concept: it is about the ability to act, the ability to exert influence, the ability to resist influence, the ability to control an environment. Our sun is powerful. It dominates our solar system. It would not be affected by the loss of any of its planets. It could be impacted by the largest comet or asteroid we know of without effect. And yet there are larger suns in the universe and one day its energy will have been consumed unless the black hole at the centre of our galaxy gobbles it up first. At a more parochial level, it is powerless to prevent mankind's probes from leaving its embrace.

It is not that power is absent from football – some clubs are more powerful than others (that is to say they can attract the best managers, players, crowds and sponsors – all of which are mutually reinforcing), only that it must express itself within mutually agreed constraints. But this is true of power generally save only that in place of agreement are the limitations of physical matter. One of the reasons we enjoy magic so much (and stories about beings with super-natural powers) is to imagine ourselves breaking free from these limitations. And indeed, individuals are enormously more empowered than they have ever been.

We can fly around the world in hours (well ahead of the now pedestrian 80 days of Jules Verne's 1869 imaginings) and travel to almost anywhere we want to within a couple of days. We have greatly extended the human life span. Children can be as much a function of choice as of biology. Millions of us have never known hunger and live in homes few could have imagined even a hundred years ago. We can talk to one another over long distances and share images of the world which have become a reality in their own right. We have, in short, gradually bent our environment to our will. If this isn't power, I don't know what is. But......

And isn't there always a 'but'. The 'but' is that power is a residual, which is why it is often so hard to pin down. It is like those things that loom large in the early hours only to have dissipated by daybreak. Take the human situation as I have described it above (and as it is in the 'developed' world, at least). Now compare it to an ant colony. Both exist successfully, utilizing their environment to their best advantage. We would not, intuitively, describe an ant colony as powerful. Does the fact that human individuals are empowered in the way I have outlined make them more powerful than an individual ant? One would certainly think so. But if humanity experienced a nuclear (or other) calamity of its own making and, like the dinosaurs, became extinct while leaving the ants untouched, which then – ants or humans - would you say was the more powerful? And that is the point about power. It is a means to an end, not an end in itself. It is a residual: that which enables a structure to function as it does.

So when we consider change we have to consider how power flows through the structure subject to change. What is perhaps unique about human systems is their loose-tight properties which facilitate adaptation. Individual consciousness enables individuals to stand outside the systems they are part of, at least to some degree. So while an army can work in a mechanistic way (like an ant colony), military failure will undermine its legitimacy in the eyes of its participants, making them more open to other structural arrangements, such as altered leadership extending even to an acceptance of the victor and the victor's systems. So while the evolved mechanisms of the ant colony may be more unbending and so enduring, those of humans are more adaptable turning an apparent mechanical weakness into an organic strength.

What we think of as power – the ability to direct a social structure made up of conscious individuals – entails at best an acceptance of the efficaciousness of a given set of social arrangements (with its hierarchy of order-givers and -takers) and at worst the inevitability of such arrangements (as is the case with the ant colony in which no other way is known). Consciousness allows human systems to learn from experience as individuals in key positions contemplate the outcomes of their actions and the actions of those with whom they are associated. Ambition might prompt some to call for a change of leadership, i.e. placing the power of the system into fresh hands.

This may be disruptive enough, but when individuals start to think that the system they are part of might itself need to be changed, that threatens to be more disruptive still. This dichotomy – the tension between the reassurance of the established order (with all its vested interests at every level of its hierarchy) and realization that the established order may no longer be working in the majority's best interests – defines the problem of change.

8

Politics

POLITICS and consciousness are intimately connected. Indeed, without the latter the former would not exist. Its antecedents, however, can be traced to awareness and volition. Animals often seek to influence one another. Two cock pheasants will duck and weave like boxers in order to establish which will hold a particular piece of territory and perhaps attract a mate into it if a hen deems the real estate attractive. The male Bird of Paradise will put on a magnificent display to attract a female although what exactly persuades a lady to go to one gentleman rather than another is not obvious.

But what we can assume is that the need to entwine two separate individuals (such as a male and a female) in the social process of procreation requires one to seek to influence the other and the other to respond, and because choice is on offer, that the selection is supportive of those characteristics which have ensured the survival of the species to date, although with just enough latitude to at least allow for the possibility of some variation which turns out to be useful.

In human society politics is the process whereby conscious individuals are woven together into a functioning whole and it starts early in life. Watch children negotiate with parents and each other and you are observing politics. It is unfortunate that we have come to think of politics as a discreet activity associated with government because it gives 'politicians' and those associated with them an inflated view of themselves. More importantly, it gives us a distorted understanding of what politics is. Let us start with children and try to break open the process.

In order to influence what happens to them, the first thing a child must do is get attention. Making a noise is its first line of attack. There then follows the start of what will be a long interaction between parent and child during which both seek to influence the other. Sociologists call this socialization – integrating the child into the social mores of the group he or she is to be part of. Naturally this entails introducing the child to a whole range of seemingly fixed relationships – if this, then that; this good, that bad; etc. Very quickly the child will come to realize that these relationships are not quite so fixed and that compliance can be negotiated.

This then raises the possibility of tangential relationships: if you do A, I will give you B. If a child beams and stops crying when it is picked up it is more likely to be picked up. Parents habitually bribe children with the offer of pleasant things in order to get them to do things they might not naturally be willing to do. Punishment might also be used to make certain acts less appealing. Sibling rivalry for affection, attention or desirable outcomes is standard amongst children and quite often they interact solely for the pleasure interaction itself brings. Boys will push and shove one another without any particular malice, simply to express themselves physically and see what outcomes follow certain actions. Girls seem to spend a great deal of time nurturing, discussing, trying out and being disappointed with or pleased with relationships.

The politics of the home, playground and school embody every facet of the political process. The use of 'triggers', 'bribes' and 'cabal building' are techniques worked out before a child reaches double figures. The trigger is that which gets a reaction: a cry from the child, a cry to 'soak the rich' or some such from the professional politician. Bribes seem to be ubiquitous in politics with parents and children at it from the word go and seasoned politicians brazenly bribing voters with the voters' own money (or better still, with that of their children or grandchildren). Cabal building, too, is as old as the hills. Children routinely say their younger siblings 'need' this or that as a way of lending weight to their own objectives. People with similar interests banding together to secure what they want has come to define the structure of democracies, although the formality of party politics may now be draining it of its spontaneity.

And of course politics is not confined to the world of children and elected representatives but operates within every single part of a polity's social structure. All organizations are formed around some objective and operate within the legal fabric which defines a polity's structural relationships. Even individuals are categorized by class with classes subject to particular legal constraints. The individual who breaks the law, for example, is classed as a criminal; individuals below a certain age are classed as minors; those who do not see the world as most see it are classed as insane and not responsible for their actions. Underlying each of these is an assumption that some actions are acceptable and others not, and that, crucially, individuals are responsible for determining which is which.

There is, of course, a delicious ambiguity in this. On the one hand how one person or organization should act upon another person or organization is deemed to be clear cut, and on the other hand individuals are held to be responsible for differentiating between 'good' actions and 'bad'. When individual ants in an ant colony go about their business they operate mechanically, save that each ant enjoys independent locomotion thereby increasing the colony's ability to find and gather food and surmount obstacles. Humans have even more scope than independent locomotion affords. They can create whole new social structures.

The drug cartels which operate within the Brazilian favelas (urban slums) operate outside the law and yet they clearly serve a need which the official social structure does not (at the very least they give young men something to do and provide them with a way to make a living). The friction between the 'legal' and 'illegal' structures is political enabling the structure as a whole to function. The prohibition in the USA against the 'production, importation, transportation and sale of alcoholic beverages' between 1920 and 1933 was a political triumph for the moralists who sponsored the legislation and gift to the criminals who met the needs of all those who regarded the legislation with contempt. As much as moralists might like it to be otherwise, life is not black and white but rich in colour and subtle distinctions. It is hardly an exaggeration to say that a fair portion of the money spent in the bawdy houses established near places of pilgrimage in the Middle Ages found its way into the coffers of the Church.

Without ambiguity there would be no politics. But before the professional politician of today congratulates herself or himself for being as slippery as an eel, we need to look closely at what lies behind this ambiguity. Putting the humane to one side, a social structure – like any biological structure – can take on whatever form works. The Roman Empire, structurally enlightened in many ways, could not have functioned without slavery or without brutally suppressing any challenge to Roman authority, something underscored by its macabre (and popular) 'games'. Human sacrifice appears to have been common amongst early Latin American cultures (Inca, Aztec, etc.) empowering the rulers and priesthoods as intercessionaries between the people and the gods. The guillotine became a symbol of the French Revolution, emphasizing the new regime's hold over even royal life and its efficiency in dispatching it. In the United States 'Old Sparky' (the electric chair) is still a powerful symbol of state power and some 1,400 have been executed since 1976 (most, more recently by lethal injection). One survey found 41% of those placed on death row were African Americans who make up only 12.6% of the general population and this reflects America's racial politics. Social structure does come in all shapes and sizes.

The distinctive feature of human evolution is the speed with which human societies can learn and adapt. That they can is thanks to the loose-tight properties which allow individuals to probe for improved arrangements, while still managing to tie those same individuals into a functioning whole most of the time. This is a trial and error process which requires a great deal of redundancy manifest, up to now, in the loss of life which has accompanied competition between polities. In the final analysis, politics is the process whereby individuals communicate about the relationships they have with one another and the world around them. If things are going well, the tone of this communication is confirmatory: if things are not going well it becomes critical, creating space for a revision to these relationships. Because of the structural primacy of the individual, this is a bottom-up process and only top-down in terms of facilitation. There is no utopia out there, only today and only a journey.

* * *

A distinction needs to be drawn between politics and government. It is fully recognized that politics, as the business of influencing choices, exists in one form or another within all organizations. However, organizations are functional entities first and foremost, designed to achieve specific ends, and government is – or should be - no different. In the United Kingdom there are 24 ministerial departments, 22 non-ministerial departments, 371 agencies and other public bodies, all with some 3 million employees (there are an additional 2.3 million public employees at local government level). It is a minor miracle that a bureaucracy this large and this complex functions at all and to think that those elected to govern actually run it is absurd. It is small wonder that the public feels increasingly alienated from its government.

And there is a further problem. On paper, a member of parliament is supposed to represent the interests of his or her constituents (between 56,000 and 73,000 people). In practice, however, the job of an MP is to get re-elected and to serve the party he belongs to as either the government or the opposition in parliament. Political parties create and sustain their identities by coalescing around one or two key ideas. Focus groups (carefully selected members of the electorate against which these core ideas are tested) are used to tailor these ideas into whatever form seems to have the widest appeal. By the time any of this makes it into legislation, the specific problems concerning constituents – or as is more likely, a subset of constituents – have long been lost sight of. As things are now, MPs have come to represent parties not people.

In comparison with the organs of government, corporations (even large ones) are models of transparency. Financial analysts comb through their financial statements, hedge funds search the context they operate within for clues to suggest things might be better or worse than the market perceives, while regulatory bodies occasionally swoop on some aspect of their activity which is held to be illegal. And all this in addition to the cut and thrust of the market place in which competitors attempt to win over one another's customers. This dynamic exerts great pressure on the corporate sector to adapt, often by spawning new companies with new approaches to meeting customers' needs.

Now consider the organs of government. To call their workings opaque is an understatement. Ever since the political sociologist, Max Weber, argued that government bureaucracy should be meritocratic and isolated from political influence (in contrast to the old system of patronage), it has almost been an article of faith that the machinery of government should not be exposed to public scrutiny. Weber's working assumption was that meritorious performance was an objective reality separate from context. There is no doubting that professional administrators (those trained in the discipline of administration) were a distinct advance on the often haphazard arrangement that existed when departments of government were handed out as personal sinecures. However in shielding the bureaucracy from political oversight, Weber threw up a barrier between governors (at least those who actually run government) and governed.

When we talk about the democratically elected government we are talking about no such thing. What we are actually talking about is the hierarchy of the party which secured the most votes at a general election. This hierarchy (in Britain at least) gets to appoint its members to various government departments as ministers (or secretaries of state), the idea being that these ministers then become the public face of the departments. But to imagine that they run these departments is fanciful. A remarkably popular television series in the 1980s was *Yes Minister* which depicted an often hapless minister with "ideas" being skilfully outmanoeuvred by his permanent secretary (the bureaucratic head of the department) so that the business of the department could continue as the bureaucracy had concluded was best.

A minister is somewhat akin to a merchant on board a sixteenth century sailing ship, which his colleagues back home are financing, telling the captain that he should head for Tidore rather than Ternate (spice islands in the East Indies). For the merchant to tell the sea captain how to sail his ship would be lunacy (although some occasionally tried). The policy governing the voyage – to bring spices back to the European markets and make a fortune, for example – would often be rather general and subject to review in the light of experience. So when a British prime minister announces to parliament (or has the monarch – as nominal head of state - announce for him) that his government intends to introduce greater choice into publicly-funded education, for example, he is expressing a rather vague objective – one of several such vague objectives his party will have espoused in the run-up to the election.

To imagine that this policy expresses the settled will of the electorate is moonshine. At best it expresses a hazy feeling that public education could do with a bit of a shake-up; at worst it expresses the ideological view of the party elite who have secured the most votes for a variety of reasons wholly unrelated to education. What it isn't is a well-thought-through plan with objective measures to gauge its success. The educational bureaucracy, in this example, finds itself managing its primary responsibility (in a manner which has evolved over time) while being charged to make changes largely on the hoof (and frequently with no additional resources).

Another feature of the present system is that whenever an event occurs that generates public concern – "this must not be allowed to happen again," the political machine simply loads the bureaucracy with the responsibility of ensuring that it does not, without ensuring that the bureaucracy has the means to comply. Glaring examples of this have cropped up in the area of child protection. Several children have died at the hands of their 'parents' and social services have been castigated for not having prevented it. Signs of abuse are far clearer ex post than they are ex ante, and social services know they will engender howls of protest if they remove children from parents having misread the signs. And in any event, finding good foster parents for children is not easy.

There exists an in-built tension within the bureaucracy between the treasury and all other departments. The treasury allocates the money to the departments without which they cannot function. An added layer of tension exists between the treasury and the taxpaying electorate whose taxes enable the treasury to function. All this is augmented by the fact that politicians are incented to promise their electors low taxes and superlative departmental performance. In the private sector, money flows to those organizations able to attract the most profitable sales. This encourages a gradual shift towards the currently most effective organizations. In the public sector money flows to departments on the basis of their existing size and what the treasury can get away with. This encourages a degree of stasis with a bias towards over-manning and underfunding.

* * *

As there will always be many functions in a polity which do not lend themselves to the approach utilized by free market capitalism the questions become what should these functions be, how should they be organized and funded, and how should their performance be monitored?

A good place to start is to model the way society works as it is. Obviously this is known, because it exists and so merely needs to be made explicit. The number of parliamentarians who have a clear idea of how their society works is probably embarrassingly small; the numbers in the general population who do will be close to zero. And we are not talking about an overly complicated model, just primary functions, how they are funded and where the funding comes from. The fact that this has never seriously been attempted exposes the shallowness of our representative democracy as it stands. The cri de coeur across the ages: *no taxation without representation* remains true and largely unfulfilled. Ignorant parliamentarians allied to even more ignorant electors is ultimately a recipe for failure.

Max Weber was only partly right to argue that the modern state needed a professional bureaucracy to run it rather than one over which vested interests exercised control, because administration is not an end in itself. The key question is whose interests does the bureaucracy exist to serve? There is no reason why the functions of the state should be isolated from public scrutiny, save a desire by those undertaking these functions for minimal exposure. Scrutiny by easily bamboozled ministers with party political loyalties is simply a smoke screen. The electors pay the bills, not the Treasury, nor government ministers, and it is to electors that the functions of government should be directly accountable. More information is made available to the shareholders of corporations than is ever made available to those who underwrite government departments.

* * *

In recent times the mechanics of a coup d'état entailed controlling the streets and controlling the media. If successful, the elimination of all opposition followed. As the life blood of conscious systems is communication, the medium through which communication takes place is central to the political process. Just as Johannes Gutenberg's printing press (1439) broke the Catholic Church's monopoly over religious information, so the internet of today has empowered individuals at the expense of mainstream media companies. In both the United States and Europe, the established order is being upset by this development. The companies that control the internet platforms are now being told by the authorities that they have a responsibility to police the content put out by individuals. *My heavens,* guardians of the status quo have cried out, we can't have people concocting the facts – that's our job!

The mainstream media, like the political parties, hold themselves out as necessary gatekeepers to ensure that what is made available to the public meets a certain standard – be that in relation to a news story or to a political candidate. Doubtless the Roman Catholic Church felt exactly the same in the sixteenth century as a succession of humanist tracts circulated across Europe and the leaders of a fresh approach to Christian worship struggled to assert themselves. However, just as back then aspects of Catholic orthodoxy appeared suspect and elements of the Church hierarchy seemed venal, so today there is a growing feeling that the established order has become self-serving and lost touch with the people it is supposed to look after.

* * *

Authoritarian regimes clamp down on extraneous communication which is considered critical of the status quo and with good reason: just as banks are vulnerable to any rumour of a 'run' so governments depend upon being considered legitimate. In Mein Kampf (1925) its author wrote: *The most brilliant propagandist technique will yield no success unless one fundamental principle is borne in mind constantly and with unflagging attention. It must confine itself to a few points and repeat them over and over. Here, as so often in this world, persistence is the first and most important requirement for success* which became popularized in the aphorism that if you repeat a lie often enough, people will believe it, and you will even come to believe it yourself.

All conscious systems run the risk of falling into this mode; of preferring blind certainty to adaptive curiosity and for a time, even a very long time (as it was for the Roman Catholic Church although not for the *Third Reich*) it may work. The world's tectonic plates appear to be shifting. With the relative power of America waning, post World War II liberalism, together with the globalization it underwrote (underpinned by the power of the United States), is losing its momentum calling old certainties into question. This is unsettling, causing people to start looking inward, a trend likely to continue until our political structures have caught up with reality

This introspection may be an illusion however. Global communication is richer, faster and more far-reaching than it has ever been. Whether we have to pass through a cathartic hell first – a draining of the swamp, to quote one contemporary politician – before reaping its rewards remains to be seen. The status quo came to believe in its own propaganda that all was well, when beneath the surface it was not. To reconnect individuals with their government our democratic systems need a fundamental overhaul. We will likely regret letting populism do the job.

9

Dear Mr Walsh

I include the following for a little light relief, although not just for that (or for the pleasure of doing so), but because we need to remind ourselves that human organizations are complex things and that running them is far from easy. The International Airlines Group (IAG) employs over 60,000 people, has revenues of around £18.27 billion and generated a profit of some £1 billion in 2015 serving over 88,000 customers. Headquartered in Madrid, but with its operating headquarters in London, it owns Aer Lingus and Iberia as well as British Airways and is largely the creation of its CEO Willie Walsh.

An Irishman, who became a pilot for Aer Lingus aged seventeen, Walsh is a tough no-nonsense CEO who has had to deal with everything the airline industry has thrown at him. His is the real world of getting things done and IAG is a success. I doubt that he would ever make it (or want to make it) as a politician. I never did get a reply to my letter!

Mr. William Walsh
International Airlines Group
2 World Business Centre Heathrow
Newall Road
London Heathrow Airport
HOUNSLOW
TW6 2SF

Sunday 21ˢᵗ February, 2016

Ref: 16002

Dear Mr. Walsh,

BA1449 – 15/02/2016:

I recently had cause to fly on one of your airlines (the cause being that you have successfully eliminated all competition on the EDI-LHR route).

My wife was carrying four items of carry-on baggage: one regulation size case for the overhead locker, one soft fabric bag, one ladies' handbag and one small paper bag containing flowers. At the desk before the sky bridge she was denied entry even though her handbag would have fitted comfortably inside her soft fabric bag and both would have fitted into the small carry-on baggage metal template - along with the flowers although doing so would likely have squashed them. The fabric bag, handbag and flowers would have fitted comfortably under the seat in front of her (which in fact they eventually did).

The flight was full. Priority boarding had been called forward, which seems to have encompassed a large number of people so that the logical process of filling from the back (especially necessary when there is only a front entrance) was thwarted. The manager on duty was taking no prisoners – rules were rules and to be applied. My wife was not to be allowed through and the crush of people trying to board meant that she was not given an opportunity to try her luck with the metal template. At that point I am afraid I blew a fuse.

The manager and I had a right go at each other and while I was bent double at the entrance of the sky bridge stuffing my own handbag into my regulation size carry-on bag with the manager standing over me (both of us by now fuming), my wife walked calmly onto the plane, where she comfortably tucked the fabric bag, the handbag and the flowers under the seat in front of her. She did struggle to lift her regulation size case up into the overhead locker as she has recently had a hip replacement and I was not there to help her. I would like to claim that I was engaged in a clever diversionary tactic but I wasn't. With other passengers filing past muttering support, I was just absolutely furious!

On arrival at LHR there was no one to work the sky bridge because, our captain told us, Terminal 5 had not been notified of our arrival. We were assured however, that he "would be filing a report." Ah, I thought, this airline is just a bureaucracy with an identity crisis - no frills and privilege - making it a clumsy behemoth.

Your countryman Michael O'Leary (who I much admire and whose airline I have used for over a decade – it does what it says on the tin) was recently reported as saying that his airline needed to "stop unnecessarily pissing people off." I rest my case!

Yours sincerely,

Robert Mercer-Nairne

PS. For your convenience I attach a reply to this letter.

Dear Mr R. Nairne,

Complaint # 1011106:

We are sorry that you did not feel we came up to our normal high standard of customer service on BA1449 – 15/02/2016.

You will appreciate that customer safety is our first priority. This dictates our cabin bag policy which our staff have been instructed to uphold to the letter. We were disappointed that you took issue with a member of the British Airways team in this regard.

With regard to Priority Boarding, it is our aim at British Airways to reward our loyal customers with certain privileges. Naturally part of privilege is being able to enjoy watching those we do not regard as 'loyal customers' struggle to the back of the plane.

As for the delay in getting the sky bridge to the plane on arrival we have looked into this and concluded that the wait was minimal, but as a gesture we have added 10 Avios to your frequent flyer number 7XY22114.

Yours faithfully,

J Prendergast
(Complaints administrator, Hounslow)

10

Cocktail party chatter

MOST of what appears in the media is little more than cocktail party chatter – the expression of opinions for effect. This makes the political posturing we are subjected to, day in day out, equally vacuous. In 2016 I often watched the Channel 4 news in which the redoubtable Jon Snow and his team (Krishnan Guru-Murthy, Cathy Newman, and others) hammered away at such topics as the Syrian refugee crisis and Syrian civil war with all the moral assurance of those who know the answers.

It amazes me how many politicians agree to be interviewed like moths to a flame, in the certain knowledge that their hackneyed, self-serving prescriptions will be frazzled under the withering glare of C4's ethical superiors. But of course the C4 news team is being no less self-serving. Its aim is to share its viewers' imagined indignity as yet another drowned infant is shown washed up on a Greek beach or eviscerated child on a stretcher in Aleppo is displayed on our television screen. 'Arise Sir Jon' or even Saint Jon cannot be far away. Populism comes in all shapes and sizes.

To be fair, reports from the field by the remarkable Lindsey Hilsum, or Alex Thomson on a good day, do try to describe the complexities behind the burned-out buildings, body bags and squalid refugee camps, but the programmers clearly feel that too much contextual analysis would be bad for ratings. Matt Frei's gentlemanly politeness comes as a welcome relief after Jon and Krishnan's impersonations of the German Rottweiler, while the lovely Helia Ebrahimi makes even the most arcane twitch of the business cycle appear alluring. One can just imagine the programme controllers calling for a little more subliminal sexuality here and a little more fecund kindness there to show that the C4 team is made up of decent people – just like you and me.

The most delightfully comical moments come when Jon and Krishnan interview some monosyllabic rapper or cutting edge artist, whose art they do their unsuccessful best to understand, with all the unctuous reverence of pilgrims kneeling before the Holy Grail. Where is Geoffrey Chaucer when you need him? By the time you get to the weather, Liam Dutton's extraordinary ability to describe one day's weather in four different ways within the space of a minute, without actually telling you something you didn't already know, leaves you gasping for air – and for a rerun of Dad's Army.

My favourite, though, is Kylie Morris, who always seems to be looking happy and slightly windswept as she reports on one Washington blooper after another – well who wouldn't be happy with a ringside seat to such a rich comedy of errors (which are not our own for a change). Having said that, C4's symbol of religious tolerance, the elegant Fatima Manji in her impeccable headscarf, does bring me close to conversion, or at least would if I could only remember what I would be converting from.

The C4 team appears to include some pretty decent, able and interesting people, just the sort it would be fun to mix with at a cocktail party. But if there are numerous cocktail parties on the go, all competing for our presence (because numbers signify success) you will tend to pick the most entertaining, the one most reflective of your own prejudices and which fits most easily into your daily schedule. So sooner or later, the chatter you will expose yourself to and be part of will be the chatter inside your own head.

In fact most of politics is the same sort of chatter, not least because politics is played through the media and the media are the chatterboxes. Today these are augmented by the *Twitterati* who use platforms created by the internet to express and share opinions. But does all this sound and fury have any bearing upon what happens in the world? Indeed, do a handful of individuals who happen to belong to a political party which happens to have secured the most votes during a five-yearly electoral jamboree actually run a country of 66 million?

Well of course they don't but it flatters us and them to think that they do. Cocktail party chatter is about our reaction to reality, not about reality itself. Even when those we don't like have been elected, we can engage in that delightful pastime of *I told you so* when things go wrong. Now does this mean that the individuals in government do not affect our lives? Sadly it means no such thing. The formal part of what we call government is a mighty blunt instrument at best.

Imagine yourself at one of these cocktail parties at which the burning issue is whether you should turn left or right when you leave the building. You listen to and participate in this vital discussion while draining down champagne or draught depending on your social status. Eventually, charged up with a sort of confused certainty, you leave the building and head either left or right with only the vaguest notion where the direction you have chosen will lead. Somewhere along the way you are tapped on the shoulder, bundled into an unmarked car and taken to a large building with many rooms where people are sitting at computer screens working: on what, you have no idea. Still dazed you wait in an anteroom until someone who looks rather like you comes in and congratulates you at becoming Home Secretary of the United Kingdom of Great Britain and Northern

Ireland.

Naturally you have thought about all manner of things over the previous weeks and months and read countless articles and position papers about the merits and implications of going left or right and watched any number of programmes on the subject. Once you were even interviewed by C4 on the civil war in Syria, a subject you knew even less about than the person who interviewed you, but a visit to Damascus as a student twenty years before had prompted your party to push you forward. At the end you had been hit by a 'surprise question': would you enter a coalition? Having no idea how a person should turn both left and right you flannelled, you ducked and you weaved in your answer for what felt like eternity until the interviewer ran out of time. Thank god, you thought, for programme scheduling.

After three years you were beginning to understand how the Home Office with its 28 agencies and public bodies from the *Gangmasters Licensing Authority* to the *National Counter-Terrorism Security Office* actually worked. Regrettably, however, you had failed to find a way to reduce immigration, a subject of mounting cocktail party chatter. A summons to the Prime Minister's office and the suggestion that you become Secretary of State for Northern Ireland would have drawn a line under your ministerial career had you not decided to take a shot at the top job. To your surprise you were elected as the candidate everyone else disliked least.

On leaving the Home Office you feel a need to reconnect with your political roots before embarking on the next challenge. Left and right have become a bit blurred you tell the doorman, Reginald, who it is clear knows as much about the workings of government as anyone. "Wanting to retrace your steps, eh" he says, "and start again?" "Something like that," you answer. Reginald shakes his head. "Won't do you much good," he elaborates. "Starting out everyone thinks left or right makes the difference, but it doesn't. Either way ends up here."

For a moment you feel you have glimpsed wisdom as through a glass darkly – Corinthians has always appealed to you, but as you turn towards Downing Street and Reginald's words drift off into the ether, you begin to dream about changing the world – and the possibility of a peerage.

11

In praise of populism

POPULISM is a dirty word in some quarters. Now why is that? Saul of Tarsus, Maximilien Robespierre, Thomas Paine, Vladimir Ilyich Lenin, Benito Mussolini, Adolph Hitler, Mao Zedong, Nigel Farage and Donald Trump (to name but a few) have all stirred up popular disquiet against establishments. Unless one is willing to accord these men supernatural powers, might it be that they were on to something?

In spite of having everything including the kitchen sink thrown at them by the great and the good across the globe, a majority of English voters chose to ignore their warnings and advice. The political commentator, William Woodard Self – that master of anti-establishment establishmentarianism - castigated the unwashed for having voted with their hearts and not their heads. What a terrible sin. Was it the communist party, or the fascists, or the Catholic Church, I forget, who tried to remove children from families for fear that familial love would corrupt political orthodoxy?

Remain lost the vote because predominantly older people in the north of England saw the communities they had grown up in change before their eyes. To them it did not seem fair that the young from Eastern Europe should enjoy the fruits that English men and women had worked for. The free movement of people from the impoverished East to the prosperous West was foisted on English communities by the European Union ideologues without so much as a by-your-leave. Instead of listening, the great and the good called the traditional inhabitants of these communities racist, sprinkling salt into their wound.

Why is it that economists, the leaders of large corporations and international bureaucrats so often praise globalization on the grounds that it will bring a shiny future and ignore the fact that for many it brings a shoddy present? Could it be because they are isolated from globalization's dark side? Well, the great and the good should not be surprised that when people are given the chance to express their frustrations they do so.

It is surely a little rich for those who profess a love of democracy to decry populism. If the great and the good had been doing their jobs properly and looking after the people who pay their salaries, we wouldn't be in the pickle we are. A little self-criticism would not be out of place right now, but history suggests that whenever the orthodoxy of the great and the good is challenged, the great and the good dig the hole they are in with increased vigour. It is not populism that deserves the dirty name.

12

Anarchy

W H E N William Butler Yeats wrote his now famous lines *Things fall apart; the centre cannot hold - Mere anarchy is loosed upon the world* he was drawing on the Hindu idea of a long cycle during which order ascends until its collapse and the creation of a new set of arrangements begins. When he wrote these lines in 1921 Europe had just undergone the First World War. The traditional hierarchy seemed to be disintegrating and Christianity with it. The Russian Tsar, his wife and five children had been murdered by the Bolsheviks, an echo of France's earlier pogrom against members of the ancient regime. Europe's great expansion had turned inward upon itself and power was shifting across the Atlantic to the United States. Economic collapse was lurking round the corner and the bovver boys of Fascism and Communism were just itching to claim the carcass.

But what exactly is the process that gives rise to anarchy? The social economist Mancur Olson (1932-1998) developed a set of ideas around how individuals within groups were incented to work. He suggested that over time a polity's wealth would be absorbed by the groups closest to the top of its hierarchy even after the contribution of those groups to the wellbeing of the polity overall had diminished. Because the gains were concentrated and costs distributed widely, individuals at large would barely notice until economic and social decay had set in bringing anarchy in their wake, anarchy being a state in which individuals are only incented 'to steal and destroy' not work cooperatively. In an equilibrium state, however, economic and social decay would not be a preordained outcome as all the members in the various components of the hierarchy would have an incentive to keep it going. So some other factor has to be in play.

Protestantism emerged in 1517 as a protest against the practices of the established order, but why then? Church practices were not new. The French Revolution took place only sixty-four years after the glittering reign of Louis XIV came to its close. Did economic and social decay set in across France that quickly? Or in both cases had decay been underway for a long time and only come to a head in the 16th and 18th centuries respectively? Olson uses the analogy of a frog in water slowly being brought to the boil not noticing its precipitous situation until just before its demise. And this gives us a clue as to the nature of the other factor at play which upsets an essentially self-sustaining situation. Social equilibriums are not upset internally but externally.

The age of the dinosaurs lasted for around 135 million years. What one means by this is that over that period a biological ecosystem existed in which dinosaurs were the dominant terrestrial vertebrate. Like 16th century French aristocrats or 14th century abbots they lived at the top of the food chain. Many sea creatures, plants and other types of animals existed alongside them in a symbiotic relationship which you could characterize as self-sustaining exploitation. Just as Triceratops horridus and Pinacosaurus grangeri were part of the Jurassic-Cretaceous landscape, so the Dukes of Burgundy (dating from the 9th century) or Abbots of St Mary's, York (dating from the 11th century) were part of the rich tapestry of mediaeval life. To suggest that they should not have existed or that the hierarchy they were part of was flawed is meaningless. What one can say is that their time passed.

In the biological world, species evolve by random variation to fill whatever space sustains them. After an extinction event (there have been many) surviving life forms battle it out in an anarchic fashion until a new hierarchical ecosystem is created and a degree of stability returns. The ability of life to adapt in this way to external trauma has been its saving grace. Consciousness has imbued life (increasingly so in humans) with something new: the ability to adapt social arrangements rather than body parts in order to secure some perceived advantage. Up to now, however, the mechanics of this process have been messy.

The Roman world was held together by Rome's military power. This superstructure supported Roman law, Rome's trading network, Rome's culture and it facilitated the dissemination of Roman knowledge (much of it gathered in from different parts of the empire). Western Europe's older Celtic culture was subsumed within it. By 285CE, however, the empire was coming under sustained attack from beyond its borders by Jutes, Angles, Saxons, Franks, Goths, Visigoths, Ostrogoths, Huns and Vandals. Recognizing the empire's administrative overreach, Emperor Diocletian began the process of splitting it into West and East (centred on Constantinople) but by 476 the game in the West was up. The empire in the East held together until 1453 when the 21-year-old Ottoman sultan, Mehmed II, finally captured Constantinople.

Under Emperor Constantine (306-337CE) Christianity had emerged as the Empire's dominant religion and remarkably, what remained in the West was the emerging structure of the Roman Catholic Church. Although secular power became anarchic as warlords vied for control following the implosion of Roman order, the most successful of these recognized the power of religion (as well as the usefulness of the knowledge which existed within its institutions) and allied themselves to it. The great Frankish leader Charlemagne (748-814) even had himself crowned as Emperor of the Romans in

800 by Pope Leo III. Church and fledgling state vowed to support one another and it was an arrangement that underpinned the politics of Mediaeval Europe for the next 700 years.

That the Pax Romana (a peace which lasted from 27BCE to 180CE) benefitted the Mediterranean world is undeniable and perhaps could have lasted much longer had two other factors not intervened. Ultimately the Roman model was an avaricious one: it depended upon conquest to sate the ambitions of its merchant and military class. It was also a soulless model – many religious practices were tolerated so long as they did not challenge Roman power. When Jews and Christians started to look beyond the Roman state, and Christian martyrs began flaunting the brutal expression of Roman power, the state's legitimacy started to lose its luster.

The adoption of Christianity might have given the empire a soul but it could not bolster Rome against the eager attention of the peoples beyond its borders, a border too long and too expensive to defend. A great wall, like China's, would have had to run from the Black Sea to the Irish Sea and this would still have left its eastern and southern flanks exposed. Like a top, Rome had to keep spinning to remain upright. In the way of a consuming-asset corporation, digesting what it needed in order to sustain its momentum, expansion eventually proved impossible. While its internal contradictions might, in time, have been ironed out (and the adoption of a monotheistic religion was a step in this direction) the pressures from outside would surely have proved irresistible.

And yet, although messy, the secular anarchy which followed the Roman Empire's collapse in the West proved to be more of a reformulation than dissipation. What emerged were secular nodes of decentralized power under a centralized belief system. As adaptive structures go, this was a clever innovation: an outcome of creative happenstance, it has to be said, not conscious design, although systemic and individual survivals were surely its driving force.

So when the overarching umbrella of the Roman Catholic Church started to fray, what was going on? The post-Roman landscape was one of saints, martyrs and pilgrimage in which most people saw their world through the stained glass and carved imagery which adorned their churches and great cathedrals. It was a world sometimes devastated by plague and dynastic squabbles. It was a world of market towns and agricultural communities visited by travelling merchants and players. It was a world in which regional magnates and bishops maintained order and kept each other in check. After the Black Death, which claimed up to 60% of the population in some communities between 1346 and 1353, it was a world of rising wages (due to a shortage of labour) and rising prosperity. But alongside these realities other changes were taking place which would transform this world.

In the 16th century, Europeans increasingly started to look outwards. The great merchant families of the Italian city states (Venice, Milan, Florence, Genoa, etc.) had long been outward looking, serving as gateways between Europe and the East for knowledge as well as trade, but from 1492 (the year in which Ferdinand of Aragon and Isabella of Castile took Granada, the last Muslim stronghold on the Iberian Peninsula, and agreed to sponsor Christopher Columbus, an adventurer from Genoa) trade across and around the Atlantic began to dominate European thinking. By the end of the 16th century, Catholic Spain had become the dominant European power with extensive possessions in the Americas.

The invention of the printing press in the Holy Roman Empire around 1440 by the German, Johannes Gutenberg, accelerated a hunger for knowledge beyond Catholic dogma. The merchant class had always been alive to fresh thinking (and even to the thinking of the ancients buried under centuries of religious doctrine) and in Northern Europe resentment was growing toward Spanish domination. Throughout much of the 15th century, the papacy had fallen into the ways of nepotism, territorial aggrandizement, sexual licence and the pursuit of artistic wonders. The perceived moral laxity of the church hierarchy gave Northern Europeans grounds for questioning Catholic (and, by association, Spanish) hegemony.

The Protestant-Catholic fracture across Europe unleashed anarchy on a grand scale. Between 1524 and 1648 wars raged continuously. Between 1618 and 1648 alone many communities lost a third of their populations as competing armies marched back and forth across a bitterly divided Germany, plundering, raping and murdering as they went. France, anxious to escape Spain's embrace across the Pyrenees and from the Holy Roman Empire in the north (controlled until 1700 by the Spanish Habsburgs), supported the Protestant cause although predominantly Catholic herself. When the dust finally settled the English and Dutch had embraced Protestantism as well as representative government (the two tended to go together) and were on their way to creating worldwide trading empires, the first of which would eclipse those of Spain and France and lead eventually to the creation of the United States of America.

Anarchy is clearly not a desirable state. However, for want of a willingness to adapt, it is just as clearly a necessary one. So the question we must answer is how can we learn to adapt less painfully? This comes up against every system's inherent drive to protect itself and, in more common parlance, the old adage that if something isn't bust don't go trying to fix it. But like Olson's frogs how do we know if disaster lies ahead when the temperature is pleasant enough in the present? Some of our best moments are invariably in those periods of calm which hindsight shows preceded a storm.

What holds a polity together is a functional hierarchy in which the great majority of its members enjoy the necessities of life (as defined at any given point in time). The energy that sustains the polity is food in the first instance and more recently fuels from which heat as an active agent can be extracted (wood, coal, oil, gas, electricity and nuclear fission). As polities have become increasingly detached from the biological environment, man-made structures and networks of functional relationships (trade networks, security networks, educational networks, communications networks, etc.) have taken on greater importance.

Because a polity's individual members are conscious agents with a degree of independent action, there has to be a mechanism which coordinates those actions. These are the incentives Olson talks about, but they are much more than that. They are patterns of symbiotic activity (even if they can be boiled down to slave and master). Once a pattern has been established it tends to be self-reinforcing (which is no more than system self-preservation). If a slave gang sees one of its own make a run for it and be brutally beaten as a result, that tends to reinforce the status quo. Nowadays most tasks for which forced labour can be used are executed by machines. That said, economic necessity can be as effective as the slave driver's lash. Many miles of America's rail network were constructed by Chinese workers willing to work very hard for very little, just as much of England's early rail network was constructed by Irish navvies for the same reason.

Armies relied on a steady flow of young men looking for a square meal, adventure and companionship with the possibility of gain from looting or promotion, when the alternative was an often uninspiring rural existence (people would not have flocked into the grimy industrial cities of the 18th and 19th centuries had it been otherwise). As one moved up the political hierarchy, the roles entailed more judgement and less supervision, requiring particular experience and ability (such as when to launch a counter-attack or initiate a merchant adventure) and enjoyed more privileges in consequence which those who held them were naturally unwilling to lose. The hereditary transfer of positions was not just down to Olson self-interest, it was also functional: destructive squabbles were reduced. Provided the hereditary pool was large enough to produce individuals able to perform the roles a polity needed to fill, being brought up to the role was also a plus (trades at all levels invariably passed from father to son because there was no other way of learning them).

So long as a polity worked – that is, sustained people at whatever level they were used to, it was considered legitimate (what else was there?), a legitimacy reinforced by cultural displays which everyone was involved in and could enjoy. The Roman circus might not have been much fun for its objects but it was hugely popular amongst Rome's citizens who could feel that they too exercised the power which held the Roman state together (the lowliest member of the family could at least kick the cat). Of course bread was essential too, and the emperors made sure it was available. Displays of salacious violence wore thin eventually and Christianity offered an alternative.

It is here that consciousness enters the picture. Our ability to imagine alternatives, however vaguely, means that a polity is an arrangement sensitive to the influence of experience, example and ideas. Even though we can think about far away galaxies, our imaginative scope is local. If things go wrong we lose faith in the hierarchy we are part of and grab hold of any passing object, idea or group that appears able to sustain us. This is when lawlessness takes hold. In his important book, *The Vanquished*, Robert Gerwarth describes how, far from ending in 1918, the First World War continued well into 1923 as those in the defeated empires – German, Russian, Austro-Hungarian, Ottoman, settled scores, reverted to racial groupings, espoused long-dormant nationalisms and devoured revolutionary ideas as they struggled to fill the vacuum left by the defeat of hierarchies whose legitimacy had been shot to pieces. Anarchy ran riot and millions died.

It might not be fashionable to say this, but it is far easier to destroy a polity than build one. The formal part of the First World War should not have happened. The German nation was becoming an industrial power house, bursting at the seams. The French resented this and persuaded the Russians to the same view. Fearing a pincer movement from east and west, Germany struck first and the carnage began. It was a colossal miscalculation and destabilized the continent. Russia quit and descended into civil war. Although on the winning side, Italy lost more than she gained and her people were left with a burning resentment. The Ottoman and Austro-Hungarian Empires had sided with Germany and were ruined by the peace whose negotiators were more interested in vengeance than stability. Could any of it have been avoided? Probably not: just look at the difficulties being experienced by the European Union today and that is after a second dose of brutal adaptive reality.

But one has to hope that we can learn because - to put it bluntly, the human race will not survive, nor deserve to unless we can. So what can anarchy teach us, beyond its mindless brutality? There seem to be five processes at work. The first might be called **functional-mechanical** and is concerned with how the political system ensures that its members get the necessities of life which they have come to expect. The second can be called **power disposition** and is concerned with who gets to hold the positions of leverage within the political hierarchy. I will call the third the **emotional driver**. This is the subliminal force within us which triggers action and can range from the steady, internalized day-to-day to the seriously provoked. Fourth is the **prevailing story** which in a general way rationalizes the status quo. Finally there is what I will call the **deep anchor**, the point at which we abandon our conscious selves to a primal self, as occurs in martyrdom, childbirth and battle.

As Gerwarth describes in his book, the collapse of Russia's Romanov autocracy unfolded in stages. Serfdom (which tied families to the land and lord they were associated with by birth) had only been abolished in 1861. But from a slow start and weak base, Russian industry was expanding rapidly and by the end of the 19th century workers were increasingly being drawn to the cities and factories. Out of a population of around 130 million across the Russian Empire, some 1.9 million were from the noble class and many of these could see the need for reform. But as it stood, the system vested power in the Tsar who really was the ultimate decision-maker and with the best will in the world could not single-handedly address the social problems industrialization was throwing up.

Russia's defeat by Japan in 1905 came as a terrible blow to the prestige of the autocracy and thanks to increasingly open communication the Tsar could not duck responsibility in the eyes of his people. Finally accepting the limitations of his office, Tsar Nicholas II (a kindly man, out of his depth from the word go) appointed a parliament (the State Duma) and oversaw the establishment of a constitution. This helped to stabilize the situation but industrial unrest continued which the state police struggled to contain. However by 1913 the climate had settled down sufficiently for the Tsar and his government to authorize public celebrations for the tercentenary of the Romanov dynasty.

Then came the killer blow. The regime decided to enter the war against the Central Powers in 1914 as much to display its European credentials as for any strategic reasons. The Tsar moved to the front to take personal control. Setback followed setback and the escalating number of troops needed to replace those killed became steadily less willing to fight. The mood in Petrograd was poisonous with the government split between centre-left and hard-left. In the background radicals, many financed by Germany whose foreign office wanted to destabilize the regime, were stirring up discontent. By February 1917 the situation had deteriorated so much that Nicholas was forced to abdicate and power devolved to a Provisional Government which remained resolved to prosecute the war.

In what turned out to be a master stroke, Germany facilitated the return from exile of Vladimir Ilyich Ulayanov (a long-time radical from a minor noble family better known by his pen name "Lenin") in March 1917. Lenin took control of the hard left Bolsheviks (radical groups that had formed spontaneously in factories across the country) and in October the Bolsheviks managed to oust the

Provisional Government. In December Russia declared an armistice with Germany and the other Central Powers (the Ottoman and Austro-Hungarian Empires) and signed a peace treaty in February the following year. In July 1918 the Bolsheviks murdered Nicholas and his family, who were being held under house arrest in Ipatiev House in the Urals, and, over the coming months, as many other members of the Romanov family as they could lay their hands on.

Civil war raged across Russia for the next four years as the Bolshevik Red Army slugged it out with the White Army, an uneasy association of socialists, democrats, monarchists and capitalists egged on by eight outside nations. Over 7 million people are thought to have died during this upheaval, mostly civilians, many from disease and hunger. Even after this anarchy was brought under control the suffering of the Russian people was not over. Under the Stalinist autocracy a further 5-10 million people are believed to have died of hunger and disease as a consequence of the government's misguided agricultural reforms. Then in World War II close to 9 million were killed defending the motherland from German incursion along with around 11 million civilians. It is small wonder that Russian literature is etched in pathos.

And Russia was not alone in misery. Following the formal end of World War I (which itself had claimed over 15 million lives) the dismemberment of the defeated empires (German, Austro-Hungarian and Ottoman) unleashed five years of score-settling between groups that had previously lived in tolerable harmony with one another, destroying millions of lives more. This bloody aftermath has prompted Gerwarth and others to wonder: had the war been brought to an end early in 1917 leaving Europe's superstructures intact, might things have been different? This possibility was raised by Britain's ex-Foreign Secretary, Henry Petty-Fitzmaurice, in his now infamous Lansdowne Peace Letter (published in November 1917 but based upon a memorandum he had circulated within government the previous year). However none of the belligerents could accept that vengeance belonged to the Lord.

What seems clear is that across Europe industrialization had altered social arrangements in the 19th century as fundamentally as Protestantism had in the 17th and that communication played an important part in both. In the latter case the shift was a shift in thinking from the acceptance of Church dogma, Church rules and Church hierarchy to a more individually focused attitude based upon inquiry and personal responsibility. Printing speeded up the dissemination and refinement of ideas. Trade had always been important but from the sixteenth century on it pulled itself clear from the shadow of Church and aristocratic power as an enabling activity in its own right, mutating as it went into industry and forms of government accountable to more than dynastic and ecclesiastic interests.

By the start of the 20th century Europe was predominantly industrial with large numbers of working people living in close communities for the first time with access to vibrant communication. Conditions were evolving on the hop and certainly without much central or even local planning (although Britain was somewhat better in this regard than many other European countries). Coloured by a symbiotic relationship between church and state, much of Europe was still subject to a predominantly agrarian superstructure, with regional landed magnates supported by local magistrates owing allegiance to a monarch assisted by a rudimentary bureaucracy and sometimes by a parliament, as well as by an army and internal police. Politics was struggling to catch up with the reality on the ground.

To take the Russian example, the **prevailing story** (the efficacy of the church and hereditary class) was becoming threadbare in the face of military defeat and industrial-urban problems it had no experience of. The **functional-mechanical** structures were no longer fit for purpose in the evolving industrial age. This called into question the prevailing **power disposition** and undermined the **emotional**

drivers which had previously led people to work within the system as it was. As industrial chaos escalated and increasing numbers of people started to be killed at the front for no discernible benefit, individuals began to throw caution to the wind and drop their **deep anchor** into vague new pools of aspiration. This anarchic cocktail just needed to be shaken so that a new order could form.

The irony, of course, is that the birth of the Soviet Union inflicted more suffering on the Russian people than the Romanovs ever did. This tells us something important about the anarchic process: it is not rational in the strict sense of the word (as when one step follows logically to the next) but exploratory and creative. It is driven by each individual's instinctive drive to survive as a collective entity not as an individual per se. When a soldier 'goes over the top' he is putting what he is part of ahead of himself. When a woman gives birth she is putting the continuity of life ahead of herself. Political dissidents feel that securing a new status quo is more important than self-preservation within the status quo as it exists. But it would be wrong to think of this as heroic altruism, although it is often heroic.

It is actually part of a powerful evolutionary drive nestling within all of us which subsumes our identity. The soldier, the woman and the dissident all become part of an adaptive unfolding mechanism without knowing what the outcome will be - because creative outcomes can never be known precisely. The soldier might be shot, the woman might die in childbirth and the dissident might be murdered, but both by their existence and their demise the systems they were part of will have been changed, perhaps imperceptibly, but changed.

There is a nice sentiment expressed in the Bible (Luke12:6) in which even the humble sparrow, sold in the marketplace for pennies, is not irrelevant to God. When Edward Lorenz (1917-2008) was trying to calibrate his weather model he discovered that the tiniest variation in the model's initial conditions (his were set by a random number generator) could lead to markedly different outcomes. This gave rise to the thought that a hurricane might have been influenced by the earlier flap of a butterfly's wings. When a status quo model breaks down because it no longer sustains those who make up the hierarchy defined by it, the chaos (anarchy) that ensues opens up enough space within the polity for other structural avenues to be explored. But it does not guarantee any particular outcome.

When the Hutu majority set out to eliminate the Tutsi minority in 1991, the inability of the Rwanda polity to function effectively caused it to turn violently inward along racial lines, an all too common occurrence when a polity wishes to refocus its energies around a simple cohesive story. The 100 day chaotic slaughter, during which between ½ and 1 million were killed (as United Nations forces stood by) was doubtless as cathartic for Hutu Rwandans as expelling Jews from the newly empowered Spain in 1492 was for the Catholics who had just ejected the Moors from their peninsula. Spain went on to become the dominant power in Europe. Rwanda is still predominantly rural and is one of the most densely populated countries in Africa with an average life expectancy of under 60 and a per capita GDP (nominal) of $769. After the genocide, Tutsi rebels regrouped outside the country and now, following a brutal civil war, the Rwandan Patriotic Front (a largely Tutsi party) dominates the government.

Anarchy is a subliminal response to failed structures. It is nature's way of righting itself but the process is profligate in human suffering. If we want to avoid such suffering then we need to work a lot harder at understanding how social structures work. What is clear is that our belief in the effectiveness of the polity we are subject to is critical to its success. While these beliefs may be influenced by propaganda (negative as well as positive), ultimately they are determined by the polity's ability to meet our expectations. If expectations were static we could, eventually, come up with a mechanical set of arrangements which worked.

Many aboriginal societies seem to have achieved this, attaining long-lasting stability. However, pressures emanating from outside a polity and its environmental network still need to be dealt with and such events are not predictable. For example, there was no way that America's native populations could have anticipated the arrival of Europeans who existed on a plane outside their field of understanding. The key to long-lasting survival is adaptive structures, but structures will only adapt if there is something they have to adapt to. What conscious man appears to have stumbled upon is the evolution of structures that do not just compete for resources but compete in how best to organize themselves so as to secure them.

This upsets the prevailing story and serves to transform expectations. It puts pressure on existing **functional-mechanical** structures, calls into question the prevailing **power disposition** and undermines the **emotional drivers** which tie individuals into the existing status quo. When the legitimacy of the prevailing structure fractures, people's **deep anchors** are untethered and a chaotic period ensues as competing groups vie to tie them to some new vision of the future. To avoid the requirement for anarchy we should recognize the benefit of endowing polities with loose-tight properties which enable individuals to create new structures to meet new needs and which allow old structures that no longer meet needs to wither.

Free market capitalism does a rather good job of ensuring this in the economic sphere, but in the social sphere we are still in the dark ages. Having millions of individuals entrust the architecture of society to a handful of party politicians might be an improvement on entrusting it to a monarch, but it is still a pretty poor system. Until *how societies work* becomes a standard part of everyone's education and the state bureaucracy comes under the control of the people it is supposed to serve rather than the status quo it actually serves, bouts of self-destructive anarchy are likely to be the price we have to pay for social progress.

13

Because we can

IT IS I think, a characteristic of things to go where they can. The aphorism, nature abhors a vacuum, speaks to this. When the rabbit was introduced into Australia in 1859 it found abundant food and came up against no serious predators. Within ten years two million or so were being shot annually without any noticeable impact on their population. When the horse was reintroduced into North America by the Spanish in the sixteenth century (the continent's prehistoric horse had died out around 12,000 years before) a number became wild and the population quickly grew, altering the range habitat. When a structure develops it keeps reproducing itself until denied the means of doing so. That seems to be the nature of the evolution we are part of.

This, of course, has relevance for human behaviour. When bankers are given access to cash and offered incentives to accumulate more of it for their employers, they will endeavour to do so until stopped. When Nazi operatives are given incentives to dispose of certain minorities they will keep doing so until stopped (or until they run out of the target minorities – job done). When soldiers are sent into battle to kill they will keep killing until they are stopped or run out of men to kill. When airmen are sent up in bombers to bomb cities they will keep doing so until they run out of bombs or until their planes are shot out of the sky. When an invading army captures a fiercely contested city its male soldiers will rape that city's women until their blood lust has run its course. When a sought-after new product is launched, people will rush to buy it until their demand is satisfied. You will have got the point by now. What we can do we will do.

A social equilibrium – in fact any equilibrium – is a structure held together by offsetting checks and balances. In the human body, the scourge of cancer occurs when destructive cells find a way of mutating and reproducing – like the rabbits in Australia – without constraint. 007 was granted a licence to kill, as are invading armies. While the mythical secret agent is constrained by the need to keep alive himself, marauding armies, like those that crisscrossed northern Europe during the Thirty Years War, move like a plague, destroying everything in their path, until they have nothing left to feed off (or are defeated by some opposing army).

These are all biological characteristics, even universal ones. So what is it that stops any one of us from running riot like teenagers on a Friday night after a heavy session clubbing? Well, the police for one thing. But consciousness has also given us the capacity to memorize the consequences of past actions together with the imagination to 'feel' the effect of sanctions. The organized brutality that has characterized the evolution of human society is no accident. Public burnings, hangings, floggings and executions, along with the threat of torture, serve as the psychological checks against behaviours that might disrupt the social equilibrium of the time.

The highwayman as folk hero speaks to the part in all of us that would just love to kick off the traces which constrain our lives – if only we had the courage. The pleasure we get from watching a Freddie Mercury or Lady Gaga perform is because we see ourselves through them breaking the bounds of everyday convention, trapeze artists flying through space like shooting stars. Deep within us lurks the energy which drove our universe into life and has been feeding the evolution of structures ever since.

What stops us pressing the self-destruct button is that property of all structure: the need to sustain itself. To form at all, a structure must possess a set of checks and balances which enable it to absorb energy from outside itself in a particular functional way. The Islamic suicide bomber and Japanese kamikaze pilot are both given the green light to violate their own structural integrity. This green light elevates a 'greater good' above their own structural integrity, the same green light that drives soldiers into battle, causes wildebeest to herd and fish to cluster as a way of limiting the effects of predation. The loss of some is acceptable if it secures the whole.

The Catholic Church took a dim view of suicide, although it was more than happy to send men into battle where individual death was the certain outcome. The man or woman who took their own life was denying the Church power over them, so such an act would naturally condemn them to horrors after death. The world of mediaeval man was rich in imaginings. In fact he lived alongside a parallel world as real as the humdrum one he inhabited, rich in demons, saints, goblins and ghouls. Witch trials were no joke. Women who were thought to have harnessed demonic powers were a threat to social equilibrium. The Church had to exercise control over the spirit world.

I have often marvelled at martyrs. How could they have endured what they did for an idea? The fundamental answer must be because they could. We all do the most extraordinary things, because we can. This is the open-ended nature of the universe we inhabit. Torn between our structural imperative and the transient energy which sustains us, we live and sometimes die - because we can.

14

Commerce

IT is as well that we understand what commerce is. At heart it is a process of transformation and an expression of evolution. At the core of evolution is the conversion of energy into matter. Matter differentiates within its logical bounds to create a platform from which new matter can form and itself differentiate to the extent possible within *its* logical bounds. A progression of evolutionary layers is evident with the most recent embodying aspects of the layer before.

All biological life converts energy into structure. Randomly differentiating structures find different ways of securing energy, which include drawing it from structures previously formed in a sort of hierarchy of interdependence. Human beings are no different. The challenge has always been to find enough energy to survive, with those characteristics that consistently secured it being the ones most likely to be replicated. With consciousness, the business of finding energy became more inventive and successful. Out of this success has come widespread organizational differentiation as it became possible to pursue an array of individual objectives.

That thousands of people can now sit in an arena and watch

their favourite performers is a measure of the distance Homo sapiens has travelled in working out how to transform the environment to his own ends. The greater part of this transformation has been the outcome of exchange between individuals and groups of individuals, sometimes directed by force but oftentimes undertaken in return for rewards freely given.

After Genghis Khan and his successors had brutally imposed order across their empire which at its height in 1279 stretched from the Pacific Ocean to the Baltic Sea, the Mongol emperors were anxious to invite merchants, scholars and performers into their cities so that these displayed the wonders of the Asian, Islamic and Christian worlds. The exercise of power so as to secure order may be an initial prerequisite in human affairs, but a delight in individual expressiveness and novelty is rarely far behind, especially if it flatters the established order.

The modern economy now transforms material from the environment into a staggering array of products and at a prodigious rate. Slave and animal power may have been behind much of early consumption, lifting at least some people out of a hand-to-mouth existence. But it was with the clever use of steam and coal power to drive mass production in the 18th century that this transformation truly gathered pace. What we call commerce is the mechanism through which producers and consumers communicate. From coffee houses in London and Amsterdam, schemes were hatched and funds raised to send sailing ships thousands of miles to collect the food-enlivening spices English and Dutch consumers craved.

Before long merchants were buying humans from tribal chiefs in West Africa and shipping them to the West Indies, packed like sardines, to be worked to death on plantations whose sugar these merchants then transported to Europe where it was devoured with increasing enthusiasm without much concern for its provenance. The flow of money back and forth stimulated innovations in banking and insurance with governments getting in on the act. Products were taxed, government debt was raised through the banking system and military force was deployed to support each nation's own trading networks. In no time governments were at war with one another to protect and expand their commercial interests.

Improved agriculture and increasing demand for men and women to work in the factories sprouting like mushrooms in the 18th and 19th centuries stimulated a rapid rise in populations and in the size of cities. Mass communication followed mass production and issues were raised. While some concentrated on production and some on consumption, others started to focus on the quality of life in these urban agglomerations which were both terrifying and exciting in equal measure. Labour laws were introduced, sanitation standards set; the trade in slaves was bought off by taxpayers and Samuel Plimsoll's line stopped boats from being overloaded. The design and production of weapons, ships, trains, planes and automobiles also accelerated. It was a helter-skelter time of free-forming structures with no one much in control save commerce as the intermediary between the desires and concerns of millions.

By the start of the 20th century the World's political systems had become all but overwhelmed by events and it was not long before mass production gave way to mass murder on a truly prodigious scale. Mass communication stirred up mass fervour of a nationalistic kind which no one knew how to rein in even if they had had a mind to. Generals planned for battles of a kind they had never fought with weapons they did not understand until it became a fight to the death between monsters endowed with a surfeit of muscle over brain. As national fortunes were squandered, commerce, for the most part, slipped into hibernation.

Trade would creep out of its cave after the war as people struggled once more to be gay. However the world's political systems were still broken and an even more devastating world war lay just around the corner. When it was finally over and many more millions had been killed, commerce took to road, rail, sea and air once more to bestow its technological wonders, an Aladdin's cave of manufactured goods and food from every corner of the globe, on war-starved consumers through new and glitzy emporia.

And here we are in a new millennium. With war-time restrictions on commerce progressively rolled back, trade reached into every part of the globe, shifting millions from an agrarian tradition into the world of mass consumption. As jobs were being created in parts of the world that had not yet industrialized, they were being destroyed in the already industrialized world by technological innovation and the transfer of work to regions with lower wages. But the consumer was king and finance came up with all manner of ways to accommodate him, aided and abetted by politicians eager to secure his votes.

Once again this helter-skelter transformation began to run ahead of the world's political systems. Mainstream media found its monopoly over communication challenged by the internet which enabled individuals to generate their own content. Advertisers were forced to transfer their allegiance to these new platforms, draining the old guard of funds and influence, and making politicians tweet and blog to get their own message across and show that they were 'with it'. But as the beneficiaries of this brave new world stroked each other's feathers and praised the globalization which had brought them high-end running shoes and iPads, the system was running out of control - again.

Encouraged to lend, government-sponsored mortgage organizations in the United States fed money to individuals who were never going to be able to pay it back. These toxic contracts found their way into a poorly-regulated financial sector eager for commissions and, in a replay of Thomas Gresham's 16th century observation that bad money would drive out good, the world's financial system became polluted. In 2008 it collapsed and had to be bailed out by Western taxpayers.

Across the developed world the now welfare-dependent casualties of technological innovation, financial dislocation and globalization started to find their political voice. Ignored by the liberal elite they sought sanctuary within parties of the so-called hard 'right' and hard 'left' just as they had once before in the depression years of the 1930s. Rather than examine their own shortcomings, the beneficiaries of the status quo set about demonizing their opponents with thinly disguised references to their ignorance.

What is clear from all of this is that the transformative power of commerce frequently exceeds the ability of national systems to keep up. Even if commerce is courted by political elites for their own ends, it has to engage with individuals every day in a way political systems do not. Monopoly commerce, even when it is an oligopoly (competition between very few) is rightly thought poorly of, but monopoly politics and its close relative, oligopoly politics (competition between two main parties), is the norm. Until this is corrected, the benefits of commerce will be squandered by the failings of politics.

15

The problem with government

IT is an illusion that someone is in charge. Why we persist in it doubtless needs a Freudian explanation. Quite probably, the thought that we may be little more than flotsam and jetsam on the ocean currents of life terrifies us. So we invent a father figure to assure us all is well, the same one we look to for salvation when it is not.

But what we **have** done is build systems to help us navigate the day-to-day of our existence. Hitherto, these systems have been defined by rules or customs which we have come to accept and be populated by individuals whose task it is to give them active impetus in accordance with their functions. The function of the soldier, for example, is to fight. The function of the general is to direct the fighting. In this example, the system is the army.

Clearly such a system cannot exist in a vacuum. Armies must be fed. Another system we developed was settled agriculture. This might consist of a paterfamilias who makes the key decisions about what to do when, his wife whose task it is to run the household and mind the children, together with any farm hands or domestic helpers who attach themselves to this family unit. Right off there is a conflict between this system and that of an army. Armies can rape and pillage, but sooner or later will run out of females to rape and land worth pillaging. Neither can they absorb all the males into their ranks without affecting agriculture. So the social systems we have developed overlap and compete for the same resources.

And there is more. Consciousness has imbued individuals with an ability to consider and – to some extent – adjust their actions. So not only do the systems we have developed often bump up against one another unharmoniously, but the individuals who power their actions are not entirely predictable. Added to that, the ubiquitous hierarchical structure that pervades all human systems endows the roles nearest the apex with increasing power (where power is the ability to act outside fixed rules) akin to a logarithmic progression, such that the role at the top enjoys a disproportionate amount. By now you should be getting a feel for the problem with government.

* * *

In the run-up to the First World War, one of the most destructive in human history, what were Europe's leaders thinking? One has to imagine that none of them had an inkling of the real horror to come. The French, history tells us, were concerned about German expansion, so they courted the Russians both diplomatically and financially, their thinking being that if Germany had to fight on both an eastern and western front she would be at a disadvantage.

Russia was in a terrible state, although the European powers appeared not to recognize this. The Russian Pacific Fleet had been utterly defeated by the Japanese in 1905 and in 1917 the entire Tsarist system of government would be swept aside. Britain, well aware that her over-extended empire had virtually become indefensible, had allied herself with Japan in the east and had resolved her colonial frictions with France in the west. The Austro-Hungarian Empire was showing signs of buckling under the weight of its ethnic divisions and the Ottoman Empire was struggling to reform its woefully outdated system of government.

The German principalities (excluding Austria) had merged to form the German Empire in 1871 with Prussia as the dominant component. From Belgium in the west it stretched all along the southern shore of the Baltic Sea to Russia in the east and marched with the Austro-Hungarian Empire to the south. By the start of the 20th century the empire was becoming an industrial powerhouse. Her volatile Kaiser had a love-hate relationship with Britain, being both envious and in awe of its empire. He appeared to be in thrall to his military advisers who suspected France and Russia of wanting to encircle Germany.

The assassination of Austria's Archduke Ferdinand by a Serb nationalist was the trigger for the war to come, although it was a war looking for any excuse to begin. The Germans put pressure on Austria to take a firm line with Serbia, a country with strong Russian ties. Russia appeared to mobilize sending troops to its frontier with Germany on its new railway financed by the French. The German high command decided to launch preemptive attacks both east and west as its Kaiser ran around like a headless chicken, wondering what had been unleashed. Britain, in accordance with its traditional policy of opposing any power seeking to dominate the European continent (and objecting to Germany's violation of Belgian neutrality) joined France.

Over the next four-and-a-half years some 70 million men were mobilized, 11 million of whom would be killed along with around 7 million civilians. The Ottoman Empire had come in on the side of the Central Powers (the German and Austro-Hungarian Empires) and would collapse at the war's conclusion. Russia would pull out of the war following its descent into revolution and civil war. Germany would eventually throw in the towel when America, with fresh troops and armaments, entered the war on the side of France and Britain in

1917. France and Britain would declare victory on November 11th 1918 although the first was all but ruined and the second almost bankrupt.

The Germans were forced to accept a humiliating defeat. The Kaiser was pushed out and the German people were encouraged to adopt a democratic system of government which would prove insufficiently robust to withstand the economic depression to come. Led by the idealistic US President, Woodrow Wilson, a League of Nations was established to prevent such wars from happening again. Twenty-two years later, in September 1939, World War II would begin, once more started by a Germany anxious to re-establish its Central European Empire.

This time the Soviet Union, as Russia had become, would prove a match for Germany by simply pouring more men into battle than the Germans could field (some 11 million Soviet soldiers were killed). Eventually the Soviets fought their way to Berlin and absorbed all of Germany's East European Empire. In the west, the German offensive started well (as it had in the east). France was quickly defeated and most of it absorbed into the Reich. Britain, however, refused to fall, although she lost almost all her possessions in the Far East to the Japanese who had sided with the Reich and its ally, Italy's Benito Mussolini.

The United States entered the war against Germany in 1941 and by May 1945 Soviet and American forces (aided by the British) had overwhelmed the Reich and converged on Berlin. The war in the Pacific was only brought to a close after the United States dropped two atomic bombs on Japan forcing its capitulation in August. All told, some 75 million people lost their lives as a result of the conflict, many due to genocide carried out by German and Japanese personnel. Only around 20 million of the dead were soldiers. At the war's end, the Soviet Union and United States emerged as the two dominant powers.

Following this debacle, efforts were made to integrate a shattered Europe and the construction of the European Union began. By 2013 almost all of Europe was part of a single economic community with many countries sharing a common currency. However, by 2016 it was apparent the currency union was favouring Germany at the expense of Europe's less productive economies. Her efficient manufacturing industry was benefitting from a lower currency than was justified and Southern Europe's inefficient economies were struggling with too high a currency – their common Euro. Without fiscal transfers and a banking union, the Euro area started to become untenable.

If these tensions were not enough, the continent was hit by successive waves of immigrants from a war-torn Middle East destabilized by ill-conceived US interventions. Britain (America's ally in the Middle East) had remained out of the Euro area and was unwilling to accept the political integration needed to make the European project work. Her quite successful economy had been attracting workers from across the European Union (under the EU's freedom of movement principle) and, when asked if they wanted to remain in the European Union, a majority of English voters (many of whom felt EU migrants had depressed their wages) voted to leave.

So here we are, once again facing a fragmenting Europe unbalanced by German industrial might. Across the continent, political parties opposed to mass immigration from the Middle East are growing in strength, and England is not the only country in which voters not only fail to see the benefit of further political integration but want less of it. People are dissatisfied with their economic prospects and afraid. The wagons are being circled: nationalism is on the rise. The prognosis for the near term is not good.

* * *

Since before Roman times, Europe has been a cauldron of

conflict, but it has also been a hotbed of innovation and change. From Greece, to Rome, to Spain, to France, to Holland, to Britain one or more of its constituent parts has spread its influence well beyond its continental borders, while at different times and repeatedly, its Germanic tribes have reshaped its character. And of course none of this was planned. Every decision taken by the men and women who shaped its history will have been seen as the right decision at the time. Even those of the twentieth century, whose consequences were death and destruction on an unimaginable scale, will have seemed correct within the context in which they were taken. Does this mean that we are either doomed to stagnate or to tearing one another apart as the price of progress?

After years of observing the natural world, Charles Darwin concluded that it was not the strongest that survives, nor the most intelligent but the most responsive to change. This bears thinking about because there probably is not a government in existence whose principals do not strive to be both intelligent and strong. Indeed, every one of the leading governments which brought Europe to its knees at the start of the twentieth century will have had this objective.

But therein lies the dichotomy. In the European jungle the leading governments all jostled for the top spot. And sometimes a government's faith in its ability was validated – for a while. After the crowns of Castile and Aragon were united, the Catholic north embarked upon a campaign to evict the Moors from the peninsula (which had fallen under Muslim control in 718CE). In 1492, the year Columbus sailed to the Americas, it was successful. Jews and Muslims were forced to convert or be expelled and Spain began its ascent, becoming Europe's leading imperial power with territories in North and South America. When the Habsburg Charles I ascended the throne (1516), he added the Central European provinces of the Holy Roman Empire (of which he was Charles V). But by the 17th century, dynastic infighting and the rise of Protestantism gradually brought an end to Spanish domination in Europe.

Europe has been the crucible of its own change because no single power has been able to dominate the subcontinent entirely. Even the Romans failed to control the region known as Germania Magna east of the River Rhine, populated by Germanic and some Celtic tribes (who would eventually sack Rome itself). Although Europe's political dialogue has been expressed through warfare, the subcontinent has not just been a playground for warlords, although these have certainly had their days, but a space within which competing polities have sought to build civilizations each with its own culture, albeit under the umbrella of the Roman Catholic Church (from 380CE at least) until Northern Europe broke free in the 17th century to follow the banners of Protestantism.

So the changes that propelled Europe to its pinnacle happened in spite of governments not because of them. This does not mean that governments had no role however. The correct conclusion to draw is that competition between polities stimulated adaptation. Indeed, without innovative governments within Europe, each competing to enhance its own polity through the accumulation of wealth, a stable status quo would likely have resulted, similar to that enjoyed by imperial China at various times in its long history. The real question is this: was the extraordinary human carnage of the twentieth century which engulfed Europe, the Far East (in particular China) and Russia a necessary part of that adaptive process?

The simple answer (and quite probably the right one) is yes. But to conclude that this validates perpetual armed conflict and the human misery that goes with it in a kind of *survival of the fittest* nightmare that runs for eternity like Dante's Inferno, constitutes an unforgivable rejection of consciousness. That the First World War represents a monumental failure of Europe's institutional thinking is now abundantly clear in hindsight: the conflict triggered social changes which were never part of the belligerent's stated objectives. Worse still, these changes (the abandonment of Europe's imperial writ, the expansion of participatory government within Europe and the economic empowerment of its people) needed a second world war to consolidate. The construction of a European framework within which adaptive decisions can be reached without recourse to armed conflict remains a work in progress.

The problem with government then is that its structure (up to now at any rate) is backward looking: it seems, almost grudgingly, to adjust to the last crisis but rarely more. Populism erupts from time to time when the people in a polity are hurting and feel that the status quo no longer represents their interests. However populism need not be anti-establishment. Before the First World War it was channelled into nationalism.

It has been a common tactic used by the guardians of the status quo to deflect internal tensions towards some external 'enemy'. And it should not be assumed that this is merely a Machiavellian ploy used by a ruling class to shore up its legitimacy (although there will doubtless be elements of this). More generally it is a logical response to external threat, be that threat some perceived obstacle to a polity's aspirations (such as encroachment by another polity) or actual hindrance to a polity's ability to sustain itself (as might arise from a succession of crop failures). The metaphor *to circle the wagons* denotes a people coming together to face down a common menace. However, if a majority do not have confidence in their leaders, populism may give rise to revolution - the rebuilding of the power structure around a fresh group of individuals. The alternative to either of these two alternatives in combatting the danger is likely to be a people's dissipation or absorption into a competing polity.

The reactive nature of government can lead to some rather crude outcomes. When the Soviet system replaced the Tsarist one, one autocracy displaced another, although the new one drew from a different pool of people (individuals chosen not on the basis of heredity but on the basis of a new political orthodoxy). This reinvigorated autocracy won the support of the majority and Russia was transformed, but no one can pretend that it was a pretty process or that a more adaptive transformation from the old to the new wouldn't have served its people better. Neither the Tsarist system of government nor the Soviet system that replaced it 'knew' how to adapt the power structure because the people who made up both polities were the same and had only experienced autocracy.

Government is not some abstract thing to be tweaked by intellectual dictate, much as intellectuals might wish otherwise. When Abraham Lincoln urged that government of the people, by the people, for the people, should not perish from the earth at Gettysburg in 1863, after America's bloody civil war, he was – as he, consummate politician that he was, must have known – stating the obvious. Government is always of the people, by the people, for the people because every system of government ultimately depends upon the tacit acceptance of a majority of those governed. That acceptance may be engineered by fear, by ignorance, by selective bribery, by false promises, or by any other underhand device open to a self-interested ruling elite, but ultimately the ship of state must float and to do so it needs all hands.

America's Southern states were fighting for their way of life and Lincoln recognized that. When his Northern armies finally secured victory he instructed that there should be no recriminations. Although he had pushed through legislation banning slavery on federal land in 1862 (the system which underpinned the Southern economy) he knew he could not override the wishes of state governments without a constitutional amendment. It was not until two years after the war (and after Lincoln himself had been assassinated by a resentful Southerner) that the thirteenth amendment abolishing slavery cleared Congress.

Lincoln's overriding political concern had been to preserve the Union. His moral position was that the Union could not endorse slavery. Even the most advanced system of government in its day could not reconcile irreconcilable positions without bloodshed. The British fared better in this regard. When the Abolition of Slavery Act was passed in 1833, Britain's slave owners were bought out at considerable cost to the public purse. Could America have done the same? It was discussed but no agreement was ever reached.

Racist sentiment remains a political issue in the United States and African Americans have still not secured the rights to which their constitution entitles them. The problem with government as it stands is that citizens assume legislators possess more power than they do. Our representatives do the minimum to persuade us they have addressed this or that issue and we are happy to endorse the illusion. So many loose ends are invariably left that even the most enlightened-sounding legislation often stands little chance of securing its stated objective.

All too often, we drive in hope looking at the rear view mirror while trying to negotiate the corner ahead on the basis of the curvature behind. If government is to improve, we the people are going to have to look forward not at the road just travelled. To do that, like navigators, we will need to improve our understanding of how societies work. And, like Lincoln, we will have to make some moral judgements. The way this might be achieved will be the subject of a separate essay.

16

What is democracy?

I STARTED this essay with the question *Is democracy possible?* and quickly realized that it is the nature of democracy itself which we need to consider. But first, two hopefully uncontentious assertions: the first is that collectives cannot run countries and the second is that no polity can function without the support of its citizens.

Pericles (495-429BCE), Athenian statesman, orator and general, is often associated with the flowering of democracy. For a period, the Athenian Assembly did consider most matters that concerned the city. The body consisted of all male citizens. Neither women nor slaves had political rights. Most administrative positions were allocated by lot for fixed terms, although generals were elected. This allowed Pericles to dominate the Assembly. Without his leadership the Assembly embarked upon some disastrous ventures (an unsuccessful invasion of Sicily being the most notable). Abandoned, resuscitated and then modified, the Athenian experiment in direct rule eventually withered when Macedonia and finally Rome came to dominate the city.

In 1863 Abraham Lincoln, as President of the recently

confirmed United States (and suffering from a raging fever), dedicated the cemetery at Gettysburg to the honour of the Union soldiers killed. He spoke for only a couple of minutes - the ex-senator, governor, government minister, Harvard president and pastor Edward Everett had spoken for two hours before him – but Lincoln's address became the most famous in American history. It included these words: *that this nation, under God, shall have a new birth of freedom—and that government of the people, by the people, for the people, shall not perish from the earth.* Pericles would have approved - and understood. Lincoln led his people, he didn't follow them.

A good leader is one who sees what needs to be done and then persuades his people to go along with it. Unfortunately seeing what needs to be done is not always obvious and what makes a good leader depends, in part at least, on the circumstances he must deal with. The only basis upon which one might imagine that a collective will make a better decision than an individual is by assuming that an issue is clear enough for a majority to adjudicate it correctly. This is only likely to be the case if the discussions preceding the decision clarify the issues in a way that was not available to an individual as leader.

Where the collective will does come into its own is whenever an elite becomes so wound up in its own self-interest that it irrationally conflates its own interests and the collective's, deeming the hardships of those outside its circle as being the necessary price of progress, survival or whatever. In such circumstances a populus might oust a leader and his cabal. What a voting system does is allow this to happen without bloodshed. But this is a long way from being government of the people, by the people, for the people. It is simply a reaction against structural failure by those entrapped within it.

The problem within our present 'democratic' systems is that opposition has become an integral part of the structure offering little more than a choice between managers. The structure itself is rarely under review. When it does come under review, as it did in the recent referendum in the United Kingdom about whether the UK should remain in the European Union, the system as a whole experiences a sort of structural seizure: *how <u>could</u> our status quo be challenged?*, it seems to say. This was the reaction of the British to the uppity actions of their Bostonian colonists before America's War of Independence (1775-1783). It was also the confused response from both the French and Russian ruling houses before events swept them away in 1789 and 1917 respectively.

However severe stress does not always lead to a structure's collapse. When the Scots born steel magnate, Andrew Carnegie, had his associate Henry Clay Frick face down the Amalgamated Association of Iron and Steel Workers at his Homestead plant, the confrontation turned violent and ten men were killed. Competition in the industry was fierce. There had been a recession in 1890-91 during which business activity declined by 22% but Carnegie had been busy making his Homestead plant highly automated for the production of top quality steel. The old trades in the plant, wishing to preserve their elite status and practices, demanded higher wages but Carnegie and Frick were only willing to pass on some of the plant's increased profitability and they wanted streamlined work practices. Both sides dug in and the union lost the battle.

The Great Depression (1929-33) affected a quarter of the workforce in America but the American structure survived, unlike the German one (where unemployment reached a similar level). The fundamental difference between the two was that the American polity believed in itself (it was new, brash and on the up) whereas the German polity was tentative (it had only recently moved to a system of representative government and its people were embittered by defeat in World War I). If it was popular suffering that caused political structures to collapse, the Soviet Union under Stalin and communist China under Mao should both have done so. But both structures were new, having overthrown earlier structures, and were supported by a conviction amongst their people (by how many of them we cannot know, but it must have been by a sizeable percentage) that the arrangements they were putting in place were the way of the future.

Would fascist Germany (which emerged out of what we call a democratic process) have survived, like fascist Spain, had it not invaded the Soviet Union? It is very likely. And would it have mellowed in response to the wishes of its people, as did Spain, the Soviet Union and China? That seems very likely too. The formation of political structure is often a violent affair driven by belief. And what underpins belief is a desire amongst individuals to experience a better life. And because individuals cluster in order to effect action, minorities frequently get crushed.

We fool ourselves if we think that democracy (however we care to define it) is an end in itself. It is not. The structures we will always want are those structures that we believe will enable us to lead good lives. This makes it imperative that we infuse belief with wisdom (the great challenge of education). And because circumstances are always evolving, our structures will need to evolve too. Designing systems with the capacity to do so without the violence and disruption that has accompanied change in the past is the challenge we face.

17

The crisis in Western democracy

D EMOCRACY, by its nature, is probably in permanent crisis. So what is new? Before considering what might be new, let us first consider why democracy is prone to crisis. The answer is because all polities are subject to internal and external pressures, whether they are democratic or not. Only when a people's environment is stable and their relationship to it is settled - a state enjoyed by countless groups for long periods (such as that enjoyed by Australia's aboriginals before Europeans disrupted their lives) - does a sense of crisis not exist.

As argued in the accompanying essay, *What is democracy?*, collectives are poor decision-makers. As a political mechanism, however, democracy can precipitate a change of leadership without too much disruption and generally without bloodshed. But what democracy can't do, as was pointed out in the essay referred to, is change itself. So if the system within which it is embedded ceases to be functional in some way, the best democracy can do is express a people's frustration in the form of *a plague on all your houses*.

This might translate into voter apathy or into support for any individual able to express the voters' discontent, be that person a

Benito Mussolini or Adolph Hitler. In the end, all government – regardless of its type – comes down to one thing: competence, which means looking after the interests of those it represents. When Genghis Khan (c1162-1227) united the Mongol tribes and led his horsemen on a rampage east and south into China and west through the Middle East across into Eastern Europe (to create what was to become the largest contiguous empire in human history) his followers were delighted. But he showed scant regard for all those he conquered.

Caught unawares by the Mongols' skilled use of equine technology, they fell like ninepins, as Mediterranean communities had to Rome's innovative legions and coastal communities would to Europe's (and particularly Britain's) transformative use of maritime power. But once conquered, the people and cities left (by some estimates upwards of 30 million people lost their lives through famine and war as a direct consequence of the Mongol expansion) became assets to be run for the greater glory of the empire. Religious toleration, meritocracy and trade were encouraged and what became known as the Silk Road facilitated extensive cultural exchange between East and West. But by the end of the 13th century the empire had already begun to split apart.

History accords Genghis Khan *greatness* but the thousands of settled communities he destroyed to gain that accolade, and in which people doubtless led decent, largely peaceful lives, barely get a mention. In the real world, *The Magnificent Seven*, who save a quiet farming community from the exploitation of desperadoes (by teaching its men how to fight, it has to be said) do not exist. The visible powerlessness of the United Nations in the face of one conflict after another is symptomatic of the powerlessness people inside our Western democracies now feel. And what do we increasingly want to do? Reach for our own version of Genghis Khan *to sort it out*, just as many Americans reach for their pistols *to sort out* street crime.

Earlier this year (2016) the Francis Crick Institute was opened in London near Kings Cross St Pancras. At a cost approaching £700 million and annual running costs of around £100 million, it will house over a thousand scientists who will undertake biomedical research into how living organisms form and function: a good news story to set alongside the mayhem reported daily from the Middle East with its seemingly intractable consequences of rootless refugee migrants and terrorists radicalized by death, destruction, religious bigotry and western hypocrisy. And then I wondered, why in heavens name do we not have a similar centre to the Crick concentrating on how societies work? Surely many more lives are lost on account of social mismanagement than because of diseases such as cancer.

Biomedical research, like pure physics, is regarded as a hard science which seems to mean science that does not have to deal with our human character. The science that does sails under the banner of the social sciences, but this branch of study has often been its own worst enemy. Having largely sat in abeyance since the Roman-Greek period, our interest in how things worked started to gather pace in the seventeenth century and has been gaining momentum ever since. Catholic dogma, which had held the field as far as describing how the world worked for fifteen hundred years, was the first casualty. But right behind were the arts - philosophy, literature, history, etc. – which the emerging breed of social scientists regarded as woolly distractions from their new god of cause and effect.

A raft of new departments started to appear in universities – anthropology, political science, economics, linguistics, psychology, sociology – each with its own language and methodology, and even some of the old fields, such as history and the law were recrafted in pseudo-scientific clothes. Unless something could be counted and forced into a chain of cause and effect, it wasn't mainstream. History ceased to be about individuals wrestling with problems and instead concerned itself with great sweeps of inevitable change. Gertrude Himmelfarb called this *the new history and the old*, making clear that if she had anything to do with it, the old was not going to go down without a fight.

Lured by its self-proclaimed potency, I chose to study economics at university and vividly remember one professor standing with his back to the class and covering the blackboard with equations. Such precision, I thought and wondered why I didn't see the same world he did. It won't surprise you to learn that I did not go on to become an economist. Although the social sciences have been humbled since those heady days of certainty, they have cast a light over many interesting things and drawn attention to the importance of method and categorization, as well as to their limitations.

But has the field improved the human condition, as studies of electromagnetism and organic cell structures have? In spite of the hundreds of millions (pick your currency) spent on social science departments around the world, I am not sure one can answer that question in the affirmative. That there can even be doubt about this is part and parcel of the crisis affecting Western democracy today. We the people have lost faith in the ability of government to solve our problems or worse – in its ability to govern at all.

* * *

Let us consider just one issue, albeit an important one: the downside of globalization. The deregulation of markets, which enabled business (especially large business) to operate on a world stage, came about following the inflation crisis of the 1970s when entrenched labour and business practices, often underpinned by governments, drove up living costs. The proximate cause was higher oil prices (engineered by the Organization of Petroleum Exporting Countries – OPEC) which pushed up the cost of living of the oil importers.

Rather than adjusting downward to this transfer of wealth away from the importers, labour unions in the West pushed for higher wages to compensate. Market rigidities (long-standing agreements preventing wages from being reduced) led to an escalating and ultimately self-defeating rise in prices across the board which only came to an end when the authorities on both sides of the Atlantic engineered recessions which destroyed thousands of businesses and threw millions of men out of work. From then on, the free marketeers were in the ascendant and the virtue of unregulated competition became the accepted economic dogma.

After a hesitant start, worldwide trade did grow and many millions in the developing world saw their standard of living rise as companies transferred production to them, exporting what they made back into the West at lower prices. Developing countries benefitted (especially China which had chosen to adopt a hybrid model of state-sponsored capitalism), Western consumers benefitted, corporations benefitted, and the free marketeers who had ascended the heights of government were able to bask in the aura of a job well done. There were, however, a couple of flies lurking inside this otherwise sweet-smelling balm.

The first was obvious to everyone but could be ignored as victors can always ignore the vanquished, aided and abetted as they are by the many who just want an end to the crisis. From the once-mighty Detroit, home to the Ford Motor Company, Jimmy Hoffa of the Teamsters Union and Tamla-Motown Records (Smokey Robinson, Stevie Wonder, Marvin Gaye, the Supremes) to the steel towns of South Wales and coal mining communities of the Rhondda Valley, Clackmannanshire and Yorkshire, men whose skills had once earned them high wages were unable to support themselves, let alone their families. Their once-mighty trades unions seemed powerless. Their cities and towns crumbled around them. Those who could leave did so. It was as if John Steinbeck's *Grapes of Wrath* had been brushed off for a new generation. There was some sympathy of course, as there was for the aristocratic victims of France's revolution, but the bigger feeling was that they had lived high on the hog for long enough. There would, however, be an afterburn to this story.

The second fly in the free market ointment was altogether less visible. Even most of those in a position to see it chose to look the other way. When everything appears to be going well playing Cassandra is rarely career-enhancing. The exporting countries in the developing world (and this included the oil exporters) were racking up large cash surpluses which their still-developing economies were unable to absorb. Much of this footloose capital ended up in the two financial centres best able to handle it – London and New York – where it had to find a return for its new owners. In the absence of any other products which needed financing, the boys and girls on Wall Street (who were nothing if not inventive) started to come up with products of their own.

At first it all looked rather promising. In London the Royal Bank of Scotland borrowed a ton of money to purchase a number of companies, including parts of the Dutch Bank ABN AMRO, briefly becoming the world's largest bank and earning its chief executive a knighthood. In April 2008 however, the bank was forced to admit that what it had bought was worth some £5.9 billion less than the amount it had paid and its slide into bankruptcy had begun (averted only by a £37 billion government-brokered bailout courtesy of the UK taxpayer).

In the United States money was being lent at a prodigious rate to aspirant home owners, something dear to the heart of both main political parties. Bundles of mortgages were packaged together to include reasonable and less reasonable credit risks and the debt rating agencies were persuaded to accord these 'products' a good score on the assumption that these packages as a whole would prove viable. Unfortunately the incentives to originate them and sell them on were more generous than the scrutiny over what went into them was effective (an unintended consequence of financial deregulation).

Only when legions of these toxic offerings (and other equally inventive financial instruments) had found their way into every part of the financial system did it start to dawn on people that Mr and Mrs Jackson of Wayne, Michigan (and thousands like them) were never going to be able to repay their mortgage. Panic set in. Financial institutions from banks to insurance companies tried to offload this tainted paper. Prices collapsed and the financial sector would have seized up entirely had not the government stepped in with – yes – generous amounts of taxpayer money.

* * *

Considering this sequence of events overall, what conclusions can one draw? The first is that globalization did increase economic activity to the great benefit of many in the developing world and to the benefit of consumers in the developed world. The second is that those in the developed world whose jobs were exported to the developing world, together with the communities they supported, suffered mightily. The third is that the deregulation which facilitated globalization led to an ineffective level of supervision when it came to mortgage-lending in the USA and to a cavalier attitude towards bank expansion in the UK. The fourth is that when the consequences of these failures surfaced it was deemed too risky to let the market dish out the necessary corrective medicine in the form of bank and insurance company failures (which would have damaged innocent and guilty alike), and governments stepped in with taxpayer money (thereby saving innocent and guilty alike).

Fifth, it is clear that asymmetric economic activity - such as when developing-country exports generate huge cash surpluses which can only be absorbed by the financial institutions in the importing developed countries - is potentially destabilizing. Sixth, while the deflationary effects of low-cost production (brought about by the use of technology to de-skill work and the export of work to low-cost areas) has benefitted those in developed countries with well-paid jobs, it has reduced the pool of well-paid jobs available in developed countries. Seventh, this shrinkage in well-paid jobs has put downward pressure on consumption in the developed world, marginalizing some of the developing world's new productive capacity and leading to a surfeit of worldwide capital – now unable to find a productive or even an unproductive use – manifest by the collapse in interest rates.

Finally, in the face of all these moving parts now grinding rather noisily against one another because of their variable lags, governments in both the developed and developing worlds are appearing incompetent. In the developed world this is opening the door to populists, each offering their own brand of miracle cure, thereby adding political to economic instability. In the developing world the perceived failings of free market capitalism and capitalism's handmaiden, democracy, is leading to a strengthening in authoritarian centralization.

* * *

To say that the crisis in Western democracy is down to a lack of competence would be true, but it does not bring us closer to the root cause of the incompetence. Whilst there are undoubtedly incompetent individuals, as there are in any field of life, at the root of democracy's difficulties is the structure of democracy itself. In the United States its structure was deliberate, being the product of some of the finest political thinkers of the age. The use of two legislative chambers (the House of Representatives and the Senate) was designed to reflect the immediate concerns of the electorate (Congressmen in the first chamber are elected for two-year terms), as well as the longer term needs of the nation (Senators in the second chamber are elected for six-year terms).

Executive authority is reserved to the President, elected for a maximum of two four-year terms. The application of the law is separate from the Presidency and Congress and ultimately falls under the authority of the Supreme Court. Supreme Court justices are nominated by the President and appointed by the Senate: there are currently nine. Overarching all of this is the Constitution of the United States which seeks to ensure a balance between individual rights, the rights of states vis-à-vis the Federal Government, that the views of the electorate are reflected in legislation, but that swings in sentiment are moderated and that the government, through the presidency, can take action.

The political disposition of the United Kingdom does not owe its authority to any constitution, but evolved over many hundreds of years. The head of state is the monarch (a hereditary position) but executive power rests with the prime minister of the day, the leader of the party with most members elected to the House of Commons. The upper chamber, the House of Lords, now consists mostly of appointed members although some hereditary members remain, and is concerned primarily with revising legislation originating in the Commons. As in the United States, the application of the law functions separately but in the United Kingdom draws its authority directly from the head of state.

There are many subtleties on both sides of the Atlantic not summarized here, but the essential principles both sets of arrangements seek to address are the same and their way of doing so is similar. Elsewhere in the world, democratic systems are comparable and all have the same glaring weakness: issues are framed in party political terms, which is about the disposition of power and not in terms of the problems to be solved. Issues are submerged within electoral soundbites and when a party is in power, are fed through the filter of political advantage. In short, the system expends more energy maintaining itself than in solving problems.

* * *

If we consider two great cities, each with around 8.5 million people, it is plain that polities do not need complex political structures in order to function. Both possess elected mayors with executive powers whose primary function is strategic – laying out what each city needs to do to maintain itself going forward. London is divided up into local authorities whose task is to deal with local issues. In New York, each district elects one individual to the City Council. In London, the Mayor's decisions are scrutinized by the 25 elected members of the London Assembly. Although party politics exist, the government of both cities is primarily geared towards problem solving.

Both cities have had to deal with change. New York all but went bankrupt in the 1970s when its manufacturing base and tax revenue collapsed, aggravated by a middle class exodus to the suburbs to escape its rising crime rate. London has only recently moved to a mayoral system (to counter the party political gridlock that blighted its administration), but it too has had to deal with extraordinary upheavals – from the Great Fire of 1666, through waves of immigration, industrial pollution and two world wars. But the remarkable thing about these two conurbations is that for most of the time they have run themselves, responding best to an intelligent, firm and focused hand on their tillers of government whenever there are specific problems to be solved. Party political whinging is held in contempt. Competence is what matters.

The United Kingdom has an advantage over the United States. It is more compact (93,000 sq. miles to 3.8 million), has fewer people (65 million to 324 million) and, crucially, has an embedded civil service. In theory, at least this last should allow the UK to devise solutions to problems that are focused on more than the next election. But the tradition is that Britain's civil service does not speak unless it is spoken to and the fiction is that it is the elected members of government who run the country (when what they most often do is confound the work of the civil service). In the United States it is frequently the state governments which come up with innovative solutions to problems while the federal government wallows in partisan gridlock leaving the President to keep himself, his state department and his military occupied spreading the West's superior form of government overseas.

The West's democratic system is badly broken. If China could just bring itself to separate its law from its political party it might even have an edge. In the meantime, we in the West are likely to stumble from crisis to crisis until we accept that we live in an uncertain world, that actions have consequences, often unseen, and that problems are there to be solved by thought, effort, trial and, inevitably, error. Party political bluster is no longer something we can afford.

18

A shared model

IN these essays I have sought to address, in one way or another, how societies work. In this regard I have tried to tie their workings into the way our universe works more generally. The essential concepts are these: what we are part of is dynamic and symbiotic, its energy transforms into structures, structures are time-limited, types of structure have evolved which serve as platforms for new types with each elaborating to the extent the physical rules we are all subject to permit, and that the loose-tight relationship between structures allows for creative outcomes (which is to say outcomes it is impossible to plan for precisely). While it is dangerous to infer directionality in all of this (for fear of elevating mankind to some unwarranted pinnacle) it is hard to escape the conclusion that consciousness (in spite of its tentative nature at present) represents an energy-matter transformation beyond the biological.

Now, turning to social structures specifically, several things have been suggested. Unlike animals, conscious beings organize themselves in a particular way. Instead of relying on instinct or on learnt behaviours, humans have embedded their thinking within structures, some of which are hard, like buildings and roads, and others softer, like laws, customs and hierarchical arrangements. The purpose of these structures is to guide daily activity so that individuals function collectively in a manner that sustains them. In effect, these structures do much of our thinking for us and so are, if you like, cerebral. However, these arrangements have to mean something to us at the level of felt experience.

Drop a Londoner into the Amazon forest and he would have no idea what to do, but an Amazonian Indian knows exactly what to do. Now reverse these roles and the Amazonian would be the helpless alien. So the second key element in how conscious beings function is the way in which they imbue their constructed environment with meaning. The Amazonian has to take the forest as a given and learn how to survive within it through experience and example. He will be subject to some tribal protocols reinforced by storytelling, peer pressure, example and ritual but the bulk of his environment (the forest) is fixed. As conscious beings have evolved, what was fixed has progressively become constructed.

However, for all practical purposes this constructed environment is as fixed as the forest for most individuals most of the time. A crucial difference is that the constructed environment contains sub-structures (and an increasing number of them) which individuals can learn to navigate and derive succour from (the wage they receive from a company, for example). This endows the whole (the extended tribe as society) with considerable adaptive capacity. Not only can individuals engage in differentiated activity (the specialization Adam Smith and others have identified as a driver of growth), but the capacity of society as a whole is greatly magnified and strengthened by the proliferation of sub-structures that seek out opportunities and can be abandoned whenever these imagined opportunities do not materialize.

Another important difference – although it only takes effect over the long term – is that consciousness requires any given set of social arrangements to be perceived by individuals as legitimate. This is somewhat nebulous, but it is important. There is not much point in the Amazonian fretting about the nature of the forest (although he might have concerns about tribal decision-making, even though its scope is likely to be limited). Similarly, for long periods of time individuals are unlikely to see much point in questioning the structure of the society they find themselves living in. Equilibrium is generally a desirable state. If you possess the essentials for life, know where you stand and can navigate within your part of the constructed environment, why feel aggrieved? It is when the structure fails for some reason and you find yourself hungry or at risk of attack that its legitimacy comes into question.

As a tribe (or collection of animals) which finds that its location can no longer sustain it will move on, so the legitimacy of a constructed environment will be questioned by its inhabitants should it fail them. Sometimes people can vote with their feet as they did in their millions when they left the perceived failures of Europe for the imagined bounty of North America, but generally the only option they have is to protest and because states in equilibrium are, by their nature, resistant to change, such protests are generally violent.

A striking feature of human society has been the preponderance of organized violence. Not enough is understood about this but both spontaneous and socially sanctioned violence have acted as destabilizing spurs to social adjustment, whether they be changes of leadership, alterations to social arrangements, technical innovations, or even revolutions in the way people see their place in the world. It also seems likely that violence (organized and spontaneous) has served to release social tensions and thereby preserve the status quo by giving it time to adjust. There must be many a union leader and corporate executive (albeit covertly) who have recognized the therapeutic value of a strike.

Alongside the growing sophistication of our constructed environment, albeit a product of the often clumsy and costly process that has prompted humans to adjust their social systems and support themselves in increasingly large numbers, must be set a mechanism conscious beings have extrapolated from the biological world – tribalism. In biology, species differentiate to produce a complex interdependent environment. Humans have differentiated themselves by adopting different identities (or roles) which are no less interdependent than their biological counterparts, but which involve little biological change. Put a crown upon a man and he becomes a king; dress him in rags and he becomes a pauper.

The differentiation in roles in itself is far from being a problem and indeed, as stated earlier, has enabled human systems to become increasingly adaptable and effective in sustaining conscious life. The problem arises, to use Marshall McLuhan's advertising insight, when the medium becomes the message, or to put it another way, when rulers come to think of themselves as being more important than anyone else. We have, gradually, come to see this and to distinguish the role from its occupant, but we are still ill-equipped to take an objective view of the role itself. Along with the rest of our constructed environment, we tend to take roles as a given.

To their great benefit (and let's even say to their credit) the English have managed to redefine the role of their ultimate leader. The monarch is still the head of state, but executive power has been devolved to the country's prime minister. There were many dynastic battles along the way and tussles between nobles and kings, but following one regicide (the execution of Charles I by Oliver Cromwell's Puritan Parliament) and one bloodless coup (the so-called Glorious Revolution of 1688 when the Catholic-leaning James II was forced out by Protestant parliamentarians in favour of his Protestant daughter and her husband, the avowedly Protestant Dutchman, William of Orange) the English alighted upon their seemingly illogical solution. The chief executive could be hired and fired and do unpopular but necessary things without besmirching the nation's symbol of itself.

Whether individuals continue to be willing to serve as monarchs, not by choice but by birth, remains to be seen, but this creative and unforeseen development is precisely how conscious systems will evolve. The French, always a more literal people than the English who are suspicious of 'logic' and prone to pragmatism, have struggled to work out how best to relate symbolic and executive power. France is now on her fifth attempt at a solution (the Fifth Republic), having oscillated between too little and too much presidential power. The glory days of Louis XIV and assertiveness of her revolution lie uncomfortably together inside her people's subconscious minds.

The problem arises when our individual identity becomes tied to this or that role. This is where tribalism comes into play. People become monarchists or republicans; communists or capitalists; Catholics or Protestants; English, French, Scots or Dutch – the divisions parallel our ability to differentiate. You might question whether assuming a national identity constitutes assuming a role, but it clearly does. A role is an identifiable set of behaviours which define an occupant's relationship with his environment. It is only different from a biological genus or species in that it is a product of the conscious mind and embodies behaviours which are more malleable than characteristics.

The British were recently asked if they wished to remain within the European Union. By a small margin (3.78%) they indicated that they did not (although it is far from clear that the decision was more than an expression of general discontent). The Scots, Northern Irish and Londoners, however, were inclined to remain within the Union but it was the English outside London who were minded to leave. This was a living example of how identity can be converted into action, often with profound consequences, even though the differentiating basis of the identity may be neither obvious nor marked. When German, French and British soldiers crossed into the no-man's-land in December 1914 to celebrate Christmas together they were allowing their shared identity to override their national one. But the machinery of nationalism soon returned and the mutual butchery would continue for another four years until one of the belligerents admitted defeat.

Systems run to their own logic (the logic of systemic self-preservation) and we need to be aware of that. When Britain's ex-foreign secretary (and pillar of the establishment) who had lost one of his sons in the early stages of the war called for a negotiated peace in November 1917 he was widely derided as a grieving old man who had lost his way and the conflict ground on for a further twelve months. At that point German records suggest the German High Command thought they could win and would have been no more inclined to settle than the British. One side had to lose. That was the rule of the 'game'. That Europe as a whole would be the loser was lost on almost everyone. The European system had all but destroyed itself.

The systems that we build hold immense power over us – we simply can't function without them, which is why we must learn to build arrangements that are better able to adapt. This requires that we develop the capacity to stand back from the schemes we are part of. The power of the Shakespearean play lies in the way it enables us to see and feel the conflicts inherent within our political (and social) undertakings, to feel the dichotomies between what the structure demands and what individuals desire. Holding up the mirror to ourselves in this way is a vital first step. The next is developing a shared understanding of what we are part of in concrete actionable terms. We have to be able to adapt our systems consciously without allowing them to fall apart. To do this we will need shared knowledge and shared values: in other words, a shared model of how the social systems we are part of work.

Let us take a concrete example. The Syrian civil war has been raging since March 2011 (it is October 2016 as I write this). The Syrian government, led since 2000 by Bashar al-Assad, son of Hafez al-Assad, who took control of the country in 1971 after decades of political instability which followed the founding of the republic in 1946, has been fighting on several fronts to retain control. Western-inspired groups, impatient with the government's authoritarian methods, resorted to armed resistance with tacit support from the West (principally Britain and the United States).

Sensing the regime's weakness, Islamic fundamentalists (spawned by the defeat of Saddam Hussein's Sunni government in Iraq at the hands of the United States), have managed to occupy much of the centre of the country. In the north, on the border with Turkey, Kurdish nationalists (suppressed by the Ottoman Turks in the first half of the 20th century) are making a play to reclaim part of what was once Kurdistan. The Syrian government is strong in the west of the country where its predominantly Alawite members are based (the Alawite sect is a branch of Islam). Russia (with a military base in Syria), Iran and Hezbollah (both Shia) are supporting the government. Saudi Arabia (predominantly Sunni) is supporting the fundamentalists. The Sunni and Shia sects of Islam have a long history of mutual hostility. Such a cocktail of competing interests would be hard to invent.

As in all wars, and particularly civil wars, it is the non-combatants who are suffering the most, regardless of their individual sympathies. The only way this suffering will cease is if order is reinstated and for that to happen authority needs to be restored.

It is hard to escape the conclusion that imperial meddling in the Middle East has caused no end of problems. Countries were created with little regard to ethnicity, leaders were imposed, community sensibilities ignored and, worst of all, especially in the case of the 2003-2011 Iraq war, functioning polities were destroyed for spurious motives and anarchy left behind. If this was not immoral, it is a challenge to say what is. Liberalism prides itself on being opposed to doctrinaire religion and conservative rigidities but its proponents seem to forget that in our constructed environment freedom without order is a bucolic illusion.

Notwithstanding that charming piece of Irish wisdom given to any lost traveller seeking direction - *well I wouldn't want to be starting from here* - what can be done and what can be learnt? The government could just consolidate around its western stronghold, but that would leave those inclined to Western democratic values caught between the government they opposed and the fundamentalists they would find even harder to live with. The Kurds in the north could probably hold their own except for the fact that Turkey seems implacably opposed to anything that looks like the rebirth of a Kurdish state either in northern Syria or northern Iraq. And apart from Saudi Arabia (and even its ruler's motives are complex) few outside Syria want to see the fundamentalists carve out an independent state of their own.

This suggests that the sooner the government can regain control over the country the better it is likely to be for the majority of its citizens. But, even with Russian help and America's tacit acceptance, is the Syrian government capable of this? And even if it is, how long would its writ run before further fighting broke out? We do not know the answers to these questions but it seems reasonable to suppose that (a) if the international community as a whole got behind the Syrian government, the fighting would be over sooner rather than later and (b) that, if the international community was willing to help a victorious Syrian government craft a more enduring set of political arrangements, the country's future would be better rather than worse and post-victory recriminations reduced. Having secured the Union, Abraham Lincoln knew full well that it would be a hollow victory if enmities were allowed to fester (as they sadly did between the black and white communities).

Tribalism flourishes in the absence of a more enlightened structure and it would be hard to pretend that the international community has demonstrated enlightenment. Hand-wringing and breast-beating are gestures of impotence that serve only to sap moral feeling: if you can't do something useful do not pretend that you can. Apartheid in South Africa was eventually brought to an end by internal and external pressure, although rule by the ANC (successor to the white-dominated government) must have disappointed many black South Africans so far. Protestant and Catholic have reached an accommodation in Northern Ireland thanks to enlightened leadership inside and outside the province, but only after countless lives were lost. Tribal hostilities can be overcome if structures are put in place which people understand and come to trust more than their tribal allegiances.

The assumption I am making is that there are solutions to problems, but only if the true nature of those problems is understood and there exists an authority more powerful than the belligerents willing to put that authority on the line for wholly altruistic reasons. America's roll-back of Iraq from Kuwait was a textbook case of the latter, but such examples are rare and this one constituted the defense of an identifiable community with a functioning government from the aggression of another by an infinitely superior power. When Poland was threatened by Germany from the west and Russia from the east in 1939 no outside authority was willing to come to its aid.

Conflicts within a functioning nation are far harder for outside interests to influence successfully. If such interventions are to be justified and stand any chance of success, they have to be combined with a genuine understanding of how hard it is to create and maintain a functioning polity. There are surely only two situations which justify intervention: (1) when a nation is being threatened by outside interests and its government asks for assistance; and (2) when a law-abiding minority within a country (and where the laws in question apply to everyone) is being systematically persecuted by that country's majority.

The question then arises who, or rather what body, is entitled to intervene at all. The League of Nations and United Nations were both conceived in hope and both have floundered on the rocks of reality. Rarely have these bodies come even close to protecting citizens caught up in conflict.

Take Syria. The government has been fighting multiple opponents. As much of the fighting has taken place within cities, the citizens in these cities have come under sustained attack whether or not they are active belligerents. Who is responsible: those trying to topple the government or the government? As every government has the duty to defend itself, responsibility lies with the government's opponents. Now we need to go back a step. What did the government do to foment opposition?

The Assad regime, like the Hussein regime in Iraq, both dominated by minority sects within their own country, took a hard line against opposition and offended Western liberals in the process. Beyond that, neither regime was overly vindictive (save to political opponents), and their countries functioned reasonably well. Saddam certainly made two bad calls: his war against Iran and his invasion of Kuwait, although it is not hard to see why he made them. Iran had long been a thorn in Iraq's side and appeared weak following the fall of the Shah and rise of its Shia theocracy and Kuwait's oil wealth must have seemed like an easy target. When Bashar al-Assad took over from his father, many better-educated Syrians with a pro-Western orientation hoped for a less authoritarian government but they were disappointed. With Western help, their opposition to the regime turned militant, and this opened the door to Sunni fundamentalists. All one can reasonably say about both countries is that neither was likely to function effectively without forceful government and neither has benefitted from Western intervention.

The flood of refugees pouring out of Syria has upset Europe (one of their destinations) as well as the liberal Western media, understandably appalled by the suffering of the Syrian people. However the liberal media's visceral dislike of the Assad regime has blinded it to a simple truth: the suffering will only end when the government reasserts control over the country, so the sooner this is achieved the better. In this regard, Russia – invited in by the government – is doing exactly the right thing. If Europe wishes to help both itself and the Syrian people, establishing refugee camps on the Syrian border with the tacit or actual consent of the Syrian government, which are fully protected, properly funded and armament free (save for the arms of their protectors) would be wholly justified.

If the Syrian government does reassert control and the civil war does end, what then? If Bashar al-Assad simply becomes a Russian stooge he will not last long (as has been the fate of successive Western- and Soviet-backed stooges before him). After a period of consolidation he will have to rebuild his country and outside support will be crucial. Those providing it will have legitimate grounds for suggesting ways to avoid further divisions, although the temptation will be for the government to eliminate all remaining opposition, real and imagined (as President Recep Tayyip Erdogan appears to be doing in Turkey following the failed coup there). This is a matter for the Syrian government and no one else. Only time will tell if the judgements it makes were the right ones.

* * *

A shared model of how societies work is a very simple idea and it is this: if a collection of people with differing sub-interests share an over-arching interest in the stability of what they are part of, they will be better-able to adapt the social arrangements which govern their collective lives to both internal and external pressures. Clearly the idea of "nationalism" – my country right or wrong – served this function, particularly in cases of external threat. With regard to internal tensions it was less effective although it did tend to set a boundary within which differences had to be settled. Guarded calls for external help to some outside power were not uncommon, however, even though they invariably floundered on conflicts of interest when outside powers demand their pound of flesh.

Both the United Nations and League of Nations before it ignored this simple logic, although the UN charter did, ostensibly, forbid it from interfering in a member nation's internal affairs. This sensible limitation has not stopped governments of this or that persuasion, egged on by those they represent, in turn egged on by their media (the *something must be done* brigade who pedal moral certainties in order to sell news) from doing just that. The most egregious recent example was America's invasion of Iraq on the trumped-up charge that Saddam Hussein's Iraq was a clear and present threat to the West.

A distinction must be drawn here between interfering in the internal affairs of a nation and helping a persecuted minority within a nation. This is not just semantics. If a nation singles out a group within it for exclusion (i.e. to be treated as if they are not full citizens), then that group has no nation and deserves the protection of any power willing to give it. Even this is not wholly straightforward in that criminals, as a class of person, are treated differentially by every nation and ideologically-driven governments have often branded as criminals those unwilling or unable (due to characteristics of birth such as Jewishness or aristocratic lineage) to comply with their ideology.

The best that one can suggest is that where a minority is being persecuted, any nation with a natural sympathy towards it should offer its members a safe haven and assist them in reaching it. In practice this has often been done, but by individual nations (or groups within them), not by the United Nations which, if we are honest about it, is a contradiction in terms. Bodies like the World Health Organization (WHO) do operate within a model that is, by and large, shared globally because disease is no respecter of national borders.

Shared models are constantly evolving. Elected governments,

for example, were a novel idea and universal suffrage was slow in coming. But just because one group of people stumbles upon a set of arrangements that seem to work for them in no way entitles that group to chase around the globe proclaiming those arrangements to be the new certainty. Firstly, any description of what they are is likely to be a misleading shorthand which ignores all the steps that led up to them. Secondly, the people being lectured almost certainly have a comparable set of arrangements masquerading under different customs and descriptions. Thirdly, all arrangements must be viewed as work in progress and so never the final solution to anything. And finally, until we develop a common language to describe social arrangements and a common way of demonstrating their veracity, verbal friction across groups will be little better than dialogues between those who are both blind and deaf: would that they were also dumb.

You can see why the default position within and without polities is a hyped-up version of whack-a-mole: by bludgeoning your opponent back below ground no further dissuasion is needed. Might is right, except that it rarely is. But when more thinking is just too hard to contemplate it seems as though it is. Conscious man has an awful lot still to learn.

19

Hierarchy

HIERARCHY is ubiquitous in human affairs. Why is that? All matter consists of structure and as we know from Einstein's equation (E=MC²) it also consists of energy. The character of structure determines how that energy is directed. To exist at all, structures must possess a boundary and so be self-contained. However structures exist in space-time and so are interdependent. But it is the space between structures (not empty but fluid) that underpins the dynamic nature of the whole. The function of a structure can only be thought of in terms of its relationship with other structures. Relationships are defined in terms of the transfer and transmutation of energy. The context within which all this occurs is evolutionary. Evolution is the accretive creation of function within space-time.

An interesting expression which one sometimes hears at memorial gatherings is *We stand here on the shoulders of giants.* It is, I suppose, a modern version of ancestor worship and an acknowledgement of what we owe the past. On this basis the universe is an inverse cone (although spreading out in all directions) with an *in the beginning* from which everything has flowed. This is our biblical and scientific story. God encompasses the rules of the universe and whereas once we sought solutions to our problems through plea, now we do so by trying to understand and apply those rules. God, as their embodiment is, indeed, all powerful. The father figure, the source, the fountainhead sits at the heart of our thinking and predisposes us to hierarchy. But there is also a more practical reason for hierarchy.

Let us think for a moment about what the biological is, that structures before that evolutionary leap were not. The most obvious distinguishing feature of biological structures is their short lifespan and independence of action coupled with an ability to replicate and mutate. This sounds like four distinguishing features – short lifespan, independence of action, replication and mutation – but each of these existed prior to the evolution of biological structures. It was only within the boundary of biological structures that they were combined (unless you include the boundary which included the universe itself).

A chemical element, such as lead (Pb, atomic # 82) is defined by its atomic arrangement (electron configuration and chemical properties). The Periodic Table (largely compiled by Dmitri Mendeleev in 1869) describes all known chemical elements in terms of their similarity (how they behave). Without the world of chemical elements, the biological could not have come into existence. Chemical elements have generally been synthesized within stars. Stars are super-heated plasma (gas in which electrons and ions can move independently) held together by gravity, consisting mostly of hydrogen atoms (71%) and helium atoms (27%). So the evolution of chemical elements could not have come about without the expansion of the universe and subsequent clustering of its gaseous nature into galaxies and stars and eventually planets (the by-product of solar collapse).

So from the origin of our universe 13.82 billion years ago, structures have come and gone, exhibited independence of action, multiplied and been transformed into other structures. But it took the favourable conditions on earth to allow simple organisms to form (essentially combinations of chemical elements), which were sensitive to their environment (from which they drew energy), were able to replicate by simple division and were sufficiently malleable to permit mutations able to populate (and create) new niches all of which over 3.55 billion years created the biological diversity we know today.

The evolution of consciousness has been underway for some time. Indeed it is part of what constitutes biology in that independence of action necessitates an organism's reactive sensitivity to its environment. Awareness entails memory albeit without reflection. A successful mutation is simply a chance chemical rearrangement which turns out to be sustainable in conjunction with its environment and other organisms. Such evolutionary symbiosis builds up memory pathways of what has gone before which are transmitted into organisms going forward. Learning by experience moved things along in an evolutionary sense in that the consequences of life enhancing and life threatening actions could be internalized within an organism and added to memory, thereby refining an organism's survival capability.

This, however, was a two-edged sword (as far as evolution overall is concerned) in that it tended to produce diverse specializations each with a narrower and narrower range of possibilities for change. The great Andean condor may be superbly adapted to the updrafts of the Andes and great ground distances between carrion, but has little scope to adapt to the changes in its environment wrought by man. That said, biology's diversity has been its saving grace. The numerous extinction events which have taken place on earth since the onset of biological life (at least six major extinctions have occurred on earth, the worst of them eliminating at least 96% of all marine species and 70% of all terrestrial vertebrates) attest to the benefits of there being many structural irons in the biological firmament – at least some are likely to survive rapid environmental change.

It took the generalist structure (one not well adapted to a single niche) to move things forward. To do so however, this structure required an organ (its brain) able to adapt to particular situations and extract the best from them. This analytic ability gradually mutated into model-building or the conscious awareness of alternatives. Whilst hardwired memory is effective (we call these instinctive survival reactions built up within species and transmitted over time from one generation to the next), it is slow to adapt and not well suited to ambiguous complexity (where the 'right' course of action is unclear). Consciousness facilitated a more nuanced array of responses and, allied with tool-making and (eventually) communication using symbols, has enabled Homo sapiens to carve out a whole new level of existence.

A crucial component in man's advance has been differentiated group behaviour (having different members of a group perform separate functions all allied to the group's success). This is a great deal easier said than done and has occupied much of man's endeavours over the last five thousand years or so, although I doubt many of us understood it as such. The first problem to be overcome is what constitutes a group. Initially I do not imagine that this was perceived as a problem: one's group was one's extended family. Differentiated group behaviour also fell naturally into male and female roles and is evident in the animal world.

Leadership roles, if one can call them that, were variable with some animal groups opting for dominant females and others for dominant males. Their functionality however, was always to do with ensuring group cohesion and the success of the next generation. In humans, the ability to conceptualize and communicate alternative survival strategies became steadily more pronounced and these included the increasing use of differentiated organization as a way of increasing the output of those commodities essential to human survival. But this increased differentiation posed a new problem: how to persuade individual humans to limit themselves to specific activities. Force by some over others was one strategy used successfully and underpinned many sophisticated societies both before and after the Roman Empire. But this slides over another human innovation with powerful implications: competition between polities (with those conquered becoming slaves to their conquerors).

But before we consider that there is a question to answer: how does one get conscious individuals to function differentially as a team? It cannot all be down to force because making people operate against their will places a heavy enforcement burden on a society (not only does the cost of supporting the enforcers have to be borne by those doing productive work, but forced labour tends to use up individuals and is invariably less effective than voluntary labour). If individuals buy into the role allotted to them because they believe it is in theirs and everyone else's interest that they do so, a system using differentiated organization should be able to work without undue force.

What this entails, in conscious beings, is everyone sharing a similar view about how their society should work. Such knowledge is built up by trial and error over countless generations and it is here that we must turn back to hierarchy. First and foremost, a hierarchy is simply a way of organizing functions within a polity. The functions reflect what people have come to assume are the things that need doing. Populating those functions has for long periods of time been done on the basis of heredity, with sons learning from fathers and daughters from mothers. But that is not enough.

A polity needs to be represented in some way. In this a leader becomes everyone's alter ego, representing the whole each has given up in order to play his or her differentiated part. Shared ceremonies further cement a sense of shared identity. And then there is the practical matter of decision-making: how does a polity consisting of conscious individuals arrive at collective decisions and iron out individual disputes? The leadership function must be overtly political, trying to tease out and guide the prevailing sentiment so that those decisions made by the leader on behalf of the whole actually stick.

In this it helps greatly if the Wisdom of Solomon is supplemented by a belief amongst those led that the leadership function is divinely ordained – that it is plugged into the whole in a way that differentiated ordinary people are not. Priesthoods, as depositories of specialized knowledge about a polity, have evolved alongside leadership roles, sometimes as entities to be consulted about life's imponderables, sometimes as co-administrators or as guardians of a polity's story about itself. At times this throws them into conflict with secular rulers whose claim to and use of the power hierarchical leverage affords them they challenge.

A modern example of the symbiotic relationship between a priesthood and a leader is how President John F Kennedy deferred to his Defense Secretary, Robert McNamara. With an MBA from Harvard and as an ex-president of the Ford Motor Company, McNamara represented the very best of America's administrative ability and its understanding of itself as a meritocratic and rational polity. To McNamara, stopping communist encroachment into Vietnam (following the French withdrawal from its old colony) must have seemed like a no-brainer.

So demonstrably better were America's values, that a little projection of power into the region would turn a natural tide. But as we know, a little projection turned into ever bigger projections until, in exasperation, Kennedy's successor, Lyndon Johnson, threw the military-technological handbook at the North Vietnamese. But this escalation so alienated his own people, whose menfolk resented being called up to fight what they saw as a pointless war in a faraway land, that it was left to his successor, Richard Nixon, to extract America from a war less about communism versus capitalism, than about a tenacious people wishing to reclaim their own polity from the clutches of foreigners.

And in any event, the Vietnamese (like the Chinese) have moved some way towards capitalism in their own fashion and of their own volition. As the West is discovering in the Middle East today, one polity's impeccable story may not seem so impeccable to a people whose own evolved story is different. The stories underpinning hierarchies can be imposed for a while like a veneer, but beneath their shiny surface the organically evolved story which defines a people's history is never far away.

This tells us something fundamental about hierarchies. While their architecture may be top-down to resolve conflicts and facilitate decision-making, their substance is bottom-up and consensual. This is hardly surprising because conscious individuals at the base of the pyramid greatly outnumber those at its top and while a judicious use of force combined with lashings of propaganda may intimidate and fool *all the people some of the time*, and *some of the people all the time*, it can never intimidate and fool *all the people all the time* (as Abraham Lincoln once pithily observed).

This is because conscious individuals delegate their power to the hierarchy in return for what they expect the hierarchy to do for them. Hierarchies are functional mechanisms. The limitations of an all-embracing hierarchy in the face of changing circumstances (principally its dependence upon the judgement of one man or woman and his/her advisors, all largely beholden to one story) has gradually been mitigated by the evolution of multiple hierarchies, each with specific functional objectives, embedded within the whole.

As with all structures, however, a given hierarchy (or cluster of hierarchies) will seek to defend itself. This has often been portrayed in class terms – as elites seeking to preserve those privileges that go with power at the expense of those the elites represent. This characterization, however, is naïve and has given rise to violent disruptions which promise more than they deliver. The challenge is how to build dynamic change into hierarchical structures – how to alter those components of a hierarchy which need altering without dismembering the whole thing and thereby plunging a polity into an anarchy which only a harsh imposition of order can reverse.

A case in point at the moment is the story of globalization and the worldwide hierarchy this story has sustained. The story itself is simple enough and, like all stories that take hold, quite plausible. In manufacturing, labour costs are a substantial part of the whole. So it makes sense for large manufacturing corporations to relocate plants from high wage cost areas to low wage cost areas. The consumer benefits through lower prices, the low wage cost areas benefit on account of the employment the switch brings and it is felt that the geopolitical environment is improved because all parts of the world are woven into the same global trading system.

The dark side of globalization is that manufacturing communities in the high wage cost areas are devastated (just visit Detroit) creating a pool of thoroughly dissatisfied individuals for whom globalization has been a disaster. Added to the export of jobs has been the import of labour willing to work for less, further undermining the prospects of these same individuals. The once proud manufacturing working class has, in effect, been disenfranchised and it is many of them who are now turning to populist leaders. And there may also have been a less obvious consequence of this story and its hierarchical arrangements which has further aggravated the situation.

Technological innovation and globalized cost-cutting has freed up large amounts of capital which have been pulsing though the world's capital markets making some financial operators extremely rich without doing a great deal for their underlying economies. Governments have generally been falling over themselves to reduce corporate taxation believing it necessary to attract businesses and the often lower cost service jobs they offer. Not only has this been financially destabilizing (the 2008 financial crisis being one likely consequence) but it has tended to reduce government revenues at a time when large scale infrastructure expenditure and worker re-education is badly needed.

It is gradually dawning on the elites of globalization – who have done rather well out of it - that they have been blind to the hurt caused to many of their national countrymen. But the scales are only falling from their eyes because these 'unfortunate casualties of progress' (omelettes and eggs come to mind) are now fighting back in the only way they know how: by turning their back on the globalization story and its advocates in favour of what to the oh so rational globalists are political clowns (Marine Le Pen in France, Donald Trump in the United States and the Brexiteers in England).

We have to get it into our heads that we are part of an evolutionary journey and that static equilibriums are an illusion. The best we can hope for are dynamic equilibriums and this requires that we keep improving the way individual consciousness interacts with the hierarchies we build (or as is more often the case, evolve). To take the globalization story as an example, there needed to be a way for those adversely affected by it to demand some offsetting initiative. To wait until frustration boils over into blunt political protest is not smart. In the cases of coal, steel and automobiles, neither trades unions nor elected representatives were able to act against the prevailing story of free market globalization. People in the affected communities, which free enterprise had created in the first place, were expected to get on their bikes and sort themselves out.

The old post-war story of state-directed enterprise, which favoured a static status quo, had been found wanting. Its conflicted pressures found their way into inflation just as the conflicted pressures of free market globalization are now finding their way into deflation, with the same adverse impact on all those who hold up the base of the pyramid. We tend to think of hierarchies as functional ordering mechanisms and lose sight of the fact that they are also opportunity-creating mechanisms. A rigid hierarchy loses sight of this, directing an increasing amount of its energy towards system maintenance even as changing circumstances make the system, as it is, progressively less appropriate.

When the economic pendulum swings against them, a coal town, steel town or Motown will fight to preserve the status quo until there is no great factory, rows of empty houses, countless abandoned shops, few well-paying jobs and an atmosphere of tattered martyrdom amongst residents kept afloat by welfare payments and old memories. Like aristocrats under communism they live in two rooms of their now subdivided mansion and survive without hope on a diet of bitterness. Even those like John Steinbeck's Joad family, driven by falling prices, debt and crop failure from their Midwestern farm in search of new opportunities in California's wine country, find many more doors closed to them than outstretched arms of welcome. But at least there were opportunities. America's hierarchy was multifaceted and its loose-tight properties were more likely to unearth opportunities for the future than a more rigid system would have been. Its harshness, however, was undeniable.

So how do we design hierarchies that can adapt to change while still maintaining their overall effectiveness? The laissez-faire option has much wisdom on its side in that evolution has unfolded creatively without a master plan (as far as we know) although in accordance with certain rules. Consciousness, however, obliges us to act with intent, so onto the rules of physics we have to add a rule or two of our own. Probably two general rules will suffice – a do no harm rule and an empowerment rule. The do no harm rule simply means that any action likely to cause harm to individuals should be prohibited by law unless those affected can be offered acceptable amelioration. The empowerment rule would require governments to justify all actions on the basis of how they will enhance the lives of those affected.

More specifically, we should delineate hierarchies and the

hierarchies within them more clearly, detailing their functional objectives and how progress towards those objectives can be measured. The chain of command and responsibility within hierarchies should be made explicit. All hierarchies should be time-limited.

Hierarchies serve many functions besides their overriding one – the objective they are designed to achieve. They offer the pleasures of companionship. They offer individuals a purpose. They provide a forum within which individuals can test and develop their abilities and compete for recognition and reward. They confer status and identity. In many respects, hierarchies share the attributes of the jungle tribe we never left. A senior politician once told me that all politics was essentially tribal, and there is much truth in this. However, these characteristics can present their own problems alongside the advantages they undoubtedly confer. The objective of the hierarchy can become buried within its social attributes – you can find poverty programmes that serve the programmers more than the economically disadvantaged, political parties that outlive their original purpose and regulators who become entwined with those they are supposed to regulate.

In addition to what has already been mentioned, two further adjustments might help us to move along a little. Education is woefully deficient when it comes to teaching children and young adults how their societies work. Along with reading, writing and arithmetic (the so-called three 'Rs'), understanding the dynamics of society must be a fundamental requirement for all conscious beings. Otherwise how can individuals make sense of and develop a critical understanding of what they are part of and which governs their lives?

The second thing is that social engineering needs to be brought into the mainstream. Architects and civil engineers help us design buildings. Social structures should be treated with no less rigour. Unfortunately, many in the social sciences have not covered themselves in glory by coming up with pseudo-science that is overtly political. It is not the job of science to set objectives but to establish relationships and measure outcomes. Priesthoods for millennia have sought to convert knowledge into power, largely by claiming to know more than they did. A free press is supposed to protect us from such things but much of the media is in the business of selling sensation rather than reasoned reporting and while bombarding consciousness with cocktail party chatter has undoubted entertainment value, it falls well short of the useful information we need if we are to nurse along the evolution of hierarchy.

20

Rectangular man

I HAVE often wondered why the rectangle is so ubiquitous in the human world and yet so rare everywhere else. If you are sitting in a room look around and notice how many of the structures have straight edges aligned at 90°. Now look outside the window and see how many non-human structures you can find that do the same.

We use the rectangular shape because it is easy to fabricate. I remember this from my brief exposure to carpentry. I was never good enough to use a jigsaw and cut all those shapes into a rectangular piece of plywood to create a puzzle. Much later I found myself involved in the manufacture of computer-controlled machines which cut wonderful shapes into metal. But even here one was dealing with an essentially rectangular concept.

There was an x axis and a y axis (the vertical and horizontal sides of a square, for instance) and the computer calculated a large number of continuous xy points, to trace out the desired shape. Now add a third axis z to make a three-dimensional space, tie the computer's signals to a bank of cutting tools and you can churn out three-dimensional shapes of great precision and considerable complexity for as long as the machine has power, sufficient cutting fluid to temper the heat generated by friction, cutting tools that remain sharp and enough of the metal to be profiled.

The computer did not create the shapes, of course. An individual did that using mathematical equations to describe the desired form which the computer would then convert into *xyz* points so rapidly that the movement of the cutting blades appeared continuous causing the figure to emerge out of the block of metal being worked upon as if by magic. I have not yet used one, but today you can even purchase a 3-D printer.

All those wonderful saints, gargoyles and stained glass windows which adorn the great cathedrals of the 13th century attest to the individual skill of the craftsmen who created them. The extraordinary fluidity of these massive structures, with their vaulted ceilings and flying buttresses, reflect the organic, trial and error brilliance of the age. The master masons, who accumulated the knowledge acquired in building them, were much sought after. The computer is still a tool in the hands of designers, but its attachment to machines as an adjunct to the profit and loss calculus, has eliminated the rich peculiarities of the skilled artisan and given us abundance. Rectangular man has prevailed.

But why does rectangular man not prevail in nature? Surely whatever is easiest will be adopted? Or does nature operate in a fundamentally different way to us? But if so, are we not of nature ourselves? The questions just keep piling up. Sometime around 300BCE Euclid of Alexandria set out the *Elements* of what became geometry. The Ancient Greeks seem to have been a well-organized, practical people, keen to understand how things worked. Their penchant for building encouraged them to consider the relationship between distance and angle and Euclid decided to regularize practice and reduce these spatial relationships to a few self-evident truths (axioms) from which many other propositions (theorems) could logically be deduced.

Straight lines became the shortest distance between two points; the square built on the side opposite the right angle of a right-angled triangle would equal the sum of the two squares built on the triangle's other two sides; the angles of a triangle will always sum to 180°; a triangle with equal sides must have angles of 60°; etc. This work established a set of truths separate from the situation being considered and so prevented a lot of head-scratching and relearning. The rules could be applied allowing the practitioner to be confident in their outcome, just as today we use computers and drive cars without knowing exactly how they work.

Most of the axioms were provable, but not all. One, the parallel postulate (that, if a straight line falling on two straight lines makes the interior angles on the same side less than two right angles, the two straight lines, if produced indefinitely, meet on that side on which the angles are less than two right angles) worried the ancients. To prove it one would have to walk towards infinity if the two lines were not quite parallel. As it happens, the axiom cannot be proved. Calculating the area of a circle (πr^2 where r is the circle's radius) was another slight anomaly because it required the use of an irregular number known by the Greek letter π (the ratio of a circle's circumference to its diameter) 3.14159..... and so on to infinity. But for all practical purposes, Euclidian geometry did the job.

In the 17th century the French mathematician, René Descartes, recast Euclid's axioms into algebraic form as theorems [the distance PQ between two points px, py and qx, qy, for example became $|PQ| = \sqrt{(p_x - q_x)^2 + (p_y - q_y)^2}$] making calculations even easier to manipulate and compute. But in spite of the Euclidian system's longevity and undoubted utility, some started to feel that it did not describe the world as it actually was. One such person was Albert Einstein. According to his Theory of General Relativity (1915), space-time was not Euclidean. The internal angles of a triangle constructed out of three rays of light would not sum to 180° because gravity would curve the beams and there is no objective way of describing the shortest distance between two points other than as a beam of light. GPS systems now adjust for this even though the distortion is very small in terms of earth distances.

Another person troubled by the disconnect between the rectangular world of Euclid and the natural world around us was the Polish-French-American, Benoit Mandelbrot (1924-2010). Statisticians had found much utility in what became known as a Gaussian (or normal) distribution. If you wanted to home in on the most likely outcome of a similar set of events, you could observe those events in the expectation that they would cluster around a central point with as many falling away to the left of it as to the right (hence the term, a normal distribution). Looking at stock and commodity prices, however, Mandelbrot found that their distribution was not normal but consistently skewed so that the most likely outcome would be to one side of where a normal distribution would put it.

This prompted his interest in non-normal distributions. With the help of an IBM computer he started plotting bound sets of complex numbers (numbers that combine different units of measurement such as magnitude and direction) so that, regardless of the iterations performed, the inherent rough shape plotted would be maintained. Take the difference between a beech tree and a fir tree. Each is recognizably different, but no two firs and no two beech trees are the same, although both sets of objects are unquestionably trees. Mandelbrot's fractal geometry (geometrical figures made up of parts which have the same statistical character as the whole) started producing beautiful shapes any of which the Haight-Ashbury crowd of acid droppers would have been proud to call their own. More practically, the jagged nature of a coastline could be approximated and the formation of ice crystals modelled.

It took 17th century advances in optics to give Galileo Galilei the tool to observe the night sky more closely than before and confirm the view of Copernicus (1473-1543) and some others that the heavens were not Geocentric (the Ptolemaic view that had held the field for 1500 years). In spite of a rearguard attempt by the Catholic Church to silence Galileo, the heavens were being seen in a fresh light. Isaac Newton (1642-1727) formulated laws of motion and universal gravity and used a reflecting telescope to develop a theory of colour by refracting light through a prism.

But just as we thought we were seeing the universe as it really was, along came Einstein to tell us that Newton's brilliant, mechanical, essentially Euclidian model did not reveal the full picture. Using partial differential equations, he concluded that gravity was a function of space-time (in which Euclidian space and time are combined) with objects like the sun and the earth stretching its fabric. Light, he predicted, would be bent by gravity and disappear inside black holes (regions in the fabric of space-time where the concentration of energy and matter is so great that light cannot escape).

As of now there is no theory which combines Max Planck's quantum world of sub-atomic particles (in which an electromagnetic wave, such as light, can be described as quanta or packets of energy possessing both particle and wave-like properties) with the macro world of space-time. However, having the Large Hadron Collider near Geneva concentrating on the former and the Hubble Space Telescope (launched into Earth orbit in 1990) concentrating on the latter, we are inching ever closer.

What is already certain is that how we see ourselves and the world around us is undergoing a fundamental transformation. We are part of something more integrated, more dynamic, more complex and more astonishing than we ever imagined. The rectangle will doubtless remain a staple for some time to come, but we are now beginning to realize that rectangular man never existed.

21

On being human

THERE are many ways of thinking about humanity which leave one marvelling at our irrelevance. There seem to be at least 100 billion galaxies in the observable universe. Our Milky Way galaxy alone probably contains around 100 billion stars and the same number of planets, some of which may not be too dissimilar to our own and support some kind of biological life. Our universe itself appears to be just under 14 billion years old and expanding rapidly such that many galaxies have already slipped beyond the time horizon and can no longer be seen. Other galaxies will merge as ours and the Andromeda galaxy are expected to do in 4 billion years. In short there is an awful lot of everything compared to us moving in ways that are not exactly life enhancing.

Then you have to wonder at the relevance of any single individual when there are currently over 7 billion of us and counting. Deserts and grains of sand come readily to mind. For good measure you can then play with the probability of evolution producing something like us and conclude that we are an utter fluke, of interest only to ourselves. It is small wonder we invented God and had him create us in his image. Our loneliness otherwise might have been unbearable.

But hang on a minute. Isn't that exactly what has happened. If we think of the term God as denoting the dynamic of the universe then we are God's product and we are in God's image, just like everything else. That does not mean, however, that there are any grounds for special pleading. What we are and the circumstances we find ourselves in are for us to handle. That said, although creative and not mechanical (the loose-tight property between structures allows new combinations to form), the universe is governed by rules.

So what are we and what aspect of us warrants the particular name human? Each of us is made up of some seven-billion-billion-billion atoms of which almost $2/3$ is hydrogen, $1/4$ is oxygen and $1/10$ is carbon, comprising 99% of the total. Our bodies include over 40 trillion bacteria microbes alongside 30 trillion human cells. Humans and chimpanzees (our nearest animal relative) share about 95% of their DNA, the deoxyribonucleic acid molecule which carries most of the genetic instructions used in the growth, development, functioning and reproduction of living organisms.

We are devilishly complex evolved structures governed by what we call the laws of physics and biology that have come into existence over 13.82 billion years on a planet which is around 4.5 billion years old and which has supported some form of biological life for 3.8 billion of those years. What has evolved uniquely in us is a brain able to analyze its environment and act upon it with pre-meditated purpose. Does this then mean that what makes us human is the ability to calculate? Well no. We are not actually that good at calculating and have already built machines that can do it better.

What we need to recognize is that we are nothing less than the whole universe so looking at only bits of ourselves is likely to lead us astray. Consciousness is about awareness, it is about curiosity and knowledge, it is about felt experience - the craving to share, it is about the urge to create and control, it is about the need to understand, it is about the desire to exist. These are all emotional things, not abstract, intellectual things. The challenge we face is in divining where these motivations come from and what their evolved purpose is so that we can weave them into a rich tapestry that enhances rather than diminishes the experience of unfolding life.

Inevitably we are going to have to move away from Earth at some point in the future and even if doing so is not imminent, it allows us to ask an important question. What bit of ourselves will we take? It is already becoming clear that our bodies, which can be repaired, replaced and regrown, are adjuncts to our sense of life so it is on understanding and developing that sense of life that we should concentrate. But while our sense of life is a personal, individual matter, our existence as human beings is social and so it is how best to organize ourselves in this regard which demands attention.

Although thinkers from Plato to James Madison have thought and written about it, social architecture is not the coherent mainstream subject it needs to be. For example, it should be perfectly normal to pick a local area and experiment with improvements to its accountability and governance. It should also be perfectly normal for social architecture to be taught in schools, not as some obscure elective, but as the subject of greatest importance to all of us. If being human means anything it surely means working on the evolution of our collective lives, not as some dry mechanical subject but as an endlessly enriching and creative one.

Our biological drivers (those evolved, deeply embedded survival instincts) need to be understood and then managed. For example, it is rather extraordinary that we still think it normal to kill one another on a prodigious scale in order to resolve disputes. Yes, we make muttering noises about places like Iraq, Libya and Syria – and then get involved in the killing ourselves, all in the name of democracy of course, while trying (often unsuccessfully) to avoid what we politely call collateral damage.

We need to take peacekeeping seriously, which means not just sending in blue-helmeted troops mostly untrained for the job, with a mandate to do almost nothing. The first Iraq war was a model intervention. Iraq invaded Kuwait and American troops sent the invaders packing. The second Iraq war was an utter disaster. Launched on a false premise, the military did what it was told to do which was to destroy a functioning state. But military efficiency was offset by political incompetence because no one had thought through how the country was to be run after its social infrastructure had been wiped out. States (even dictatorships - perhaps especially dictatorships) are delicate organisms. Supporting them one minute and then destroying them the next is extraordinarily stupid.

To a visitor from another galaxy, it would be hard to escape the conclusion that part of being human was belligerence. But look beneath the surface and what one would see are social organisms fighting for if not dominance, then certainly survival. Humans have created a whole new ecosystem populated by polities of various shapes and sizes, all competing for resources. And what underpins the structures of these different polities are sets of ideas which seek to legitimize them in the eyes of the conscious individuals who make them up. Ideas, in the broadest sense of that word, and how to express them are at the heart of what it means to be human.

Most animal species have worked out how to resolve conflicts amongst themselves (in the main over which male should be permitted to propagate the next generation) without inflicting fatalities. Humans have done this in the field of commerce and to a large extent in choosing leaders, but have been extraordinarily unsuccessful in the field of intergovernmental relations. And if one looks at this specifically, larger, expanding polities are more likely to wage war against smaller polities than the other way around, except when a social ecosystem becomes crowded and matched polities tear into one another, presumably because they possess no overarching structure to mediate between them. In such situations, evolved intelligence has clearly been outgunned by evolved biology.

Notwithstanding how disgusting the treatment of humans by humans can be, it is worth dwelling on what lies behind it. Straightforward killing is a facet of our biological nature. The excitement of the hunt is palpable and draws on that instinct to capture prey for food and so to survive. As instincts go, it has a far longer lineage than Moses's tablets urging us not to kill. More complex and in many ways more intriguing is the urge to inflict pain (and its converse, the urge to have pain inflicted upon one). Explanations are somewhat tentative, but watching some male birds virtually gang rape their female opposite number probably provides the clue. Domination and submission are integral components in group dynamics. When filtered through consciousness, the urge to let go and the urge to control can become elective and not merely instinctive.

Of still greater interest and importance is the use of cruelty images in the governance of hierarchies. The public flogging of miscreants on board sailing ships was considered essential in maintaining order amongst these small communities of men living cheek by jowl. English and Scots magistrates (known as sheriffs in Scotland) frequently regarded a good hanging to be a useful expedient when it came to maintaining public order, especially in instances of mass protest. Absolute fairness was often a secondary consideration. Likewise, the threat of torture (the more gruesome the better) could have a chilling effect on any tempted to challenge the status quo.

Uniquely, human beings possess an imagination (the product of consciousness) which can build a cause and effect model, linking its components to actual feelings: *the sheer thought of it sent shivers down my spine.* The brutality of the Roman Circus played to the natural sadism of both males and females and to their sense of schadenfreude (the pleasure derived from another's misfortune), as well as emphasizing the hierarchy's power of life and death over its individuals.

Politics is, in large part, the management of instincts as they manifest themselves in the conscious realm. An aspirant leader might appeal to the sectional interests of the cohort he or she is attempting to dominate by vilifying a minority: *they are not one of us*. This is a blatant appeal to species (or sub-species) identity. Jewish identity is enhanced by the prohibition against marrying outside the 'faith'. Unfortunately this projection of 'we are special' can evoke a strong reaction by 'outsiders' to expel the self-proclaimed 'alien' in their midst. Racism draws on a deep instinct to protect those most like ourselves and is probably little different from our immune response to cells not recognized as being part of our own system. Appeals to class loyalty and such like are all attempts to manipulate this instinct for political gain.

What is interesting, however, is that when a leader has consolidated power she or he very often wants to attract diverse groups and the special products or talents they possess to his or her 'court' in order to enhance its wealth and prestige. The break as to which way this instinct goes (the instinct to exclude versus the instinct to embrace) seems to be entirely functional. An expanding polity feeds on the diversity it attracts in a self-reinforcing cycle. In a contracting polity the instinct is to get rid of all that is not essential to its survival. When the infant United States of America had a continent and its resources to exploit it readily absorbed millions from overseas, but when economic hard times hit, the welcome mat was withdrawn. During the Great Depression, California posted vigilante groups along its border to keep out migrants fleeing the pitiful state of farming in the Midwest, searingly captured in John Steinbeck's *The Grapes of Wrath*.

Another facet of group identity is a sense of fairness and injustice. Tying these into basic instincts is more complex. When early

Christians were attempting to establish themselves, Saul of Tarsus (who was to become St Paul) chose to open Judaic monotheism to all who acted with Christian sentiment and not just to those who followed Judaic law. Why should God's grace be granted to the rule-bound, he wondered, and not to all who sought God's love? In *The Grapes of Wrath* Jim Casy attempts to organize against the exploitation the desperate Midwestern farmers are subject to when they reach California and is savagely beaten for his attempt. Both men are spurred on by a sense of injustice and attract those whose survival is threatened by it.

Consciousness enables men to articulate their fear and to construct what they think is a remedy that is actionable. This is really the point at which the biological and the cerebral diverge. From an evolutionary perspective this represents a significant new departure. Rather than wait for random variations to throw up something that works, as in speciation (when a structure which has managed to survive in a particular way – in a particular association with its environment – reproduces itself to the point of not being able to do so with an ancestral structure that has taken a different path), consciousness allows for deliberate attempts at generating plausible new structures. Although survival is the 'decider' in both cases (as it always is in evolutionary differentiation), the medium of consciousness (of manufactured thoughts and imagery) represents a new kind of structure (as did the evolution of galaxies out of gases).

Humans, therefore – and certainly at the moment – straddle the biological and the cerebral (the conscious world of thoughts and imagery), being driven sometimes by pure instinct (biological memory) and at other times by conscious intent (the belief that certain actions will lead to specific outcomes). All one can say is that human history is littered with miscalculations. But it is out of this process of trial and much error that we have reached the position of dominance that we have, although at great cost to ourselves in terms of individual human lives. Our scientific acumen (often biologically driven, it has to be said, by competition between us) has brought us close to self-destruction. Understanding how to manage our evolution is proving far harder than understanding the physical workings of our universe.

I have avoided the "L" word up to now because *love* is all too often waved around as being akin to some universal prophylactic against the "E" word *evil* and its agent the "S" word *sin*. But the great religions represented a remarkable attempt by our forebears to overlay our biological dynamic with a cerebral one. Judaism, Catholicism and Islam were constructed around a full appreciation of our biological nature and all three religions set out to channel our 'animal instincts' into cooperation on a large scale. Inevitably, perhaps, the powerful identities created by these belief systems threw them against one another as each vied to dominate the cerebral space they had created. Being the most exclusive, Judaism has come to define far fewer than the other two.

The third largest religion in the world is Hinduism and, like Buddhism, Shintoism and Confucianism, is primarily focused upon where humans sit within the cosmological order and how they should behave rather than being deeply exercised by dogma. But as with the monotheistic faiths, these religions are concerned with the structure of society as well as with right and wrong behaviour. In this they offered much more than the gods who represented facets of the human experience and were approached to help with this or that and to serve as bridges to the unknown. The conscious mind demands more than a random sequence of possibilities beyond its comprehension and control. So it manufactures hypotheses about how the world works and about how human beings should work within it.

Individuals have a range of needs, beyond those of being fed, watered and housed. How to be protected in order to live is a fundamental biological memory and an essential facet of structure itself. The drive to procreate and safeguard the next generation is frequently a more powerful instinct than individual survival and has doubtless empowered countless armies in battle as well as legions of mothers through the rigours of childbirth. Which is not to say that innate human curiosity – the desire to find out what will happen if…. – hasn't played its part. You often hear about young men approaching war anxious to find out how they will react under fire.

The feeling we identify as love probably springs from our instinctive desire for group solidarity as well as from the nurturing instinct primates display towards their young. To love and be loved unreservedly is a cathartic 'letting go' in that all other concerns, with their inevitable conflicts, become secondary. Perhaps pure hatred offers a similar release and is on display when soldiers finally capture a city and run riot within it. Balanced love entails concern for the wellbeing of the whole even to the extent of recognizing the impermanence of all equilibria and the need, on occasions, to let go and allow the system one is part of to find its own level. This is what we mean by 'nurturing individual freedom' even as we hope beyond hope that those so liberated will 'make the right choices'.

As humans we are an offshoot of biology. As the carriers of consciousness we have assumed a responsibility for where evolution goes next. Working out how to interact with one another, recognizing when biology is the driver and learning how to override it if necessary or channel it in directions of our own choosing, is likely to be our ongoing challenge for some time to come. We have to learn to respect structure and the order it brings while at the same time being willing to experiment with different approaches, often in parallel. Perhaps most crucially, we need to concentrate on the here and now and empower people to improve their lives. In a creative universe, ringed with uncertainty, driving towards someone's vision of utopia runs counter to the evolutionary process and will end in tears.

René Descartes' (1596-1650) dictum *cogito ergo sum* (I think therefore I am) may have only got it half right. **To feel what one thinks** is the true burden consciousness bestows upon us. Because knowledge is conditional it is transitory. Only feelings anchor us in the present to our past and to our future.

22

The space between

I F I was writing a physics treatise, this chapter would be a page or two of mathematical equations. Instead it will be several pages of words. As a language, mathematics is very precise whereas words (like 'God' and 'Big Bang') allow more wiggle room and so can finesse complex things. With that caveat, I want to explore some very basic relationships using words as symbols rather than mathematics.

Where we are at the moment in our fundamental thinking is that our universe started its present life when an extraordinary concentration of energy reached a critical mass and expanded outward leading to the differentiation we see around us today. So one's first question might be, what is energy? Einstein had it as being 'Mass' times 'the Speed of Light' squared ($E=MC^2$). But as useful as that is, it is not quite good enough.

Conceptually there are two problems about the origin of the universe. The first is, what is energy? The second is, how is the universe bound? The first arises because energy is transparently dynamic and this dynamism must be triggered by something. The second arises because the concentration and subsequent expansion of energy implies that it be bound by something and we don't know what that something is or what lies outside it. At present energy is deemed to consist of four fundamental forces: gravitational, electromagnetic, the strong nuclear and weak nuclear. One certainly can imagine that the act of gravity pulling electromagnetism inward would generate huge tensions and that at some point these tensions would reach a critical point bringing about a reverse into expansion.

One can also imagine that, for the differentiation that has accompanied this expansion to occur, something like the strong and weak nuclear forces would be required, or else how would tangible matter (as atoms, etc.) evolve? But then we come up against it. Does this mean energy is an irreducible composite and what does that which lies outside it mean and conversely, how is what falls within its boundary connected? This brick wall has led physicists to chase various speculations, from there being multiple universes, or a fifth dimension, all the way to particles being viewed as one-dimensional strings. Quite reasonably, it caused our forebears to think in terms of there being a prime mover. The problem for physics, as it was for descriptions of God, is that, if the point of origin is a singularity (a one thing), the rules of physics break down, just as in religious terms we are left wondering what created God.

Now let's take a new tack and come at the problem from a different direction. The process of evolution suggests that, while the universe is interconnected, it is not mechanistically connected. What I mean by this is that the universe appears to be a creative entity, not a Newtonian one of fixed relationships like a car engine. Einstein wrestled with this and came up with two hypotheses. In the first (his Theory of Special Relativity) he suggested that the laws of physics were the same for all non-accelerating observers and that the speed of light within a vacuum was the same no matter the speed at which an observer travelled.

The implication of this was that space and time were a continuum and that events occurring at the same time for one observer could occur at different times for another observer. In his second (the Theory of General Relativity) he proposed that the gravitational effect associated with massive objects would distort space-time. Today we can watch events that took place in the early universe (billions of light years away) and observe that light takes longer to pass a large object than a straight-line calculation would suggest because its path has been bent by gravity.

Einstein's insight loosened up Newton's rather rigid arrangement and turned the universe into more of a living thing than a mechanical thing. In the Newtonian world you could pull a lever at point A and its effect would be felt instantly at point B. In Einstein's world an action taken at point A would have to ripple though space-time before having any effect at point B. Without this looseness (this space between) evolution's creative process would not exist. Think of it this way. Two members of the same family are connected and can influence one another, but the outcome of that influence is not wholly predictable.

In trying to define the nature of this space between one runs into yet another problem: is it actually space as in nothingness or more akin to a variable relationship like the force of magnetism (or gravity) which diminishes as one moves away from the source? And this takes us back to the nature of the universe itself. As it expands and the bits that make it up are pushed further and further apart, such that the relationship between them (the force that once combined them) diminishes on a continuum towards infinity so that – for all practical purposes – the space between the bits is eventually tantamount to 'nothingness', are the bits still part of the same thing or have they become new original things in their own right without any known creator? The problems inherent in theology and physics turn out to be the same.

Physicists once assumed that the universe would eventually stop expanding as the force behind the original expansion diminished allowing gravity to pull all the bits back together again in what was sometimes referred to as the big crunch, at which point the cycle would repeat. However measurements suggest that, far from slowing, the expansion is actually accelerating. Given finite energy and the forces associated with it, this should not be possible: where is the expansion boost coming from?

This has given rise to the hypothesized existence of dark matter (matter that does not react to electromagnetic radiation and is thought to comprise some 27% of the mass-energy of the universe as we know it) and dark energy (thought to permeate all of space and make up around 68% of the energy in the universe as we know it) whose constant presence does not diminish in the way the force of gravity does and so has come to accelerate the pulling apart of visible matter as the force of gravity has declined.

It has to be said that these two components (rather like the Holy Trinity in theology) are required in order the make the mathematical model of the cosmos work. Neither dark matter nor dark energy have actually been observed, only inferred, although there is no denying that the insights derived from our mathematical model of the cosmos have proved useful: but so too, to the ancient Egyptians, did the 4,500-year-old calculations of the priests at Giza. How much of what we think we know today will have to be revised in future, only time will tell. But for now it makes sense to look at human affairs from the standpoint of the knowledge we currently possess.

* * *

Our current thinking seems to be that Homo sapiens first evolved in Africa some 200,000 years ago and then radiated outward across the globe from there. Around 10 to 2 million years before the present (BP), apes were our common ancestor, developing a propensity to walk upright around 2 million years BP. There seem to have been a number of Homo species, such as Homo neanderthalensis, now all extinct. Neanderthal man became extinct 30,000 years ago and probably diverged from Homo sapiens 470,000 years before that. To what extent Homo sapiens and Homo neanderthalensis interbred is still a matter of conjecture.

The process of natural selection, whereby random variations in a population lead some members of that population (sharing that variation) to branch out and populate environments compatible with it (such as dark skin in strongly sunlit places and paler skin elsewhere) certainly offers an explanation for human diversity as it did for biological diversity generally. The interplay between the environment and genetic transfer through sexual reproduction encourages differentiation, a general pattern evident in the evolution of matter as a whole.

The way humans arrange themselves must be subject to the same selection process so that these arrangements themselves become a new ecosystem. The polities able to sustain themselves most effectively will predominate, at least until the environment changes and arrangements which were once effective cease to be. However the interplay between environment and arrangement is more complex than that between (for example) a type of bird and the environment that bird is best adapted to. Take the Inca people of South America. From what we know, they developed a system of communication using roads along the Andes which enabled them to manage food production (and, critically, storage) so that techniques could be optimized and supplies moved to where they were needed whenever the region's weather extremes adversely affected harvests.

The Inca system required a people spread out along a large mountainous area (the western foothills of the north-south Andes chain) to abide by a common set of customs. Pathways had to be maintained, farming techniques improved and disseminated, harvests in bountiful years stored and in the lean years equitably distributed. Not only did there need to be a ruler able to make decisions for the people as a whole, but the legitimacy of that ruler (along with his court bureaucracy) and the customs he represented had to be affirmed and reaffirmed during all the time it was not obvious to individuals what the benefits of compliance were. This was not only achieved by force (the Inca king used his army to expand his rule) but through social intimacy and the rituals which brought it about.

In one variant or another, these components – a system providing economic security delivered by a hierarchy underpinned by some force and a belief system supportive of its functional arrangements – lie at the heart of all human systems. But these systems are not machines in a Newtonian sense, but confederations of separate individuals only linked by something every bit as ambiguous as dark energy. When in 1532 Francisco Pizarro, with 168 armour-clad soldiers steeped in the techniques needed to drive the Moors out of Iberia back into North Africa, one cannon, 27 horses and a royal warrant granting him the right to exploit a land the Spanish monarch had never seen, entered the Inca kingdom, his adversary had no idea what he was up against.

Like the Vikings who used their beautifully designed longships to penetrate and partly colonize a poorly-defended Britain from the 790s and the Normans who managed to take over that country in 1066 after an audacious raid across the Channel, using their castle technology to then dominate it, Pizarro did not share the priorities of the Inca people and was bent only on conquest. Offered gold by the Inca king in the hope that Pizarro would leave them alone (as the Anglo-Saxons had offered gold to the Vikings), the Spaniard simply double-crossed the king and killed him. Without its head the Inca Empire crumbled, paving the way for South America to become part of Catholic Spain.

In this sense, human arrangements are machine-like. Get yourself into the driving seat and you stand a good chance of being able to run the show, but the analogy cannot be pushed too far. The Inca machine had human flaws. The Inca king, Atahualpa and his brother, Huascar, were at loggerheads and the king also had to control tributaries whose own leaders held ambitions. These were divisions Pizarro could exploit.

Perhaps driven by simple curiosity and buoyed up by a sense of his own omnipotence, Atahualpa decided to leave his army of 80,000 and meet with Pizarro accompanied by only a small retinue. Pizarro's men easily dispatched the retinue and Pizarro imprisoned the king who offered the Spaniard his weight in gold in exchange for his freedom. While the gold was being assembled Huascar was murdered which gave Pizarro an excuse to murder the king and offer Spain's support to Manco, the dead king's remaining brother.

If you are led to believe that an Inca king is a god, it is not hard to imagine the Inca people imbuing the Spanish and their new ways with a similar aura. Pizarro worked with Manco for long enough to insinuate himself and his men into the Inca system and by 1572 the Inca Empire had become part of Catholic Spain. It is hard to imagine a machine being overwhelmed by such ruthless political cunning. Individuals held together by consciousness are vulnerable to such manipulation. By being flexible and exploiting the space between Inca individuals (the divide and rule strategy deployed by empire builders from the past to the present), Spain's conquistadors, like the Vikings and Normans before them, were able to leverage a small technological advantage into effective political control. And of course the Spaniards possessed a psychological advantage as well: they *knew* they came from a more advanced civilization.

* * *

So what makes one civilization more advanced than another? What was it that the probably dirty, undoubtedly smelly and certainly rough-looking Spaniards had that the Incas did not? Yes they possessed a cannon, some horses and wore armour, but as interesting as these accoutrements undoubtedly were, could they really have been enough to cow an entire people? What they also had, that every fairground huckster offering some miracle cure purports to have, is knowledge.

The Spaniards knew that they came from a place that possessed bigger cities, a religion that expressed itself through more magnificent buildings and machines, such as sailing ships, of far greater sophistication than anything the Incas possessed, and it was surely the projection of this knowledge that held the Inca rulers back from killing off their visitors there and then. The conscious mind craves knowledge and is hungry to unlock the secrets of the universe in order to quell the uncertainties which surround it. Just as Lenin drew on Marxism to persuade an anxious people that by following him they had nothing to lose but their chains, so Pizarro was able to persuade the Inca people that his God was more potent than theirs.

In the 1970s a new god appeared on the scene. The previous god of regulated capital and government intervention had become associated with sclerotic economies and stubbornly high rates of inflation. The new mantra urged governments to pull back so that free market capitalism could drive forward productivity by allowing competition to eliminate inefficiencies (often associated with state-supported monopolies) and in doing so accelerate economic growth. Born inside the hallowed halls of America's financial centre and its academic outposts, this new religion eventually conquered the political establishment and, on the back of American military power, was exported around the world as globalization.

Its adherents achieved considerable success. Inflation was curbed, global trade increased, the growth in government deficits moderated and developing nations became home to international corporations whose products were devoured by consumers in the developed world. By the start of the twenty-first century unfettered capital markets had become the new orthodoxy. The hope and expectation was that millions in the developing world would be lifted out of poverty into a worldwide middle class whose synergy of interests would underwrite global harmony. But as the new millennium got underway, things started to go wrong.

The first stick to be poked into the wheel of this optimistic trajectory came from an audacious attack on the World Trade Centre in New York by Islamic fundamentalists tired of Western domination which killed almost 3,000 people and injured over 6,000, followed four years later by an attack in London which killed 52 and injured 700. Then in 2008 the New York capital markets imploded. Over-abundant capital, a consequence of the developing world's inability to absorb the returns generated by globalization, found its way into reckless lending to the American housing sector which light regulation failed to spot in time.

Bad debts, which had been skilfully marketed as sure bets to institutions hither and yon, surfaced across the financial sector because Joe Public, whose wages had been undermined by the developing world's lower labour costs, could not meet the obligations he had been persuaded to take on. To the fury of those taxpayers who had seen their jobs exported and had not been the beneficiaries of globalization, they were forced to bail out the Western banking system to avert what would certainly have been a worldwide depression rather than the deep recession which followed the calamity. But the high priests of the new free market orthodoxy were shaken and belief in their message undermined.

And here's the thing about the 'space between'. While we might prefer stability and the social equilibriums which ensure this, the nature of our universe is that structures are only loosely connected and sit within a dynamic whole such that the creation of new permutations are an inevitable part of the process. At best our understanding of what is going on at any point in time is partial, even though our desire for certainty leads us to claim otherwise. The mistake the high priests of globalization made (as have high priests of other orthodoxies before them) was to assume the universal validity of their assumptions.

Our historical interventions in the Middle East were certainly self-interested but they were often high-minded as well and globalization was an entirely valid hypothesis. But I think it was George Orwell who said that ideology serves power not truth, and so it is when the high priests of the day start to ignore the casualties of their programmes and insist on orthodoxy rather than adjustment. Our past hubris is catching up with us. Individuals will attempt to colonize the gaps in our thinking, for better and for worse. An ephemeral stability will turn into actual instability and simple solutions will once again be offered and sought. But like the presence of dark energy, there will always be a lot more of what we don't understand than what we do.

23

The nature of things

UNDERSTANDING the nature of things (*TNOT*), even in the most general terms, should make it easier for us to manage our affairs constructively. Many would say that we already do, but I would argue otherwise.

In support of my position I would simply offer up the wars and less-ordered bestiality (with apologies to animals who generally do not exhibit it) which has scarred and still scars our human world. To those who say don't be naïve, that *is* the nature of things, I would say – it may be, but does it have to be?

I do accept, and have myself argued, that competition between humans has stimulated technological and social innovation, such that Homo sapiens has come to dominate the planet. The vast numbers of us killed by our own kind has been outstripped by the numbers our systems have come to sustain. So let's keep up the competition and the killing that goes with it, the Dr Strangeloves and General Buck Turgidsons amongst us will doubtless counsel, because it is only through culling the weak that our species will survive.

* * *

This argument grew out of the scientific determinism of the 19th century when God-centred Man had finally been replaced by Scientific Man and Charles Darwin's landmark work, *The Origin of the Species* (1859), was being interpreted by every political charlatan as justifying the survival of his lot at the expense of some other lot. Karl Marx's masterly critique of capitalism, *Das Kapital* (1867), became the bible for those wishing to elevate themselves to the pinnacle of a new social order. So certain were they of their prescription that they felled all those less certain about the way their societies were being managed. It was *Who Dares, Wins* (the motto of Britain's Special Air Service, the SAS) on a grand scale. Luckily, not everyone fell for it.

Darwin's genius lay in the way he layered example upon example in support of his very simple idea about how plants and animals evolve. To the disgust of some religious hardliners, his logic showed how something as complex as a human being could evolve from an ape by natural selection (the process whereby organisms better adapted to their environment tend to survive and produce more offspring). And this was without any knowledge of genetics, the mechanism by which traits are passed from one generation to the next. Suddenly the strongest leader, like the strongest stag, appeared to have a scientific justification for assuming the powers of a dictator, logic quickly applied to those in possession of the strongest ideas (as certified by themselves).

As intuitive as this seemed to many, it suffered from the *Post hoc ergo propter hoc* (after this therefore because of this) logical fallacy. The plants, birds and animals that Darwin recorded as being so well adapted to their environments told us nothing about what these environments would be in the future. It is true that species become interdependent and so in this way help to construct their own environments (just as human beings construct the environments we call cities), but the only thing which will help a species survive into the future is its ability to adapt because the future lies outside its control. So to talk about *the survival of the fittest* – an expression Darwin did not use – was at best a popular misunderstanding and at worst, self-serving nonsense.

What was undoubtedly true was that those groups of humans best able to exploit their environment would prosper (as is the case with any species). But of course, there is a catch to this. If, like the South American condor, you become supremely well adapted to a particular environmental niche, such as the steppes, valleys and foothills of the Andes mountain range, a change in that environment (for the condor it was the arrival of farmers) might place you at a serious disadvantage. A comparable situation in the human world was that of the *ancien régime* aristocracy in France, which the absolute ruler Louis XIV had reduced to little more than a collection of peacocks.

Capable only of displaying their finery, many aristocratic families could do little more than blink in confusion and lose their heads to the scientific killing machine invented by Joseph-Ignace Guillotin when popular support for their position evaporated. In the spirit of the age this proved to be a forerunner of a certain chamber that used Zyklon B (hydrogen cyanide marketed by I G Faben AG) to kill another group of earmarked humans on an even greater industrial scale: the wonders of science indeed.

* * *

That part of the nature of things that we perhaps understand less well than we should concerns the transition from one equilibrium to another. Structures, by their nature, tend towards equilibrium simply because to exist at all a structure must endeavour to maintain its distinct presence within its environment. What we think of as an ecosystem (or biosphere) consists of numerous semi-autonomous interdependent structures (plants, microbes, insects and animals) which are more or less in balance with one another. We do not know exactly why the age of the dinosaurs came to an end 66 million years ago, but the evidence suggests that one or a combination of environmental change[s] upset the balance that then existed.

Dinosaurs themselves came to prominence after the Triassic-Jurassic extinction event around 135 million years earlier, when some 34% of all marine genera disappeared and, except for plants, land-based extinction was even greater. Again this was almost certainly due to environmental disruption although we are still not sure of what sort. The typical pattern is that an event occurs or a change takes place in the face of which existing structures struggle to survive until a point is reached (quickly or over a prolonged period) when a number are overwhelmed and the whole balance is upset. Following a period of turmoil a new balance is established around a new set of interdependent structures, all of which will have existed in some form in the earlier period of stability. With the dinosaurs out of the way, warm-blooded mammals started their ascent.

Several things can be taken away from this pattern. The first is that periods of stability (when interdependent structures have found a balance) can last for a long time. The second is that some external jolt is needed to disrupt biological equilibriums (periods of balance). The third is that the universe we live in consists of loosely and variably interdependent structures of finite life, such that destabilizing changes are a normal part of its dynamic and hard to predict. Fourth, biological diversity has proved to be a great strength in that when environmental change has undermined some structures other biological structures have managed to fill the gaps they leave. Fifth, the impulse to exist propels structures to inhabit any environment from which they can secure the energy they need to survive. Sixth, random and often very small variations endow structures with a propensity to differentiate. Seventh, differentiated structures interact symbiotically. Eighth, classes of structure tend towards equilibrium. Ninth, the loose-tight properties of the universe we inhabit make it a creative, not a deterministic enterprise.

The evolution of consciousness – the ability to imagine outcomes and devise strategies to secure them – has put man on a new evolutionary trajectory. Hitherto evolution's powerful forward momentum has been backward looking: what worked came into existence. Conscious man is subject to all the propensities outlined above (one through nine) but, by and large, we have been blind to their influence over us. This accounts for much of the self-inflicted turmoil we have subjected ourselves to.

There does not seem to have been anything inherent in consciousness alone that would account for man's domination of the biosphere (planet Earth's biological infrastructure) although an ability to dream perhaps does explain his albeit slow but nonetheless perceptible detachment from it. The longevity of tribes living largely unchanged in harmony with their environments indicates that conscious structures are as prone to attaining equilibrium states as anything else. So the next question is what 'jolted' Homo sapiens out of equilibrium and onto the helter-skelter path he is now travelling down?

As far as we know there have been no serious, generalized environmental disruptions to upset the balanced existence of Homo sapiens in his Stone Age state (the state of several isolated tribes still in existence today). The evidence suggests that conscious man, the generalist, started moving away from his point of origin in Africa. The supposition is that increasing numbers drove groups away from their jungle womb into areas that required somewhat different survival skills. The choice between attacking other groups to gain access to their resources or colonizing new territories in search of new resources was most likely a pragmatic one. Doubtless there was always a certain amount of low level friction between groups, but so long as there was new land to be filled, the line of least resistance would have been the one taken.

Only when some areas were discovered that lent themselves to a settled existence and some groups worked out how to apply themselves in this way (such as the farming culture which began to develop around the Nile Delta over five thousand years ago) did Homo sapiens begin to craft an environment to suit himself rather than live off one that already existed. A nomadic life hardly required more complex social arrangements than jungle life, but to craft an existence out of one spot which was munificent, although not continuously so, would have required a degree of forward planning as well as more nuanced social arrangements than those of the extended family.

Social elaboration – the development of priesthoods, rulers, administrators, armies and craftsmen alongside husbands, wives and children – follows the pattern of differentiation mentioned above (as the sixth characteristic of *TNOT*). To have to create the circumstances by which food is produced (rather than taking it from the jungle as required or even following it across the steppes from one pasture to the next) requires knowledge about how food grows (not just about where it grows) and the patience to wait for it to do so. Knowledge could have been accumulated over long periods of time by observation. The patience to apply that knowledge however, and await the outcome, would have required a degree of collective commitment: a shared belief that doing so would work and produce a better outcome than a family could secure for itself by wandering off and foraging.

Those eking out an existence around the Nile Delta would have been well aware of the hostile nature of the desert round about, serving as an incentive for them to stay put and cooperate. They would also have been confronted by the character of the Nile itself with its often variable pattern of flooding, bringing both danger and bounty in the form of enriched soil. Slowly they would have come to terms with this and what became the civilization of ancient Egypt would gradually have formed.

To meld a sizeable number of families together into a working whole requires a degree of organization, with individuals assuming roles and interacting in predictable ways as would have been the case within an extended family, but on a far larger scale. The innovation arising out of consciousness lies in its allowing a people to manufacture a shared vision of what they are and how they should function using symbols, with the Egyptian pharaoh becoming a kind of exaggerated paterfamilias and the priesthood guardians of knowledge and the interlocutors between the known and unknown. The growing productivity of the Nile dwellers' farming techniques would have made possible an elaboration of roles, such as skilled craftsmen, engineers, administrators and soldiers, culminating in the enriched hierarchy responsible for the pyramids, still a wonder to our eyes today.

The first, second and third characteristics of *TNOT* affected ancient Egyptian civilization. There were certainly periods of stability. However any run of poor harvests undermined the authority of both the pharaoh and priesthood and so undermined the shared vision that held people together. Mayan civilization in Central America seems to have experienced a collapse in the 9th century CE when its agricultural system failed to meet the needs of its people. Similarly crop failures in France contributed to the collapse of the French monarchy in 1789.

Great leaders such as the pharaoh Khufu (2589-2566BCE), the Mayan Siyaj K'ak' (c378CE) and Louis XIV of France (1638-1715) were undoubtedly beneficiaries of systems that were working but it would be an exaggeration to say that they were chiefly responsible for them doing so. Whatever else they are, social arrangements are functional entities which sometimes appear to be well attuned to their circumstances and at other times are not. When things move towards the latter end of the spectrum leadership positions are contested which, although an adaptive mechanism, increases instability and may or may not lead to an improved outcome.

As human agriculture became more productive, humans started to concentrate in cities, their own manufactured jungles. The great Scottish thinker, Adam Smith (1723-1790) once famously remarked that *there is a lot of ruin in a nation*. What he meant was that once established, a social system will keep throwing off its bounty (albeit at a depleted rate) even when maladapted to its circumstances (either through outdated design, poor leadership, bad luck or all three), just as a plant or animal will struggle on in poor conditions. Unlike a plant or animal, however, a social system consists of a set of functionally integrated institutions overlaid by networks of individuals who not only manage it, but lay claims upon it.

The singular characteristic of consciousness is that collections of conscious beings can come together under the aegis of a shared story, construct a hierarchical system which is capable of supporting them and then treat that system as if it were a resource which subgroups of them can exploit. Five thousand years ago Ancient Egyptians constructed a unique social system to support themselves. At its base was food production. At its apex was a pharaoh who represented a sophisticated conception of what the Egyptian people were, how their lives should be ordered and what their relationship was with the universe as a whole.

Since then the wealth of the Egyptian people has come under the control of numerous outside powers – Persians (525BCE); Alexander the Great's Ptolemaic Greeks (332BCE); the Romans (30BCE); the Islamic Caliphate (642); Ottoman Turks (1517); Napoleon's France (1798); the nominally Ottoman Muhammad Ali Pasha (1805); the British (1914) - before becoming a republic in 1953. Throughout all of this the region's people have continued to think of themselves as Egyptians and their productive systems have continued to feed them (with some improvements by outsiders), but, instead of expanding their own civilization (which had long since attained an equilibrium – the eighth *TNOT*), its surplus has been drawn off to augment the civilization of others (the creative impulse and ninth *TNOT*).

A social system's superstructure (its governing system and symbols) can fail without destroying what has been created, making it possible for an outside superstructure to impose itself and extract the wealth which had previously supported the old hierarchy. This is a variation on the benefits of biological diversity (the fourth *TNOT*) in that although imperial expansion enforces change (such as when Rome absorbed first Greece and then Egypt) it only thrives by not destroying all the functional elements of what is already there.

Trade – exchange between polities- is another channel through which new ideas move between social systems and transform them. But such challenges to identity are not always welcome. The Soviet Union and before that the Chinese Imperial Court were reluctant to encourage trade as it implied that other systems might have desirable things that their system did not and so be superior (an impossibility). When American GIs came to Britain in the Second World War and plied British girls with gifts of nylon stockings and chocolates not available to the English Tommy it caused friction, just as the arrival of hard-working Poles has upset the locals in some English cities because their own young have left to find opportunity elsewhere and they no longer recognize the communities they grew up in.

In the 19th and 20th centuries, when Europe's emigrants flocked to New York in search of a better life, they may have stuck to their own linguistic ghettos but were still looked down upon by the tribes who had preceded them. Identity – our story about what we are – is a central component of the conscious mind (we would quite literally go mad without it). However the immigrant's reconstruction of it speaks to our propensity to differentiate (the sixth *TNOT*) while still interacting symbiotically to create great cities like New York and London (the seventh *TNOT*).

The creative nature of our universe arising out of its loose-tight properties (the ninth *TNOT*) plays out in a particular way within social systems populated by conscious beings. The structures that we create (our human jungles) become environments to be exploited. When a bird travels great distances to breed and feed it too is exploiting its environment except on a very small scale (such as its nesting colonies) it has not created that environment. Settled communities, however, are productive structures created by conscious effort which require individual input and tie individuals to them. A farm must be farmed and the farmer needs to farm in order to survive (just as factories need human input to function and the humans who make them function need what they are paid for doing so). But the productive surplus which pays for the organizational component of these communities constitutes a fruit to be picked by any group capable of assuming the organizing function.

When the Romans embarked upon their great expansion they were not faced with an empty environment, but by many hundreds of self-sustaining communities. Like corporate raiders they used their superior military technology (supported by their senatorial system of government) to take over these communities and reorientate their surpluses toward Rome, increasing them where they could through the use of improved administrative, farming, engineering and trading techniques. After each conquest a fresh flow of slaves and products was fed into Rome's system, benefitting the capital's people but also the Roman Empire's elites, including those elites in the conquered territories willing to accept Rome's authority.

History is replete with examples of elites (those in control of surpluses) seeking to extend their reach, motivated by the impulse to inhabit any environment from which they can secure the energy they need to survive (fifth *TNOT*). The Norman conquest of England overlaid perfectly viable communities with a fresh hierarchical arrangement. Again and again, people are found to pay for their own subjugation for want of an effective structural component to keep predators at bay. But of course this dynamic is at the very heart of all structures populated by conscious beings. The fight for the keys to the kingdom may be fought more often at the ballot box today than on the battlefield, but the process is much the same.

It is not always easy to see what the benefit of this process is, although if there was no benefit human numbers would have decreased rather than increased, and human wealth (measured in terms of the freedoms available to individuals) would have declined. The Romans brought the *Pax Romana* to the Mediterranean world (27BCE – 180CE) during which ideas and trade flowed. The Normans bequeathed to England an effective system of centralized administration, previously lacking. And yet, as already mentioned, the self-inflicted cost in human lives of these and other improvements has been depressingly high. Why have the two gone together and must they? This brings us to the crux of the matter.

If social systems (like all systems) tend toward equilibrium and an equilibrium state is one in which no further significant change occurs, then, barring some external jolt, there is no intrinsic reason why Stone Age man shouldn't have continued into the present, except for one thing: the ability of conscious individuals to imagine better. Now think about the nature of such imaginings. These range from disgruntlement to the construction of imaginary utopias (such as those of Plato, Thomas Aquinas and Thomas Moore), as well as from the construction of a flint-headed spear to the Apple iPad. By their nature, these imaginings pose a challenge to the status quo, to how we see ourselves, to the prevailing story which ties us, as conscious beings, together.

Now think about how these imaginings get adopted by the prevailing social structure. Initially with a great deal of skepticism and rightly so: why contaminate a working system with an innovation whose outcome cannot be known? And this is where the ability of conscious beings to form differentiated groups comes into play. If enough people see an advantage to themselves in adopting the innovation (from the launch of a Crusade to the development of a search engine) the disruption can begin without anyone having a clear idea as to its impact on the prevailing structure. This simple dynamic is the genesis of both formal conflict (extending to corporate takeovers and waged wars) and chaotic conflict, such as when order breaks down (as in regulatory collapse and civil wars).

The only way for these disruptive transformations to proceed without deadly conflict is if all participants accept a framework – much easier said than done. However, one thing in particular has caused us problems: our belief that we can control the future. We cannot. The best we can do is keep making incremental improvements and adapting to circumstances. As to what constitutes an improvement, that too runs into our lack of forward knowledge – we can make intelligent guesses but we can never be sure. We do, though, have one ace up our sleeves.

Survey after survey indicates that humans have remarkably similar values, most of which can be compressed into *do as you would be done by*. That we so often don't do as we would be done by suggests systemic failure. In fact it has almost become an article of faith that our systems should be devoid of moral content (be morally neutral). What this means is that subgroups within social structures can hide behind systems – the *I was just doing my job* fallacy – which merely serves to elevate the system onto some high moral plane. This is an abrogation of our individual selves as conscious beings.

While it is certainly true that we must rely on our systems to do much of our day-to-day thinking for us – it is not practical to start from first principles every morning – it should be a legal requirement for all legislation to specify its objective, to state clearly how that objective is to be achieved and over what timescale, and to show how its success or failure is to be measured. Thereafter it should be open to anyone affected by the legislation, or by the actions of any person or body empowered by that legislation, to challenge its moral coherence.

As to what is or is not moral, that can surely be left to juries and to courts and built up over time. What cannot be allowed to continue is for our social systems and the actions they facilitate to continue functioning in a moral vacuum predicated upon some vague notion of future benefit or past precedent, often as cover for sectional self-interest. What we always need to know, and should always be required to ask, is what will it do to people today? Past and future are important but the present is reality.

24

Economics

ECONOMICS is important, but not that important. Let me explain.

Rather too much was made out of the 19th century French revolutionary war cry *Liberté, égalité, fraternité*, not least because we do not always wish to be fraternal, liberty has its limits and the one thing we will never be (if our evolutionary trajectory is to be sustained) is equal. That said, there is quite clearly a level of wellbeing none of us should fall below. Establishing what this level should be has proved both politically contentious and complex. However the concept is simple. If a polity's GDP is 'X' then a% should be returned to its citizens for their daily needs, b% should be used to fund collective services (such as infrastructure maintenance, healthcare, government, internal security and defense), c% should be invested in projects for future benefit, d% should be invested in pure research and e% should be spent on individual incentives. How these levels should be set is not simple.

But let us step back for a moment and look at these elements through another lens, the lens of a small, self-contained jungle tribe. So first, what is this community's Gross Domestic Product (GDP)?

The total value of goods produced and services provided in the community during the year (its GDP) is '**X**', the amount needed to sustain the community. The reason we have to call it '**X**' is because no monetary value is assigned to this community's goods or services. This demonstrates the first problem with economics: it is a prisoner of monetary values.

Now we could try to fudge the issue by creating monetary values. Let's assume the community is forty people and that each couple has two live dependent children at any point in time so that there are twenty adults. This means that the community has 10,512,000 available minutes every year (60 x 24 x 365 x 20) within which to sustain itself. So let's call that its GDP.

During a typical week the men will sleep, go hunting, kill some animals, attend to their weapons and construct dwellings when necessary. The women will sleep, forage, prepare food, keep an eye on the children and maintain their dwellings. Everyday communication will be punctuated from time to time by a formal meeting at which collective decisions are reached and special events celebrated. Of the total GDP, each adult contributes 525,600 and draws out the same amount. Supply and demand, that much-loved economic matrix, is in balance.

Is this *liberté, égalité, fraternité*? Well it is as close as we are ever likely to get to it. However the *liberté* is constrained by what the forest will provide and by the collective knowledge of the tribe about how to extract from the forest what it needs (in effect, this knowledge is a large part of its capital stock ('**c**'). *Égalité* probably does not describe these twenty adults very well. For a start, the division of labour (another economic 'insight') will have happened naturally and the women will doubtless do what women do today – mock the men as they loaf around between bouts of hunting aware that what they produce by way of goods and services uses up more minutes. As for *fraternité*, I doubt if there would be more of that than there ever is amongst any group of close-knit interdependent people with the usual little jealousies, slights and misunderstandings.

So how did we get from there to the *ancien régime*, with its enormous palaces, secular and religious, flotillas of servants, thousands of farmed acres and rigid social arrangements? The cuckoo in this nest, of course, were the cities in which a growing merchant and professional class chafed at being excluded from the narrow hierarchy of power that culminated in a monarch who acted like some mysterious divinity, a *Wizard of Oz*. And there were many Dorothies and Totos who wanted to pull back the curtain and unmask the gentleman who was pulling the levers that governed their lives. Unfortunately for the French king and his courtiers, these curious French masses were a lot less polite than Dorothy from Kansas.

Karl Marx, amongst others, made a spirited attempt to plot how we got from there (our jungle tribe) to here (the *ancien régime*), but his scientific determinism, together with his emotionally charged terms (exploitation of labour, false consciousness, etc.) ended up making his argument as political as it was analytic. Marx had an agenda. While recognizing that science itself has an agenda (it assumes that the universe is not only amenable to scientific enquiry, but will divulge its secrets to it), what can reasonably be said about the trajectory from there to here?

The most obvious thing is that nineteenth century France was far larger and far more complex than our jungle tribe of twenty adults and twenty children. Also the French lived inside a largely manufactured environment whereas the tribe drew on the jungle, as it was, to provide them with all that they needed in order to survive. The French polity depended upon an agricultural system which had to generate a surplus, unlike the tribe which extracted from the forest only what its members needed. This French surplus sustained a hierarchy which could project power against other polities (such as the British) in a scramble for resources as well as direct power internally in support of itself. If farmers produced only what they needed, the hierarchy would collapse, a dynamic no different from that which existed in ancient Egypt.

Whilst some of the agricultural surplus sustained the government, consisting of monarch, aristocracy and its allied religious establishment, some also leached into the cities where merchants and artisans created a trade in products which members of the establishment found desirable. In this way, cities became centres of activity only loosely under the control of the rural hierarchy. What Marx was certainly right to emphasize was the importance of capital, although looking at it through economic eyes distorted his vision. The tribe possessed capital – its collective knowledge about how to survive in its forest environment which it passed from generation to generation.

The capital of the *ancien régime* lay in its enormous infrastructure, built primarily on top of a rural economy. It is all very well to say that the rich iconography of the church and lavish display of the aristocracy were devices to suppress the lower orders, but it would be just as reasonable to say that they were the colourful embellishments of a polity which needed the upper echelons to behave as they did. Remove all the cathedrals, the palaces, the armies, the banquets, the sumptuous clothes, the art, the cities and one would have been left with little more than subsistence farmers. In fact one would have been transported back to something approaching Western Europe when the Roman Empire pulled out: reversion to a localism vulnerable to marauding warlords.

The Catholic Church in Western Europe survived Rome's departure, indicating that it was more than an establishment pillar. Indeed, the Empire's adoption of Christianity as the state religion in CE380, when there had been many other religious practices to choose from, makes clear that what Saul of Tarsus (St Paul) created out of the life of Jesus had wide appeal. But by the end of the nineteenth century religion was coming in for a good deal of criticism as an establishment tool:

> Those who toil and live in want all their lives are taught by religion to be submissive and patient while here on earth, and to take comfort in the hope of a heavenly reward. But those who live by the labour of others are taught by religion to practise charity while on earth, thus offering them a very cheap way of justifying their entire existence as exploiters and selling them, at a moderate price, tickets to wellbeing in heaven. Religion is opium for the people. Religion is a sort of spiritual booze, in which the slaves of capital drown their human image, their demand for a life more or less worthy of man.

Vladimir Ilyich Lenin in 1905, after Karl Marx.

In the fourteenth and fifteenth centuries the Italian city states, such as Florence, Venice and Milan were already operating on a different basis. Trade underpinned their wealth, and the wealth of their leading families (the Medici, the Doge and the Sforza) not agriculture. In Venice, the Doge was even elected, albeit from the city's leading merchant families. It was no accident that the pursuit of knowledge accelerated within the merchant class, it being in their interests to learn new techniques in the fields of money, trade and navigation. By the sixteenth century in Northern Europe, the tired nostrums which had underpinned the old order were further challenged by Protestantism, a more muscular, individualistic approach to religion than Roman Catholicism had become.

By the middle of the eighteenth century, the Industrial Revolution was under way in Britain and this also served to broaden the capital base away from the land, although many landed magnates were no shrinking violets when it came to using new machinery to improve agricultural productivity. In effect, what was happening was the creation of new hierarchies, challenging the one based exclusively upon control over land. To argue, as Marx and his followers did, that capital exploited labour, just as the old landed class had done, adding the wrinkle that the pursuit of profit would ultimately be self-defeating at which point the masses, guided by the enlightened ones (such as Marx and Lenin), would rise up and create a communist nirvana, was an economic *argumentum ad absurdum*, although for a while it certainly served as a rallying cry of great force for change in countries still locked within an agricultural hierarchy.

Most of the journey from a jungle tribe to a 21st century city took place without 'economics' and it certainly was not 'scientifically determined'. It evolved. All one can say for sure is that evolution builds on what has gone before, sometimes rebuilding from an earlier point when a particular path reaches a dead end (as the structure of the *ancien régime* clearly did). The dynamic nature of our universe precludes any static equilibrium, other than over the short term. Our jungle tribe could certainly have persisted for a long time (as the existence of a few isolated tribes today attests). But the loose-tight properties which characterize the universe mean that, although structures are driven to achieve stability, the interaction between them leaves open a door towards creative development whenever disruption undermines a status quo.

What knocked some jungle tribes out of their 'happy equilibrium' we do not know. In the main, animals that have evolved to fill a particular niche stick to it. As the quintessential generalist, Homo sapiens doubtless wandered into less supportive environments than the jungle and used his conscious ability to make the best of what he found by acting upon it. This adaptive technique was an evolutionary leap – rather than wait for random biological variations to prove viable in a given environment, change the environment. This required not only the use of analytic brainpower but also teamwork, and this required increasingly sophisticated communication.

As bands of humans grew in size, thanks to their ability to

organize themselves in order to better exploit their environments, they inevitably bumped into one another and this set in train a competitive dynamic which is still with us today. Just as it makes no sense to say that a hive or colony 'exploits' its worker bees or worker ants, so it makes no sense to say that the Roman Empire exploited its slave labour. As a viable organizational component, slavery was widespread at the time. What it does make sense to say is that conscious individuals held in a slave state might reasonably wish not to be so held.

Horses, cattle, chickens and pigs have all been co-opted into the systems humans have developed, but to date, none have thought to complain and most are treated reasonably (even when they are ultimately eaten) because it is in the interests of human beings to do so. The Roman Empire was rocked by three slave uprisings (135-132BCE, 104-100BCE and 73-71BCE, known as the Servile Wars) which, if nothing else, reminded Romans that the slave system they depended upon was not without cost. Slaves working in households were treated a lot better than slaves consigned to work in the mines, doubtless something domestic slaves were well aware of. Horrified by what he saw as the exploitation of industrial labour by something called 'capital', Marx completely overlooked the ability of labour to organize itself. 'Capital' was not organizing anything, people were.

Consciousness injected one other thing into the human dynamic. It enabled individuals to stand outside their situation (imaginatively at least) and wonder how it might be improved. No doubt part of the appeal of St Paul's Christian message was that faith alone would secure a place in heaven, so no matter how dismal the daily grind, a believer could look forward to better times. Lenin and Marx before him were certainly right in their cynical view that the hope for a better future was a balm against the trials and tribulations of the day-to-day, but there is scant evidence that it stopped people trying to do better for themselves in the here and now. In fact it was this desire – to do better for oneself and one's own – that helped push social change along.

It is certainly the case, however, that larger groupings of people required more rigid and more explicit functional hierarchies than the jungle tribe needed in order to sustain itself. To look upon the opulence of elite lives at the height of the *ancien régime* as some sort of economic failure is no more logical than saying the same about Ancient Egypt's great structures. To sustain between 1 and 2 million people within a hierarchy, as the pharaohs of the Old Kingdom had to do, required forward planning and a division of tasks. To coordinate these activities there had to be not only an effective bureaucracy, but a powerful shared ethos. The Great Pyramid of Giza was a mark of success, not failure.

When Louis XIV moved the government of France from Paris to the magnificent Palace of Versailles in 1682, it was a gesture of French ambition and greatness. But in just over a hundred years (in 1789) his descendents would be forced from the palace by a revolutionary mob. What had gone so spectacularly wrong? Believing it would improve efficiency, the king had centralized government. He reversed Henry IV's 1598 edict granting French Huguenots (Protestants) religious freedom. He had also embarked on a protracted war (the War of the Spanish Succession). During his reign there was a severe famine (1693-94) in which some 1.3 million lost their lives (out of a total population of around 20 million), made worse by the state's need to raise taxes to pay for its hostilities.

At the time of his death in 1715, France was heavily in debt, suffered from too narrow a tax base (the Church and aristocracy were excluded), had embarked upon a competition with Britain which would last for the next one hundred years (culminating in Napoleon's defeat at Waterloo) and had drawn responsibility for government into the hands of one man. By the time Louis XVI ascended the throne in 1774 the *ancien régime* was no longer fit for purpose. This had as much to do with economics as did the collapse of Egypt's

Old Kingdom in 2181BCE, dragged down by a prolonged failure of the Nile to flood and the resulting dismal harvests. Economists can count and sometimes explain, but economics cannot cause things to happen any more than two plus two causes four.

Over countless millennia, priesthoods have laid claim to special knowledge and then demanded tribute by asserting that they possess the keys to the future. The remarkable journey from the jungle tribe to our great cities of today happened organically, thanks to countless decisions by individuals seeking out the best for themselves in the face of uncertainty. Grappling with challenges they sometimes sought out, but often did not, they have ended up inside a variety of collective structures. These, some have occasionally loved and others occasionally loathed, but in the end have always changed. There is an awful lot that economists can't count which we should not imagine they can. We face a creative future not a certain one.

25

Education

EDUCATION has four primary functions: to socialize, to prepare, to differentiate and to empower. Socializing a child is the process of exposing him or her to the values and 'view' of the polity they are destined to grow up in. Preparing a child entails giving him or her the skills they will need in order to function within their society. Differentiation is the mechanism whereby a child's capabilities are matched to their society's functional requirements. Empowerment seeks to enhance a child's sense of self-worth. As with all classifications, there are overlaps, ambiguities and conflicts.

Much has been written about education over the years by people who have been more involved in it than I. So here I want to focus on one cohort – children from dysfunctional families – because what is difficult often forces into the open issues which more benign situations disguise. With this objective, two things must be grappled with at the outset. How does one identify a 'dysfunctional family' and on what basis do the children of such families justify special treatment?

So let's start with the second matter as the first follows from it – on what basis do the children of dysfunctional families merit special treatment? It is generally accepted that a person's home life affects their development. As the quality of a child's home life is not something any child can control, simple equity requires that a poor quality situation should be offset in some other way if possible. Then there is the social dimension. Children brought up to the drum of bad social habits are more likely to exhibit those same habits later in life. Lastly it seems sensible to ameliorate the negative effect a child with bad social habits has on the education of children whose social habits are closer to the norm.

As sensible as these criteria sound, they throw up one big problem: they hang on how bad social habits are defined which takes us straight to the question, what does one mean by a dysfunctional family? It is easy to envisage an Orwellian state in which any deviation from the party line (from the status quo) is deemed anti-social. The Soviets, after all, consigned dissidents to mental institutions and the Nazis gave families who did not subscribe to the Hitler Youth, the Nazi Party's paramilitary organization, a bad time. And we have all seen photographs of smiling Chinese children waving Chairman Mao's little red book and read about Puritans and Catholics fighting each other over what to pump into children's heads.

The truth is that all societies have a body of opinion which defines them and which they seek to promulgate to the next generation. Following the Second World War, a battle of ideas raged in Britain (and still rages) about the merits of publicly funded selective schools versus publicly funded comprehensive schools run by local authorities. The focus recently has turned to parental choice – that is, offering parents state-funded options other than schools run by their local authority. Selection sought to separate children at an early age on the basis of an academic test (the *11-Plus*) so that those showing academic promise could be given a more focused education, with university as a likely destination. Proponents of the comprehensive approach argued vigorously that this reinforced social divisions and penalized late starters. The choice debate pits those who support comprehensive schools run by local authorities against those dissatisfied with these local authority monopolies. In the meantime, privately funded education has gone from strength to strength, taking a disproportionate number of university places (and ultimately, the better jobs), while penalizing those unable to avail themselves of it.

In such a visceral atmosphere it is hardly surprising that the children of "dysfunctional families" attract little attention, except when they prove to be such a nuisance that they have to be 'excluded' from mainline comprehensive education. And of course an added problem is that a "dysfunctional family" is likely to have a negative effect on children long before they reach school age.

So let's look at the problem from a different angle. What lies behind dysfunctional families? And at this point I am going to have to make a stab at a definition. In the past when there was less mobility, greater job security and more tightly knit communities, gossip kept most people anchored to a common set of values. In the main these values centred on men working to support a marriage and the children it produced. Not all marriages were happy and any children generated out of wedlock were usually spirited away. And while community life was supportive (children played with other children in the street and could go to visit 'Auntie Lil' when their own mother was pregnant again and at her wits' end because her Stan was drinking the holiday money), it also threw a tight circle around expectations – boys would expect to work in the local factory and, after a spell gutting fish, or whatever, girls would expect to marry one of them and settle down to rear a family.

But all of that has largely gone. Lifetime employment in the same community, let alone generational employment (sons following fathers into the local factory) is the rare exception. Expectations have been untethered – anything is possible is the new mantra, even though it is not. When the employment that has sustained communities has been exported or made obsolete by new technologies, men are encouraged 'to get on their bikes' and look for work elsewhere. And, thanks to welfare payments, girls do not need husbands to support themselves and their children (although men are required to help them produce the child). The shift is every bit as great as took place when men and women left rural lives for lives in the burgeoning cities of the industrial revolution. And don't imagine they were leaving bucolic heaven for grimy hell. The new cities might have been dirty and dangerous but they were also exciting and offered new freedoms.

So we are where we are. Communities are optional. You get to pick and choose which ones to belong to or end up in some parasitic community, such as a drug gang or prostitution ring, by default. And along with the balkanization of communities we have ended up with something of a pick-and-mix in values too. The social arbiter is no longer the local church minister or wagging tongues but long-running programmes such as East Enders on the television or The Archers on the radio, both blind to their audience and easily turned off.

The collapse of communities is almost certainly a more direct cause of dysfunctional families than poverty. Many wealthy families are dysfunctional, if by dysfunctional one means children growing up without any clear values: stressing the importance of work, the need for self-discipline, the desirability of truth-telling, the significance of knowing right from wrong and the value of compassion – all traits which can be found amongst the economically less favoured and entail a resistance to biological desires which in nature are generally tempered by competitive equilibrium. Religion clearly provides a set of values which are transportable (the Jews have been transporting theirs for generations), but with the decline of both religion and geographic communities there is little to stop individuals from behaving in ways one might deem dysfunctional – that is to say acting only so as to secure short-term personal gratification regardless of any external impact.

While one might find it abhorrent that a woman can be indifferent to how her current mate treats a child from an earlier coupling, her reaction is not unnatural. House martins, for example, will leave a late brood to starve if the time to migrate comes before their chicks can fend for themselves and in periods of scarcity birds of prey will readily jettison one of their two young. Biology's survival instincts have evolved over thousands of years and are deep-seated. The real question is, why has consciousness given rise to sentiment when there is no such thing as sentiment in biology?

On this basis a dysfunctional family is merely a product of individual characteristics and external conditions and is only dysfunctional because we deem it to be so. Of course it is not hard to see why. If all families were made up out of males and females more interested in their mates of the moment and whatever sensual pleasures they could garner, in between securing the basics of survival, the species would likely find itself on the fast track to extinction. With biological constraints removed (or at least greatly reduced) consciousness has had to overlay our instinctive feelings with a new set of manufactured constraints (which we call morality): discarding an unwanted infant ceases to be a normal act but one which affronts our sentiments.

However, we should not allow ourselves to escape the conclusion that a dysfunctional family is the product of a dysfunctional system, notwithstanding the fact that some individuals will be prone to react to their environment more in this way than that. The psychopath, for example, seems to be one who is inherently and often aggressively anti-social and, as evolutionary variants go, may not have much utility, but as it is managed variability which has given us the edge, it is our systems we should examine before hiding behind individual 'failings'. That said, blaming individuals for their 'failings' is one of the ways we manage our collective behaviour. Our freedom to act may come down to whether we abide by our biological instincts or override them by calling upon some stronger emotional appeal. The martyr who chooses to be burned alive rather than abandon a belief manages to do just that. Our manufactured moral carapace has been hard won.

To expect any education system to be able to counteract the influences of a dysfunctional family on a child is surely fanciful. Not only has the child of such a family been witness to years of variant behaviour before arriving at school, but even while at school, this only accounts for a portion of his time. It is tempting to want to remove children from dysfunctional families entirely – and occasionally this is done – but identifying the line beyond which such action can be justified is likely to leave a lot of children on the wrong side of it and doing so is certainly not without its own problems (both moral and practical) in any event.

Liberalism – the view that individuals should be equally empowered to follow their own star, versus conservatism – the view that individuals should be free to enjoy (for good and ill) the fruits of their own decisions, sound similar but approach life from different perspectives. Liberalism evolved in opposition to the rigid hierarchy of the *ancien régime,* based as it was upon heredity (from monarch on down) and conformity to Catholicism, itself also steeply hierarchical although essentially meritocratic. Conservatism evolved largely in opposition to liberalism's penchant for social engineering, conservatives being skeptical about communitarianism's ability to foster peace on earth and good will amongst men. The French Revolution's claim to be the herald of *liberté, égalité, fraternité* had turned out to be so spectacularly wrong in practice that men like Edmund Burke (1729-1797) sought to emphasize the importance of traditional relationships which had evolved over centuries (often most clearly crystallized as property rights) in keeping capricious governments at bay.

Unsurprisingly, this difference of approach found its way into education. In essence, the state-funded, local authority-controlled comprehensive school sought to recreate the community that modern life had wrenched apart. By drawing all families into a shared experience, the hope was that the comprehensive school would foster a set of shared values (the *liberté, égalité and fraternité* that had eluded the revolutionaries). The problem, however, was that the wider community within which the comprehensive school sat was not homogeneous. Some parents craved the old grammar school system (whose roots went back to the 14th century), others preferred to avail themselves of private education, often with a particular religious orientation. Comprehensive schools were also perceived by some to reflect the political orientation of the authority controlling them and this was not to their liking.

Inevitably, the children of dysfunctional families are the most likely to create problems within schools. Private schools and selective schools can expel them without any further obligation (or not accept them in the first place). Comprehensive schools can exclude seriously disruptive pupils, but the state still has an obligation to educate them. Although a small number overall (those permanently excluded are only around .06% of the whole), disruptive children are an ongoing problem and those with special needs (not linked directly to family difficulties) soak up extra resources local authorities don't have.

It is hard to escape the conclusion that the comprehensive system, as noble as its underlying idea was, is not suitable in all situations. It was not designed to handle the child of a mother addicted to crack cocaine partnering a male with no interest in whatever child she might have (by him or anyone else). Such a child should be removed from harm's way at the earliest opportunity. A high-quality, state-funded boarding school with a pre-school component able to look after its children full time (that is during holidays as well as term time) must surely be a solution worth considering.

The existence of such a facility would make it easier for social services to act and might even be welcomed by dysfunctional mothers in their more lucid moments, save for any diminution in the social payments they would otherwise have received. This brings us to an issue not directly related to education: what responsibilities should be attached to having children?

In order to drive a car legally on a public road one is obliged to pass a test. In the past, a child was deemed to be the product of a marriage and if a woman was unfortunate enough to produce one outside marriage it was invariably spirited away to a relative or to some church body which might put it up for adoption. Today, marriage is optional and women with children are given state support, making the state a surrogate parent. At the very least, this should give the state the same legal responsibility (and rights) as a parent of that child. Unless actively involved, the biological father is irrelevant.

Our revolt against Church dogma has blinded us to the fact that the Church (and custom before it) had over two millennia's worth of experience in handling the relationship between men, women and the children their union produced. Liberalism's concentration on the rights of individual adults has been at the expense of the individual's obligations towards social wellbeing. It seems somewhat perverse that, while marriage for the purpose of creating a family with children has become optional, gay marriage as a testament to the love between two individuals is on the ascendant. It is this aspect of liberalism that conservatives find hard to fathom. Somewhere in all of this the right of a child to be brought up in a stable, supportive (and hopefully loving) environment has been mislaid.

At the start of this essay I said that education had four primary functions: to socialize, to prepare, to differentiate and to empower. Socializing a child, I suggested, was the process of exposing him or her to the values and 'view' of the polity they were destined to grow up in. Preparing a child entailed giving him or her skills they would need in order to function within their society. Differentiation was the mechanism whereby a child's capabilities were matched to their society's functional requirements and empowerment sought to enhance a child's sense of self-worth.

Now let's consider what awaits the child of a dysfunctional family and here I must come clean and define a dysfunctional family as one in which the child is not the primary focus of at least one and preferably two parents. The values such a child is likely to absorb are selfishness, wantonness, anger and neglect with an overlay of survival cunning. To take what one can get, when one can get it must appear to be a guiding principle. Authority is most likely held in contempt but feared.

The skills offered to such a child in school must appear almost entirely irrelevant. He (and if it is a she the poor girl is probably already being abused by her mother's current lover) will already have linked up with one or two other boys in a similar situation and may be part of a gang more relevant to him than school will ever be. The skills of the street will be what he learns, not the skills of the classroom. Within his gang he will find out what he is made of and where he fits into the pecking order and it is the gang that will empower him, offering emotional support, prestige and purpose. All human beings have similar needs and they will have them met, one way or another.

In evolutionary terms, dysfunctional families will be a product of their environment and individual character. It seems to be an unsurprising fact that dysfunctional children are most likely to come from dysfunctional parents, although to call them 'dysfunctional' may be a sleight of hand that partially at least, excuses the rest of us: we (or our forebears) have created the environment which nurtures their behaviour. Liberalism is a product of economic success in that economic success makes a range of lifestyles possible, so we should not be surprised if a number of these lifestyles appear self-destructive. But while we might think that a few failures justify the freedoms we enjoy (including the freedom to make a complete cobblers of our life), it is surely hard to justify inflicting those failures on children.

That said, to offset the harshness of removing children from their biological parents, the boarding schools to which they were sent might sensibly have adjacent self–catering accommodation to which their mothers alone could come. This would at least offer these women a chance to claw their way back to some sort of normality.

To expect a state-funded, one size fits all, comprehensive system of education to meet the needs of the diverse types liberalism has made possible must be a tall order, even a contradiction in terms. Evolution has demonstrated time and again strength in diversity, so long as it can be accommodated within a single dynamic framework. Solving problems should always take precedence over ideological conformity and this applies as much to advocates of choice as it does to defenders of standardized community education. But when it comes to 'dysfunctional families', radical intervention is surely called for: their children deserve nothing less. There is, however, one thing we can thank them for. Dysfunctional families lay bare the limits of liberalism, although before conservatives crow too loudly, it is the diversity born out of liberalism which has enriched all our lives. But in helping people to find their own way, conservatives are often better progenitors of liberalism than liberals themselves.

26

Us

WE are capable of more extreme brutality to our own kind than any other species. I sometimes wish that liberals (whose values I admire) would read more history of the kind they probably consider distasteful and spend less time imagining that they are above the brutish fray. They are not. None of us are. Because we are conscious beings with imaginations, terror is a potent weapon and its expression a cathartic inversion of our own fears.

Anyone could write page upon page describing atrocities that have happened in the recent past and which are probably being perpetrated somewhere on somebody by someone right now. The genius of the Roman state was to institutionalize brutality. Faced with the tit-for-tat violence between Whites and Reds during the Russian civil war of 1917-1922 (I always love the use of the word civil) – which included skinning alive, burning alive, burying alive, dismemberment of the living and gang rape: in short, anything you can imagine – Lenin, the Bolshevik's great puppeteer, concluded that more terror was needed, not less.

All property was to be taken over by his people's soviets and any complaining members of the bourgeois middle class or property-owning peasantry (yes, the class existed) were to be taken out and shot. And these were the lucky ones. So disruptive was the war and these policies that for many, death by disease and starvation was the best they could hope for: the worst did not bear thinking about. Feodor Batyushkov, professor of philosophy, died from eating rotten cabbage; S. Bengerov, professor of history and literature, died from hunger; V. V. Rozanov, another philosopher, starved to death after scouring the streets for cigarette ends to sate his hunger. Millions more, whose death went unrecorded, suffered the same fate. But Lenin's logic was impeccable.

There could exist no space outside what was coming to be called communism. So foul was the certainty which awaited any who tried to locate that space, that other imaginary world, most would even come to recoil from their own slender thoughts of it. The efficacy of such a system can be readily demonstrated. The Democratic People's Republic of Korea has applied Lenin's recipe with conspicuous success. A polity of around 25 million individuals - 1.2 million of whom are in military uniform with a further 8.3 million classed as military associates (reservists, paramilitary, etc.), entitled to the impoverished country's meagre privileges - is run by its hereditary Supreme Leader (an unpleasant self-obsessed thirty-two year old) along Leninist-Stalinist lines.

Hermetically sealed from the outside, North Korea's citizens are told that they live in a paradise whose occasional blemishes (such as bouts of starvation) are a necessary price to pay in their country's heroic struggle with the demon West. The fact that everyone living in South Korea, which has followed a different path, is far richer and freer is something they are not allowed to know. The lives of any who try to find this out are traduced beyond repair. On the other side of the equation, a citizen's loyalty to the regime determines access to responsibility, opportunity and food. The terror gauge is held at high, however. Not long after Kim Jong-un took over from his father, a vice premier of education was spotted sitting in a disrespectful manner during one of the new Supreme Leader's monologues and was subsequently shot (after interrogation revealed other counter-revolutionary crimes). A gesture *pour encourager les autres* no doubt, of which Lenin and Stalin would have approved.

What one can say about the North Korean regime is that it is a step beyond anarchy and its people are doubtless thankful for that. When the Soviet system collapsed and free market economics were introduced under Boris Yeltsin, it caused great upheaval and there were many who yearned for the days of Uncle Joe Stalin. It also demonstrates that a polity can exist on a diet of state control, internal propaganda, isolation, a judicious use of incentives and the ever-present threat of terror. Like a tribe lost within the jungles of Borneo, fearful of what cannot be seen but content with what is familiar, there is no reason why the DPRK can't continue to exist until some external change upsets its equilibrium.

What do these two characteristics – our obsession with terror and our preference for the status quo – say about us? They are probably two sides of the same coin: identity. To possess imagination is, in many ways, a fearful thing. As far as we know, animals do not reflect but react in accordance with their evolved drivers. We also are imbued with evolved drivers which we call instinct. Imagination is a comparatively recent development and can be used to trigger those drivers. Tell children a scary story and they will imagine ghouls and goblins and feel afraid, and then asked to be told it again and again.

Shakespeare's great art was to describe the goings-on of his time in such a way as to make his audience experience them from the relative safety of the auditorium (to be sure the Globe Theatre had its share of pickpockets, drunks and chancers, but that was part of the fun). A person could imagine themselves in battle, as a leader, lover, murderer or ageing clown; feel anger, disgust, compassion, fear and leave the venue cleansed of repressed emotions (the Aristotelian catharsis). In the pantomime we hiss and boo on cue, certain that we know who is good and who is bad. Much of education is about building a mind map of our world. Academics use the word to 'socialize' which means to teach individuals how to function within society. The implication, of course, is that much of our world is man-made and that instincts will be insufficient to see us through.

The problem, of course, is that instincts are what motivate us so the trick is to channel our emotional drivers along socially acceptable pathways. But these pathways are often far from precise and require judgement to interpret. Now this is where another important characteristic comes into play, one which we share with all systems: our use of habit, repetition or pattern. Most of what we do each day is a repeat of what we have done on previous days. If we had to work out what to do each moment from first principles we would get nowhere and our poor brains would explode with the effort. So we follow patterns which we have learnt and which work, and by 'work' we mean provide us with our day-to-day needs: food, shelter and companionship. And this is why the people of North Korea (and the rest of us for that matter) soldier on.

We hear a good deal these days from corporate and political minders about managing expectations. Most of us most of the time are just too busy getting by to worry much about the rights and wrongs of anything. Certainly if some perceived injustice affects us directly, and this usually means something negative outwith our expectations (such as finding less in our pay packet), then we start to question the status quo. But generally the status quo is our friend. However, a human innovation which springs from our ability to imagine has been the development of heightened expectations. Indeed, the consumer society is largely predicated on it. Sometimes cruelly, although not altogether inaccurately, advertising is described as the art of persuading people to purchase things they do not need.

But before MAD men get a bad rap for this, politicians were way ahead of them. Back as far as Pericles (495-429BCE) and beyond, a crucial instrument in a leader's box of black arts was how to manage the expectations of his followers (to ensure that they continued following). Moses (1400-1201BCE) was often challenged as he led his sometimes unruly band of Israelites to the Promised Land, an imaginary place some might say their descendants only recently found. But the hope of a better tomorrow has driven countless numbers of people forward. When America broke from England, Thomas Jefferson and Benjamin Franklin proposed using an image of Moses leading the Israelites to freedom on the new nation's great seal. And after his death, countless eulogies referred to George Washington as America's Moses. Human progress has been a product of imagination.

Imagination, however, is a mercurial creature capable of assuming many shapes. It can build a world populated by fairies. It can ignore the rules of physics and travel faster than the speed of light. In the hands of a master dream-maker it can build a Reich that will last for a thousand years. It can even imagine hell, heaven and the end of time. Lenin was not wrong to want to rein it in with terror. But fortunately, in the right hands, it can even turn its back on fear. Through the ages men and woman have been willing to endure the unimaginable for a cause, for the right to say 'no matter what you throw at me I do not and will not share your view of the world.' And like the little boy who, in standing up to the playground bully, getting beaten half to death for his stance, breaks the monster's spell over his less critical classmates.

It wasn't until 1956 in a speech to a closed session of the Twentieth Party Congress of the Communist Party of the Soviet Union that the then First Secretary, Nikita Khrushchev, felt able to criticize the excesses of the Stalinist era. When he was finally ousted from power he was not shot but pensioned off. It had taken forty years for the Soviet elite to feel sufficiently secure not to want to devour its own. But it would be another thirty-five years before Lenin's soviet system was finally abandoned. One man's utopia generally turns out to be most other men's hell.

Individually we have little more going for us than a sparrow and in some ways, less. The sparrow has evolved like everything else in our biosphere and occupies a niche within it. The biosphere feeds off its environment and itself. The sparrow devours seeds and insects and may become a meal for the sparrowhawk or cat and typically lives for around three years (although can live much longer), producing copious broods along the way. There are numerous types of sparrow and they can be found in colonies all over the world. Raise the camera high above a city and individual humans look no more distinct than any one of these ubiquitous creatures.

Individual humans only become distinct because of the leverage our evolved social systems give them. But why should a person who runs faster than anyone else over a particular distance be singled out and rewarded? Why should a person with a particular turn of mind, which enables him or her to become an 'expert' in some obscure field of little relevance to anyone outside it, be set for life within a university? Why is some of what we call art and its artists more highly esteemed than others? Why is human history peppered with heroes and villains (with the two often conflated)? Sparrows come and go each year in their millions without any undue regard for their individual merits. Why do humans love reading obituaries and novels describing how other humans deal with the dilemmas they face? How can we talk about the 'Me generation' with what almost amounts to a straight face? How, as a species, can we talk about the sanctity of human life and still kill vast numbers of our own kind?

What accounts for our fascination with the character of a murderer and our aversion to the idea of tailoring individuals to any blueprint? How can we think so much of ourselves and so little of anyone who happens to belong to a group we despise? How can we feel something in the morning and its polar opposite in the afternoon? How do we have the gall to talk about the risks of AI (artificial intelligence) surpassing our own as if our individual intelligence amounts to much? Albert Einstein may have had an aptitude for mathematical problem-solving which he imposed upon the physical universe, but he was a poor husband, an indifferent father and doubtless would have been the first to admit that he added little to the sum of human happiness. So why do we call him a genius?

Of course all this comes down to individual consciousness and its offspring, imagination. If you were a fan of Freddie Mercury (the lead singer in the rock group Queen) you will have felt supercharged by his utterly outrageous, over-the-top and yet beautifully lyrical performance. For a short while you will have been carried away from the constricting banalities of daily life on a blazing beam of raw energy: an end in itself. It is that moment when you are utterly captured by a Miles Davis riff. After Pope Urban VIII heard Gregorio Allegri's *Miserere mei, Deus* he was so taken by its celestial beauty that he decreed it could only be performed with papal consent.

We still talk about an empire which stretched from the Pacific Ocean in the east to the Mediterranean Sea in the west begun by Genghis Khan, the Mogul warrior, even though its construction embraced great cruelty and disrupted countless stable communities. In the way that we are captivated by a pure note, so we are by the exercise of power. It is like watching a flame: energy freed from the shackles of matter. Today we are horrified and fascinated in equal measure by Leni Riefenstahl's undoubtedly brilliant propaganda film, *Triumph of the Will*, which shows the Nazi Party's Nuremberg Rally: thousands of disciplined men pledging their allegiance to the vision of a leader. Religions the world over have been built out of our desire as individuals to let go, to find certainty amidst the uncertainty of existence, to abrogate responsibility for our future.

Are these two things – lauding the exceptional and losing ourselves in the moment – related? I think they are in that both address our sense of limitation and indicate our deep desire to overcome it. Even the homeless tramp is finding a way out of the human jungle and its man-made rules, something a sparrow never has to contend with. When the notorious Harvard psychologist Timothy Leary (1920-1996), for a while the high priest of America's 1960s counter-culture, urged his followers *to turn on, tune in, drop out*, invariably with the help of the mind-altering drug LSD, he was only following in the footsteps of shamans and their eager disciples going back millennia. Imagination has given us the ability to think that there could be an existence different from our own and the desire to find it.

This evolutionary innovation is undoubtedly a powerful adaptive tool in that it prompts us to try alternatives even when the status quo is satisfactory by any objective measure. In what way, for example, is the life of an inhabitant of São Paulo, London or Shanghai today better than the life of an Australian aboriginal before Europeans arrived? The latter, like the sparrow, lived in harmony with his natural environment, the former lives in a man-made environment that could spin out of control at any moment, taking millions of lives with it. But of course there is a crucial difference. The Australian aboriginal was not bent on shaping his future, other than in the spirit world, whereas we – albeit clumsily – seem intent upon doing so. However, for a majority of the citizens in São Paulo, London and Shanghai the consensus would probably be that we are doing a poor job of it.

If utopias are a dangerous pipe dream because the future is unknown and can only be something we all create in the present, we are left with process. And if we are going to prevent people clutching at pipe dreams, process requires them to be empowered so that they can participate in the decisions which affect their lives. It is a dangerous illusion to imagine that empowerment is achieved by allowing individuals to vote periodically for who, from a stitched-up list of candidates, should represent them, or occasionally to vote on specific issues about which they have limited knowledge (as was clearly the case with the referendum about whether the United Kingdom should remain in the European Union).

What the great ideologues of the 18th, 19th and 20th centuries went on about were variations of the French revolutionary war cry *Liberté, égalité, fraternité* when what they actually meant (and Lenin at least left no doubt about this) was that the revolutionaries should make the decisions for everyone else. It amounted to little more than the replacement of one aristocracy by another and because its fresh face promised everything, one which was not even constrained by the tradition of past experience. That change was necessary was abundantly clear. But to have to wait until war, failure and starvation drove people to anarchy before it happened served no one.

The conundrum, as it often is, remains how to maintain a competent stability while at the same time facilitating change. And because we are not talking about change for its own sake but change that is creative and so cannot be fully understood in advance, it has to arise out of a synthesis between different interests (which, of course, does eventually emerge out of anarchy but at a high cost and lopsidedly – i.e. in the direction of the newly dominant power). To achieve this – combining a competent status quo with a willingness to change it – requires agreement on all sides that the process will be fair. And by 'fair' one must mean a process that will not enhance one group's interests solely at the expense of another group (the zero-sum assumption behind such slogans as *tax the rich and help the poor*), but rather one that enables a judicious rearrangement which enhances the interests of both.

To work, this requires four elements to be in place: (1) an overarching set of values which essentially boil down to an acceptance that the function of society is to enhance the lives of all its members; (2) a shared understanding of how societies actually work together with a high level of technical competence in this regard; (3) a diverse array of hierarchies which serve as nodes of excellence offering many opportunities for individual self-fulfilment; and (4) the mechanical means whereby concerns can be brought to the surface, plans put in place for their resolution and structures developed to monitor progress. Free market capitalism does a remarkably good job of reconciling economic interests so as to enhance social wealth, but would have been impossible to design in advance and requires continuing adjustment as unforeseen problems arise.

In our calmer moments we probably feel that society's primary function is to enhance the wellbeing of its members. But all too quickly our intentions get hijacked by sectional interests. Consider poverty. That poverty still exists in wealthy societies is, quite clearly, a disgrace. But it is possible that the 'poverty industry', if I can call it that (all the schemes, departments and initiatives which exist on the back of poverty) has served to embed poverty in society rather than help to eliminate it. Poverty is having insufficient funds on which to live. The reason for this can be down to economic failure (an absence of accessible jobs paying a living wage) or personal circumstance (disability, temporary unemployment, reaching retirement age, poor planning, etc.). By all means keep the targeted payments to ameliorate the ill effects of personal circumstance, but give everyone a stake in the economy they are part of through a dividend paid for by a tax on corporate sales. There is only one way to eliminate poverty: get more money into people's hands. Values without effective action are morally corrosive.

Ensuring that everyone has a shared understanding of how society works seems such an obvious necessity one has to wonder why we are nowhere near achieving it; in fact why it is not even discussed as an objective. Could it be that knowledge is power and that those who have it are its jealous guardians? Could it also be that the academic profession is so tied up in the maintenance of its proliferating silos that it has lost sight of the bigger picture: namely that what we do for ourselves must also work for the betterment of the whole? Social engineering should be used as naturally as civil, electrical and mechanical engineering or architecture. If we are serious about empowering individuals then our educational and academic institutions need to refocus their activities substantially.

Self-fulfilment is a state we all aspire to. Being useful helps us to achieve this as does becoming good at something. The proliferation of roles within society not only facilitates adaptation, it also increases the opportunities open to individuals. As roles are invariably nested within hierarchies the chances of being at or near the top of one increases the more of them there are. It goes without saying that if hierarchies are to proliferate (many of which will be in the private sphere), work must not be allowed to dominate our time. To this end we will have to go on learning how to work smarter. One might never become a tsar but to head a parish council or football club for a year or two will give us a better understanding of the social dynamics we are subject to. It will also mitigate those feelings of powerlessness which can come our way and make it more likely that we will properly admire the exceptional rather than improperly worship it.

The mechanics of getting people's concerns translated into viable action plans which are then monitored is of the utmost importance (and is a useful area for the academic profession to sink its teeth into). Our current party political system is a little like allowing workers to spend their wages but only in the company store. The internet has disrupted many things and it will soon disrupt the party political system of representative democracy. We really don't need intermediaries any more. Like the Catholic priesthood of old, which stood between individuals and all things spiritual, taking its cut along the way and living very well, its time has passed. Special interest advocates empowered to legislate, certainly – elected by those whose interests they serve. And yes, we need someone able to direct the bureaucracy toward solving the concerns people flag up and strong elected mayors would achieve that – if you doubt this examine the history of New York since it emerged from lawlessness, chaos and bankruptcy. At the national level an elected president (able to appoint a small cabinet of his or her own choosing) would serve just as well as the present arrangement.

I want to end with the media because it is through the media that we communicate and display our natures – for good and ill. Before the First World War the recently empowered popular press was at the forefront of war fever (*England expects every man to do his duty* was the banner headline across the Daily Express) and there were similar sentiments on the other side. Europe was in the throes of destroying itself but the media seemed as blind as every other social mouthpiece. Should one expect a society's media to be any more enlightened than the society it is part of: probably not.

But if we are going to move to a more self-critical, more nuanced, more creative approach toward our collective futures, the media must play its part. To merely beat the drum which accords loudest with the prevailing sentiment might be good for sales but is unlikely to be good for wisdom. As a matter of standard practice every broadcast should make space for the best of opposing views. Truth is very rarely a one-sided affair even though our conscious imagination and sense of identity often prompts us to think otherwise.

27

Boredom

I suspect that a great many of the things humans do and have done were (and are) the result of boredom. Watch cows in a field and it seems that they spend most of every day eating. Even though grass is abundant, they need a lot of it to keep going. Lions, in contrast, have to hunt and, although many hunts end in failure, one kill can keep a pride going for a while so its members have time to watch and to socialize. Biological structures work to many rhythms but in the main they are kept busy eating and procreating. Humans, on the other hand, have been so successful in finding ways to extract the energy they need from the environment that they have created plenty of time for other activities.

For the upper echelons of society this latitude has been considerable, allowing the men in particular to plot and lead armies while the women ran homes and schemed. Some, of both sexes, resorted to the discipline of religious practice in closed orders to fill their day. Mankind's economic juggernaut has proved so effective that large numbers of people in society now have time to spend on entertainments such as themed eating (and over-eating), visual stimulus (from computer games to football matches), shopping, physical recreation and travel, to spending hours on the internet searching for knowledge, communicating, bandying intellectual points back and forth (to what end is not always clear), gossiping and tooting their own trumpets. Indeed modern man has more time than the members of any other species to engage in discretionary activities and these activities constitute the character of what we call our civilizations.

Of course this freedom of action throws up an interesting set of problems because all actions have consequences. When bored leaders enjoin bored young men to fight with them for some advantage (egged on by bored politicians who want to feel that they are at the centre of important things), there is a risk that their campaign will end not well but badly. The wife who cuckolds her husband or the husband who seeks sexual fulfilment from someone other than his wife might bring about less than pleasing reactions. So this freedom we have created for ourselves requires us to balance short-term gratification with an action's longer term consequences.

Because there are so many discretionary actions all with their own possible outcomes, we have had to come up with rules to help us choose. We have classed killing for pleasure as murder, unless it is done within the confines of an army encounter. Even killing in self-defense is discouraged in favour of allowing 'the authorities' to deal with the matter. And we have worked ourselves into a frenzy about the sale of sex for money, unless it is part of a marriage contract. We have even concluded that the speeds at which we can travel in cars on roads is better mandated, rather than being left to individual discretion.

Not being machines, however, we can break any one of these rules and so a range of punishments has been built into our social structures in order to increase the likelihood of us abiding by them. These vary from social disapproval to incarceration, even death. However, enforcement itself entails consequences, both in terms of the cost of redirected effort and in terms of the way individual initiative is dulled, thereby reducing a society's ability to adapt. In the shanty towns of some great cities, for example, the young alleviate boredom by resorting to petty crime. In this way some of the well-to-do's surplus wealth is siphoned off into the coffers of those who have no other opportunities, and further drained to support enforcement which itself becomes symbiotically dependent on the shanty towns.

Just as species feed off one another in the biological world, much of the activity in the human world is symbiotic: the writer writes; the critic critiques; the villain breaks rules for gain; the law-enforcement officer tries to catch him, also for gain; health services depend upon the unhealthy; welfare programmes depend upon the needy; armies need enemies; production requires consumption. Indeed societies are sets of interlocking arrangements by which individuals fill their time. But it is easy to get stuck inside any one of them.

Because they are expressions of our moral sense, these arrangements should be thought about. And as the energy we need is increasingly generated by our systems without any direct input from us, our choices will grow, making the pursuit of novelty for its own sake an abiding temptation. That leaves our inner selves as a rich and often unexplored land. The outward and inward are kindred spirits and should be fused better than they often are. Strange to say, but how we alleviate boredom will determine our future.

28

Armies

A R M I E S of the future will need to be fundamentally different from armies of the past. But first, let us remind ourselves what the purpose of an army is. At the opening of the film *Patton*, which I hope is based on fact, the great general is shown addressing some new recruits with these words: *no dumb bastard ever won a war by dying for his country. He won a war by making the other dumb bastard die for his.* It was this kind of candour that won Donald Trump the US presidency and engendered palpitations within the establishments both men found frustrating.

For the warrior, kill or be killed is the simple purity of battle. There is no political double-dealing, no diplomatic double-speak; there are no shades of grey, no tortuous splitting of hairs; it is just a question of winning or losing. The late, great Cassius Clay, who became Muhammad Ali, captured the world's hearts not just because he won but because of how he won: with nobility. There was not an ounce of pettiness in him. No hint of vengefulness: just exuberance and that same generosity of spirit which drew us to Karol Wojtyla as Pope John Paul II.

That the business of killing can be portrayed as noble makes little sense on the face of it. And indeed it is not the killing that is noble but the willingness to die for that entity (generally one's country) which bestows nobility. The marches, the memorial ceremonies, the accolades are all saying the same thing: that it is noble to give of oneself, body and soul, for your community. You accept that you are the dumb bastard willing to die for your country while sincerely hoping that you will be making the other dumb bastard die for his. It is a deeply conflicted construct and yet also a measure of a people's prowess.

A soldier in a Roman legion could take pride in Rome and its empire but when neither evoked such pride something was lost. A man is proud to fight for his family. That needs no justification. That is a measure of the biological imperative we are subject to. Families then become communities and communities become nations and the biological imperative is stretched to embrace something less tangible: a regiment, a flag, a body politic. Being proud of what one is fighting for entails a cerebral overlay. One has to have a mental image capable of triggering that elemental feeling which prompts one to fight for one's own. As every sergeant major knows, in the heat of battle one's fellow dumb bastards become one's family.

All the hoopla heaped upon a fighting force leaving for battle is designed to ensure that it does the very best for the collective whose bacon it is being sent off to save. When the bodies start returning, flags are draped over their coffins partly as a token of collective thanks and partly as a reminder of what the collective expects from those still fighting, or who might be asked to fight in the future. An army is an expression of its society's inner soul. As such, we should wish it to express the best in us, not the worst.

* * *

Soldiering, like the law or medicine, is also a profession and soldiers take pride in it. Surviving the initial training is a cause for celebration (as it is meant to be), bonding individuals to each other and to their regiment while imparting essential knowledge. The regiment becomes one's tribe and one's fellow recruits one's surrogate family. The satisfaction gained from doing something well (even if it is the perfect drill manoeuvre) serves to bind the individual to the body he is part of. Corporations have learnt from army practice in this regard.

But there is more. The context within which an army exists is important and might serve to enhance or detract from its cohesion and effectiveness. If the polity directing the army is considered corrupt or incompetent, morale will suffer and might even prompt its officers to mount a coup. And this highlights another characteristic of an army: it is both dependent and powerful. As a formal organization within a polity, it relies on the polity to sustain it. Food has to be sourced, clothes made available and equipment supplied. In this sense it is dependent on the community it serves.

However, as a self-contained hierarchy with the ability to exert force, it can take over its community as well. All polities are therefore mindful of their armies. Both communists and fascists inserted a political hierarchy alongside their military structures and in Britain members of the Royal Family are traditionally made heads of regiments to ensure the army's loyalty to the state, just as in the United States, the President is that nation's commander–in–chief for the same reason. And, as an ordered hierarchy capable of exerting force, an army is sometimes the only structure capable of holding a chaotic polity together.

That said, armies are not entirely biddable. In the First World War, elements of the French army were close to mutiny so fed up were the men of being forced to undertake suicidal advances which invariably got them nowhere; and in Russia, when faced with military defeat and domestic chaos, soldiers once loyal to the Tsar started to disobey orders, opening the door to Lenin's revolutionary soviets. Soldiers come from communities and are understandably reluctant to turn on them, which is why commanders try to use men who are not from an area they are attempting to dominate.

When the glamour of soldiering is stripped away, however, war has traditionally been a dirty business and civilian populations are often the hardest hit. Starvation is to be expected, the physical degradation of towns is commonplace and the mistreatment of inhabitants by soldiers charged up by hatred and fear is all too normal. The battlefield, where some semblance of heroism and valour was once possible, is a thing of the past. Today wars are largely urban affairs in which civilian and soldier are hard to tell apart. The armies of the future will have to be designed differently.

* * *

The first necessary change is a cultural one. General Patton's homily needs to be retired. The army of the future must be designed to protect life, not destroy it. From this flows all manner of other changes in tactics and weaponry. If empire-building is ruled out of bounds, armies have three legitimate functions: defense of the community they come from, assisting in civil emergencies and quelling aggressive flare-ups between groups. A fourth legitimate function and a twist on empire-building entails assisting with mankind's colonization of planets other than the Earth.

It is a great shame that the European Union is stumbling at the moment, as the best protection against warfare is the establishment of large regional groupings that make warfare the least likely option. It is hard to see why North America would want to go to war with itself or why any other power would want to go to war with it. Even Japan's audacious, albeit misguided, attack on America's Pacific fleet in Pearl Harbour was intended to keep America out of Japan's war in the Far East. The friction between Russia and Europe at the present time has as much to do with the European Union's rather clumsy expansion into Russia's sphere of influence as it does with any great desire inside Russia to conquer Western Europe. But of course World Wars start from just such miscalculations.

Wars have more often resulted from weakness than from strength. A chancer spots an opening and goes for it, as Saddam Hussein did in Kuwait. The certain knowledge that some greater power will intervene would have a deterring effect, just as the presence of an effective police force deters crime. But until the world organizes itself in such a way as to make lines of demarcation and the consequences of breaching them clear, armies will be used to advance narrow political objectives.

Communication today is almost instantaneous. The residents of Nether Wallop (a parish in Hampshire) can be made to feel guilty and to wonder why their government is not doing something about a conflict 3,000 miles away. This kind of media pornography is profoundly unhealthy. Planning for such eventualities needs to be carried out long before events on the ground make such interventions necessary and require the cooperation of those involved. Much of the turmoil in the Middle East today can be traced to earlier interventions by outside nations for less than benign reasons.

Perhaps the residents of Nether Wallop do have some cause for guilt, but not for the reasons they imagine. The humanitarian impulse is better expressed through carefully constructed programmes and protocols. Instant outrage from the safety of one's living room is little different from the shock of a person seeing a body fall from a tall building: understandable but of little use, unless it prompts a quest for the whys and wherefores.

* * *

If we truly want a body of men and women able to handle civil emergencies, that is capable of calming conflicts, which can defend us from evil doers, and is able to project the best of ourselves, not the worst, we need a top to toe reformulation. Should we not move from regiments to functions? And does it really make sense for the three services – air, sea and land, to be quite so distinct (what about outer space)? And should what we call intelligence (keeping our ears to the ground) be quite so covert? Secrets can be taken out of context for political advantage. And besides, if people are asked to commit to a course of action, they should know upon what basis. Bad reasons are not made good by being hidden within a national flag.

The creation of a European military organization seems to be anathema to many in Europe today even though it would save large amounts of money and improve overall effectiveness. It would enable Europe to help parts of the world dogged by instability. It would also allow for a more focused approach toward defense and space exploration. The only logical arguments for wanting national armies in Europe is if European nations wish to go to war with one another or want to project national spheres of influence beyond their borders.

* * *

Did the events of the 20th century not cure us of that lust? Not if media drum rolls are any indication! And this is the problem with armies. They can be utterly professional, populated by men of the highest standards and be armed with tools to establish order in the least destructive way – but they remain the creatures of the communities that supply them and the playthings of those community's politicians. So until *we the people* get a grip and sort out our objectives, our armies will remain the confused, strung-out things that they are at present: underfunded, overstretched and with the potential to do more harm than good.

29

Legislators

T H E architecture of a modern democracy is roughly this: a constitution (or customary practice if no formal constitution exists) is meant to encapsulate certain general principles to which everyone subscribes; laws are enacted by legislators who are supposed to represent the people; a judiciary free from political pressure is supposed to interpret the law without fear or favour; a bureaucracy exists to apply the law in an even-handed manner; the executive function of government (making decisions about what to do when, where and how) is generally allocated to an elected official such as a president, although will be constrained by a country's laws and constitution which in some particulars can impose the need for parliamentary approval.

As a polity is a forced coalition of sometimes divergent interests, the political trick is to try to reconcile these interests as seamlessly as possible, while at the same time ensuring the efficient functioning of the polity overall and maintaining its structural integrity in the face of outside pressures. Naturally these objectives embody potential conflicts, not least because future outcomes are uncertain but also because the members of a polity might have differing views about what that polity should be.

Legislation (the making of laws) is both technical as well as emotional. The technical aspects are concerned with clarity, interpretation and implications (what does the legislation mean, how will it be interpreted and will it affect the functioning of any other part of the system?). The emotional side of legislation arises out of the fact that legislation generally interferes with the actions of some to the advantage of others. However there is another aspect of legislation which is often overlooked, namely the context within which it takes place. A polity is not an abstract intellectual construct but an evolved entity. Even the United States of America, whose founding fathers set out to create something new, was made up out of individuals with deep familial connections and centuries-old traditions.

Acknowledging that legislation can disadvantage some to the benefit of others, a guiding principle (implicit even if it is not explicit) has to be that the polity as a whole will be improved by the legislation. However, as outcomes are always uncertain, the natural evolution of arrangements (what people choose to do by free association rather than state direction) should be treated with considerable reverence. For example if, after looking at all the objective evidence, a government concludes that a major infrastructure project is likely to be of great benefit to a polity going forward, the communities adversely affected by the project should, wherever possible, be relocated as communities. Scattering individuals, even with generous financial compensation, will be socially degrading.

A case in point was the legislation that led to an acceleration of globalization. Across Western Europe a period of state direction (a continuation of the heavy state control exercised during World War II) had led to economic rigidities, government over-expenditure and high inflation (as politically-connected unions struggled to maintain the wages of their members in the face of a massive transfer of wealth from the oil consumers to the oil producers) which caused a realignment in political thinking toward less state control and greater market freedoms. The wealth flowing to the oil-producing countries of the Middle East could not be absorbed by their economies and so was recycled through the Western banking system, finding its way into United States government-backed mortgage securities and the overseas expansion of Western corporations into developing economies where the cost of labour was significantly less.

The legislators overseeing this change could point to a collapse in inflationary pressures as the entrance of low-cost producers put downward pressure on a range of consumer products aided and abetted by a collapse in union power as manufacturing jobs were exported. But as the citizens of developing nations benefitted and worldwide consumption accelerated, whole communities in the West, previously underpinned by well-paid manufacturing jobs, were devastated. If this wasn't enough, the surfeit of footloose petro-money led to a decline in lending standards and a build-up of unsupportable debt in the form of mortgage-backed securities to the very people whose ability to service it was being eroded by the export of their jobs into the global economy.

Legislation to regulate (during and immediately after World War II) and then legislation to de-regulate in order to spur economic development and curb inflation were both justified. However legislators had no easy way to deal with the unintended consequences which arose from both sets of legislation. Changes in political direction generally require great effort (to dislodge those interests vested in the prior status quo), such that subtle acknowledgements of prior strengths are not easy to entertain any more than is a recognition of potential flaws in the new.

The nature of political dialogue, which is largely party political, is chiefly to blame for this. Its Hegelian character (of assertion, counter-assertion and perhaps an improved understanding somewhere down the road) embraces all aspects of society so completely (just as ethnicity or nationality sometimes does) that it might seem impossible to circumvent. However if it is the case – as I think it is – that rationality divorced from feeling is a flawed concept (2 + 2 may = 4, but so what?), we need to improve the process whereby collective understanding comes about. Party political slanging matches (during which truth is asserted as polar opposites) only serve to corrupt public discourse and weaken trust in those institutions which are the cornerstone of civil society.

Political parties came into existence naturally and for perfectly good reasons. The mercantilist tradition held that a nation should accumulate wealth by protecting its own. The free traders, however, argued that overall wealth could be increased if nations were allowed to trade freely with one another, each playing to its strengths. That the globalization/anti-globalization debate has resurfaced, indicates the contingent nature of these positions. It is easy to see a liaison developing between environmentalists and mercantilists, as the base assumption of both is that we live in a world of finite resources, with those advocating unfettered free trade and the continuing development of the natural world (or its rape, depending on your point of view) on the other. But to ingrain these positions into the political system so that debate has to be framed in these terms makes little sense and by simplifying discussion can do real harm. So how can we take parties out of politics?

In practice, political parties have been less than steadfast in their views. Britain's Whigs, for example, started as anti-Catholic, pro-Parliament and protectionist, with their opponents, the Tories, being supporters of the monarchy and inclined towards free trade. However the Corn Laws of 1815-1846, which imposed tariffs on imported grains to the benefit of landowners (generally Tory supporters), were opposed by the Whigs who were currying favour with the rising industrial and middle classes.

That people pushing an agenda should want to come together so as to foment action is obviously natural and it is understandable that the issues of the day (those things that concern and affect people) should give rise to factions. But that factions should mutate into parties able to dominate power, which tends to be the way within our present democratic systems, is something that should concern us. The Nazi Party came to power through the electoral system after all and the United Kingdom Independence Party (UKIP) managed to channel popular discontent into a single issue (that Britain should leave the European Union) largely unrelated to the cause of the discontent.

So let us consider an alternative to the party political system which presently empowers legislators. Societies are broad coalitions of overlapping interests each of which has concerns unique to it. Supposing we could categorize these interests in some sensible way (male, female, juvenile, farming, manufacturing, services public or private, military, community, etc.) that reflected the complexities of our society. Next, let us have each of these interests appoint an individual to represent them in a legislative assembly. The task of these individuals would be to advance legislation that assisted their interest and to put a break on legislation advanced by others that might affect their interest negatively.

At the moment lobbyists have to be hired by interest groups to inform legislators regarding areas they probably know nothing about. Party political legislators are chosen on the basis of their ability to secure votes and their willingness to follow the party line, neither of which are legislative qualifications nor grounds for expecting them to be well versed in any one area. The range of issues a constituency representative presently has to deal with is very wide and this dispersion and consequent lack of focus is unlikely to lead to systemic change, if such is necessary, whereas concerns channelled to a specialist would be much more likely to do so. The dynamics within a legislative assembly populated by specialists would surely be more constructive than one divided across party political lines.

There would inevitably be deals done between specialists - if you vote for or against this change I'll help you etc., and if thought undesirable could be dulled by secret voting within the chamber. But the pros and cons of this would have to be considered. One would also want a specialist to be able to appeal to a constitutional court on the basis of whether a legislative change passed by the chamber cleared the "greater good" hurdle. For instance, a minority activity like fox hunting has been banned by the UK Parliament because most legislators dislike the practice, but merely disliking a practice should not be grounds for banning it.

The initial reaction to this proposal will probably be "what about the will of the people – we can't have 'specialists' running the country!" But think for a moment. How is the 'will of the people' actually expressed under the present system? Some of the best work carried out by legislators is in respect of problems their constituents bring them. However this generally consists of directing a constituent to the 'right department' (along with a formal letter *from the MP*) where the problem can be addressed. While useful, a specialist legislator could do this just as well.

A second useful activity legislators engage in is through their committee work which peruses the functioning of particular areas within society to see if fresh legislation is needed or existing legislation needs amending. But again, specialist legislators could do this just as well.

The *will of the people* is one of those expressions that hides more than it reveals and elections are an extremely blunt instrument for revealing it. In the main, elections measure the mood of the people with regard to how effective they think the government of the day is in addressing the problems that concern them. The saying that elections are lost not won, is probably close to the truth. If people's lives are moving along reasonably well, they are likely to vote for the status quo, which makes sense. However to turf one lot out so that another lot can have a shot at running things better makes less sense although it can herald a radical change in direction – such as from state intervention with a national bias to the liberalization of markets and global free trade.

The trouble with having a new team embark on a radical change in direction is that it is almost always disruptive because the new team does not know what it is doing, other than in a general sense, and so has to learn on the job which means making mistakes that hurt people. When Margaret Thatcher's Conservatives took over from James Callaghan's Labour administration the United Kingdom was in a mess with high inflation and endless strikes. To break inflation and break the power of the trades unions to strike for ever higher pay (the two things fed into one another) the new administration resorted to a scorched earth policy. Interest rates were raised, the economy was sent into recession and a process begun whereby the state was got out of running the country's key industries directly so that they could be exposed to competition.

The strategy succeeded - eventually, but not before large swathes of Britain's manufacturing industry was destroyed and millions thrown out of work. The Labour Party's historical ties with the trade union movement and its direct involvement in the coal and steel industries as the government in power had prevented it from responding to post-war Britain's need to modernize in a timely fashion (as defeated and devastated Germany had been forced to do). The sudden increase in oil prices engineered by the Middle East oil cartel (OPEC) was the external shock that brought these matters to a head. Not only did the Labour government lose control over the unions, but the union leadership lost control to factory floor shop stewards who responded to their members' economic frustration by calling them out on strike with monotonous regularity. It looked as though an anglicized version of Lenin's workers' soviets were trying to take over government.

The problem, of course, was that Britain needed to adapt. Socially, the post-war Labour government did a remarkable job with heroic improvements to the welfare state even though money was desperately tight. But the state-directed wartime economy just did not work in peacetime because commerce had to compete internationally. This entailed embracing new technologies and rationalizing old industries like coal, steel and automobile manufacturing, none of which could easily be done by managers who had to secure approval from political masters anxious to protect jobs and wages. Margaret Thatcher's government had to do in five years what should have been done far more deliberately than it had been over the previous thirty-five and the impact was devastating.

How do you tell coal miners, whose industry had been at the heart of Britain's industrial revolution, that they and the communities they had supported for generations were no longer required? This really is the nub of it. How much easier is it to blame change on impersonal market forces than take an educated guess about the future and act accordingly? And it was not as if there had been no writing on the wall. From a peak of 1.2 million in 1923, employment in the industry had already fallen to 800,000 by 1945, and by 1970 it was standing at just 300,000. But the miners still had power. Without their coal, power stations were unable to function and by withholding it, the miners could bring the country's activities to a halt (gas-fired power stations were only just coming on stream). So why should they not have gone down without a fight? Isn't the future supposed to be what we make it after all?

With hindsight it appears that most wars achieve little in objective terms – after the carnage, life goes on. One might even wonder what revolutions achieve. France and Russia no longer have monarchs, tsars and aristocracies, they have powerful presidents and industrial oligarchs instead. Even as Britain's miners were going down, her North Sea oil workers were on the way up. So does it all come down to shifts in power and if it does, is there a better way of managing these transitions? Or is confrontation necessary before humans can accept the legitimacy of altered power relations?

A legislative chamber populated by individuals appointed by a country's vested interests would only be able to defuse such confrontations if there existed a mechanism for resolving power disputes, and part of such a mechanism would itself require power. The Roman Catholic Church held the ring in Europe for the best part of a thousand years (from Rome's departure to the Protestant Reformation). It could not stop dynastic conflict nor prevent plague but it did provide a remarkably enduring framework for life. Its ultimate sanction was excommunication – the threat of expulsion from the Christian family in this life and the next.

The authority of the Roman Church only worked because people believed in its authority. From the Protestant Reformation forward we seem to have been searching for a new authority. It is not easy to put one's finger on exactly what this authority is – perhaps because we have not yet fully identified it - but its shape is coming into view. If one had to pick one word to describe it that word would probably be *reason*, although like the tenets of Christianity it has more often been honoured in the breach than in the application. Marx prided himself on his reason, but Marxism became the most unreasonable of ideologies. The problem is that we are only gradually coming to understand how human society (and the universe it is part of) actually works, so humility is a good starting point although power and humility make uneasy bedfellows.

The concept, however, is quite straightforward: we need an evolving model of how our world works to which we subscribe and accept (I will discuss the nature of this model more in the following essay). This is not such an outrageous suggestion as most of us broadly accept the law and its consequences. The legislative chamber I have tried to describe would, in effect, be a practical expression of such a model. Identifying the vested interests in a society from which representatives would be appointed is a model-building exercise. The interaction between them would constitute the model's dynamic.

There would, of course, need to be a baseline against which all decisions could be judged and Christianity in its true, practical, non-ideological sense, would serve this function well. The ethos within the chamber would need to be one of problem-solving and, while this would inevitably lead to altered social structures, the pursuit of utopias would very definitely not be any part of the body's remit.

As it stands, our democratic systems do a rather poor job of representing people because the prerequisites of *party* interfere. As politics is always about vested interests, why not go directly to them? For example, the homeless are not represented at all, so give them a dedicated legislator (although they would likely need help in appointing one and the charities which specialize in this area could fill that gap). Similarly prisoners are not represented, and they should be. Society is like Rubik's Cube. It has to fit together even when the lowest common denominator is no more than geographic space, but it is the richness of the permutations that counts, with each block a vested interest.

Recently Jonathan Rauch wrote a perceptive piece in *The Atlantic* (*What's ailing American Politics*, July/August 2016) in which he suggested that the inability of the party system to discipline its members and so force consensus was to blame for America's political malaise. Reformers had eviscerated the old pork barrel process in which deals were done behind closed doors with long-standing committee chairmen doling out or withholding 'pork' as a means of getting things done. Now, he suggested, external activists were trashing this system of political compromise by threatening to unseat legislators unwilling to follow their narrow, purist line. Shades of the Reformation, I thought, during which activists used legitimate criticisms to undermine the entire social system - a dangerous game.

Unlike Rauch, I do not believe the party system can be put back together again (nor do I think it should be). The system has served its time and by and large has served it well. But now we need to tie the legislative process directly to the complexities which characterize society as it has become. Vested interests should be allowed to speak for themselves and because none can predominate (even dictators are a lot less powerful than they appear) solutions will emerge and society will evolve. The will of the people has always been a mirage.

30

The model

TH I S is really the nub of it. Previously (*Notes on the dynamics of man*, 2010) I have talked about the *tension matrix* as being the mechanical components of society (including us as individuals) held together in our conscious world by something I called *the story* – essentially our individual view of how we think the world works. In the biological world elements are interlinked within a shared space by reciprocal arrangements which have evolved over time. As biological structures have mutated to take on greater independence of action, this reciprocity has become looser and increasingly governed by instinctive reactions. The development of consciousness – the ability to reflect and model outcomes as a prelude to action – has been a natural extension of this and given human society a great adaptive advantage.

The ability to adapt successfully to circumstances is a sine qua non of survival for the generalist. The shark, as a specialist, has changed little over the last 100 million years because it can feed on almost all the other animals in its broadly stable aquatic world. In contrast, the genus Homo is barely 10 million years old and Homo sapiens is thought to have mutated out of Homo erectus only around 2 million years ago. Being a poor hunter by virtue of his shape, Homo sapiens has increasingly applied his brain to the task of survival and devised social arrangements to help him do so. Success has pitted groups and subgroups of humans against one another and it has been this dynamic which has reinforced and accelerated our adaptive capability. The question we must grapple with today is this: can we continue to be successful without killing our own kind in the process and without over-exploiting the non-human environment on which we depend?

Although social competition has been a great spur to our development, it has hardly been premeditated. In the absence of competition, many human arrangements have remained stable and unchanging for long periods. Our success in coming up with arrangements that can secure life from diverse environments has sometimes led to an increase in human numbers and brought us into contact with other groups similarly motivated (as occurred around the Mediterranean after we mastered sea transport and again with the onset of the industrial revolution). This dynamic has spurred further social innovations as groups and subgroups have competed for resources. But there has also been another interplay at work.

In the biological world the symbiotic interaction between species has been crucial. Not only has this been a driver behind differentiation (as species have mutated into a wide range of environments) but it has served as a crucial mechanism behind biological adaptation (through which biological structures as a whole have survived and proliferated). The drive which causes interdependent species to compete is clearly deep-seated and predates consciousness (which is, to repeat, *the ability to reflect and model outcomes as a prelude to action*). And unless these deep-seated drivers could have been overridden by consciousness to advantage, consciousness would have possessed no utility and could hardly have survived.

The ability to reflect and model outcomes as a prelude to action allows us to override our instinctive (biological) drivers, at least in theory. In practice it is hard to do. Not only are we up against millions of years of evolutionary history, but the future is unknowable. The trick we have learnt is to tie emotion (the expression of our deep-seated drivers) to intellectual direction. Wars become exercises in biological survival in which a group (such as a tribe or nation) assumes the character of a species and pits itself against another such group. Conscious individuals on both sides are corralled into action by expressions of uniqueness and the need for collective action to protect it. This emotional overload drowns out individual reflection and the posturing on both sides reinforces the posture of both (akin to the symbiosis evident in the biological world).

For as long as there has been recorded history, the European sub-continent has been riven by war. This self-induced instability has ultimately been about power, which in turn has been about control over resources. That Europe today is much the same as it was geographically three thousand years ago (that is to say in terms of its climate and basic resources), while its human population has probably increased by a factor of over 50 (such estimates are speculative although the magnitude of the change is hardly in doubt), tells us how successful the generalist has been in organizing himself and his environment to his advantage. But without the spur of competition for resources, notwithstanding the countless millions killed because of it, it is hard to envision how this would have come about.

Before we become too self-congratulatory, it is worth remembering that, when the rabbit was introduced into Australia by Europeans, their number increased exponentially (in some regions to plague proportions) because they had no natural predators. So just because consciousness has enabled us to overcome most threats to human life (save from ourselves), the exponential increase in our numbers should not be seen as any more than a natural phenomenon. Yes, we've been clever at times but the hard part – evolving with conscious intent rather than by accident – still lies ahead. The accident which has brought about our numerical triumph could as easily bring about our demise.

* * *

We have made progress in coming up with ways of competing which do not entail human bloodshed. Free market capitalism has been one such innovation as have our democratic systems. The first empowers individuals to provide and purchase goods and services in a dynamic way (i.e. so that the goods, services and their providers mutate over time according to taste and expertise). The second facilitates changes of government without bloodshed in accordance with shifts in the public mood and goes some way towards legislating according to people's needs. Free market capitalism, however, has proved more dynamic than what we call democracy.

The reason for this is that, unlike democracy, free market capitalism operates within a fairly simple, clear framework. Groups of individuals are at liberty to come together and attempt to come up with ways of providing goods and services that other individuals might want and to attract other people's money in return for a share in any profits their enterprise might generate. Over time, these naturally occurring structures and transactions have been incorporated into law so that the rights and obligations of the participants have become explicit and remedies for failure laid out.

As time has passed, these groups, together with their products and services, have come and gone, grown and shrunk and greatly enriched people's lives. Along the way, competition for custom and for the profit this might generate has spurred innovation and transformed society. The same biological drivers which power warfare have been redirected to power commerce.

Democracy has also evolved but in a more hesitant fashion, not least because the transaction between citizen and structure has been far more obtuse. What is offered at each election cycle is a bundle of things, some of whose elements can be contradictory, that express a mood more than a specific package. And where they are specific, as in the offerings from single issue parties, the trade-offs necessary to implement them are rarely mentioned. Whatever political grouping engineers enough electoral support to gain power has to deal with the situation as it is. So in the main, what changes are personnel and emphasis, with the structure of the state remaining essentially intact.

Political parties do come and go and are, in any event, coalitions of individuals with broadly similar attitudes towards certain key issues, but, as these issues are often historical (and have long since been resolved), the difference between the larger parties is generally less than it seems and they make out. The net effect is that elections have become plebiscites on party leaders, not on the effectiveness of the state. To say that this system represents the views of the people is only true (if it is true at all) in a very general sense. Its chief virtue is that it makes it harder for any leader and his or her clique (and their ideology, if they have one) to become embedded within the system, although the similarity in background of the political class as a whole may result in existing state systems being given undue benefit of the doubt. It is for this reason that revolutions, when they occur, usually come as a surprise to the guardians of the status quo.

And lest we forget, the status quo is not in itself a bad thing: far from it. Most of us most of the time crave order and certainty. Indeed it is a fundamental characteristic of all systems that they must seek to defend themselves. The problem, of course, is what to do when a system no longer serves its constituent parts. What we need to achieve is a dynamic status quo. Let me give an example from the capitalist universe. There was a time in the 1960s and '70s when the mainframe computer ruled the world. *Big Blue*, the nickname given to IBM (International Business Machines), the leader in the field, was regarded with a mixture of awe and fear. But then in 1976 along came a couple of young entrepreneurs, Steve Jobs and Steve Wozniak.

In a garage they configured a computer using the recently developed microprocessor which would put some of the mainframe's computing power onto an individual's desktop: no longer was it necessary to make an appointment (if you could) to access a bank of computing machines housed within an air-conditioned room inside some large institution. Their *Apple* personal computer exists to this day and the company Steve Jobs founded (which has spewed out a raft of innovative products) is still going strong and we have all become the richer for it.

Big Blue could see the writing on the wall for the mainframe and in 1981 came up with a personal computer of its own (the PC) but contracted with a tiny upstart company to provide the machine's operating system. By 1994 this operating system was ubiquitous in PCs made by other manufacturers around the world and Microsoft had sales of $4.6 billion, over 15,000 employees and was becoming as feared and revered as IBM had once been. Today, companies like Google and Elon Musk's Tesla Motors are transforming how we live. Contrary to the dour predictions of Karl Marx, capitalism has delivered.

But while the political system that has facilitated capitalism's success deserves great credit it has also sat astride some glaring failures. In the main, these failures have been of two types: there have been some spectacularly unsuccessful foreign adventures and it has overseen some large pockets of substantial social hardship (in 2016 around a seventh of the US population was eligible for food stamps on account of low wages or unemployment). Although seemingly unrelated, both types of failure have their roots in America's vision of itself.

The nation's undoubted success since the 19th century has persuaded its leaders to try and impose its model on polities far and wide, regardless of these polities' own histories. The laissez-faire attitude held to be behind this success (which gives individuals the freedom to contract with one another without undue government interference) has fostered a deep suspicion of anything that smacks of government-directed social engineering (socialism).

That two such diametrically opposed outcomes – imposition on outsiders and aloofness toward insiders – can spring from the same model is rich in irony and suggests that the model might be incomplete, poorly understood or misapplied, even all three. And in any event, as all models which seek to capture the complex present in relation to the unknowable future can never be more than best guesses, based upon the information to hand, it behooves us to build mechanisms which keep feeding us that information.

* * *

If one digs deep into the democratic model one has to conclude that it is about individual empowerment. And as it is this and this alone which has given individual consciousness its unique position in the evolutionary journey, state structures can have no other justification than to facilitate it. Empowerment, however, is not just about being able to vote every so often for individuals who may or may not be attuned to our needs and on issues that are less than clear. Ultimately it means enabling individuals to lead fully engaged lives within the polity they are part of. So when America invaded Vietnam or Iraq for ideological reasons (by no stretch of the imagination did either polity pose a threat other than to America's vision of how the world should work) it put its own people at risk and most certainly did not empower those it attacked. Similarly, when the pro-globalization button was pressed in the 1980s, the voice of those Americans who would be negatively affected was not heard. Internally and externally the system was blind and deaf – and some might add dumb.

And this is not to pick on The United States. When the German Chancellor, Angela Merkel, allowed over a million predominantly Muslim immigrants from the war-torn Middle East into her country, she was doubtless acting for noble (as well as perhaps economic) reasons. But because Germany is part of the European Union which is built around the principle of the free movement of labour, every single one of these immigrants could, in due time, have ended up in another EU country. By unilaterally making a decision on their behalf, she was disempowering the citizens of these countries, a high-handed act which no doubt helped persuade a majority of British voters to vote to leave the EU.

That Communism, Fascism and whatever North Korea calls itself have proved to be utterly disempowering for many millions of people and that there may be occasions, such as in World War II, when the threat to one's own values is real and must be countered directly, ideological imperialism is generally better fought by example than by force. Vietnam would have adjusted (as did the Soviet Union and Spain) and Iraq was in a far better state under its ruthless leader than it is today under its corrupt, Western-supported mish-mash of a government. That globalization is a good thing is probably true, but to ignore those adversely affected by it is folly. That the mess the West has made in the Middle East and the war-weary emigrés this has created is a tragedy goes without saying, but for Western leaders to try to make amends by forcing the dispossessed on their own people without their consent merely adds one bad call to another.

The glaring truth is that we expect too much of our political systems as they are presently constituted. We need a new model.

* * *

The dilemma political theorists always face is how to reconcile the need for executive action with the need for a system that is responsive to individual needs. In times of crisis, individuals are inclined to turn to whatever leader they think will be most likely to lead them to the *Promised Land* and to accept a suspension of the customary checks and balances that traditionally regulate the use of power. In 1942, Americans of Japanese ancestry were interned after the Japanese nation launched its raid against America's Pacific fleet at anchor in Pearl Harbour. Between 1899 and 1902, When the British went to war with the Dutch South African Republic (the Transvaal), which they coveted, Dutch families were interned in concentration camps (where over 4,000 women and more than 22,000 children died) and their farm land was salted, so as to deprive the Dutch fighters (the Boers) of resources.

The logic of war generally supersedes the logic of civilization and the survival story can be applied by leaders and their followers even when the matter of survival is moot. Building structures that can tell the difference is one of the challenges we face as is, on a less elevated scale, knowing when to allow executive action and when not. There is both a technical aspect to this as well as an educational one – if individuals are to be involved in decision-making they must not only know the available facts but also the context within which any action taken will be played out. Take, for example, the second Iraq war (2003-2011) in which the United States and Britain (to a lesser extent) were involved. In both polities elected representatives endorsed the action based upon spurious intelligence (the Iraq regime was not a threat to either Britain or the United States as claimed) and without any serious discussion about what would follow from a successful invasion of that country, which was always assumed.

Not only was the electorate ignorant but so too were their representatives and there was little incentive to remedy this ignorance – the Iraqi people voted in neither the United Kingdom nor the United States and what was there to lose from a little adventure in a faraway land dressed up as a moral crusade? The United Nations was supposed to stop such folly, but of course it failed to do so because the United Nations is a contradiction in terms. The only way such disasters can be prevented (and remember that the first Iraq war [1990-91] was an unalloyed success) is if such actions have to clear a rigorous checklist.

Imagine, then, an upper chamber whose primary task is to apply such a checklist to all actions proposed by an executive. It would operate more like a Supreme Court than a senate and need only a small number of appointed members (say six of each sex). Its mandate would be established by a polity's constitution and seek to rule on (a) whether any proposed executive action would likely achieve its primary objectives; and (b) whether the negative consequences of the action, be it successful or not, could be justified on grounds other than political aggrandizement.

Over time such a body would build up a model of what was and was not acceptable executive action and force a polity to consider the rights of individuals both within and beyond its borders. In the matter of globalization, which was a consequence of deregulation, such a body would likely have flagged up the need to strengthen the regulation that remained as well as the need to ameliorate the negative consequences on those communities negatively affected. When a polity has its tail up in a particular direction there is always going to be a tendency to ignore any possible downside.

* * *

In the essay *Legislators*, the proposal made was that individuals should appoint (or elect if you prefer) specialists to represent their vested interests. For example farmers would want one to speak for the farming industry, mothers would want one to represent mothers, children would need one, as would teenagers, manufacturers, deep-sea fishermen, educators, etc., etc. The US House of Representatives has 435 members and the UK House of Commons 650. What is being proposed is that a polity is modelled so that its vested interests are made explicit, together with their interactions. To be able to identify between 435 and 650 components (types of vested interest) would surely allow for the construction of a reasonably sophisticated model.

The objective is to tie individuals, as defined by their interests, directly to the legislative assembly without having to go through a political party. The model of how society worked would be dynamic and by being explicit would make it easier for legislators and those who appoint them to understand the necessary trade-offs. For example the representatives of the low paid and the unemployed would have no function other than to work with their colleagues to improve the lot of both cohorts. Gradually the emphasis would turn to problem solving, and away from party political advantage. Bit by bit our collective understanding of how human society actually works would grow.

* * *

The final part of this model-building process concerns education. The great monotheistic religions – Judaism, Christianity, Islam – did a very important thing: they provided an all-encompassing framework within which individual consciousness could exist. Unfortunately they also professed exclusivity and served to pit one against the other. But as I have said elsewhere, systems, by their nature, seek to defend themselves. The great innovation of science was that, while systems of thought had to be coherent they also had to be open to change whenever the facts they assumed turned out to be more complex than had been thought.

The great religions took no prisoners in this regard: you either swallowed whole or not at all. It is for this reason that for a great many they have lost their allure. As our understanding of how the world works developed we found that religious dogma often made no sense. But more than ever we need a shared understanding of what we are part of for the simple reason that to solve our common problems we have to understand how we work collectively as conscious beings. If we do not, we will be thrown back on our biological drivers which have no moral sentiment other than existence, and that is the existence of biological life as a whole, not any single part of it. If we become extinct, biological life will move on and attempt to reassert itself in other ways.

Politicians often talk about empowering the people, but more often than not what they really mean is empowering themselves at the people's expense, like accountants who claim that only they understand the tax code or lawyers who assert that only they understand the law. Of course politicians, accountants and lawyers have done and do useful work, but they are rarely in a hurry to do themselves out of a job, any more than were the Catholic priests of the 16th century who guarded the gates to heaven and hell. And academics are no different. Each discipline burnishes its importance with a language of its own. Too often knowledge has become a Tower of Babel, incomprehensible to all instead of what it should be, a beacon of light.

The aphorism *knowledge is power* is true particularly when the basis of that knowledge is how to work the system. We are all guilty of seeking to burnish our own exclusivity but this is a bad habit we must break and doing so has to start in the classroom. Every individual should leave school with an understanding of how we think human society works so that all of us can tap into the same model and be part of the same hypothesis. Is this a new religion? In a way I suppose it is. Certainly it is no less important.

* * *

So what would a reformed polity look like? Well, initially, polities would look pretty much as they look now: what is currently working should always be treated with respect as the actual trumps the theoretical. A suspension of parliamentary activity would probably not be noticed because government is exercised by the bureaucracy. The change would be multifaceted. There would be a lower chamber populated by representatives of a society's vested interests (elected by those interests). There would be an upper chamber whose task would be to guard and update a society's model of itself as well as to test legislation (proposed by either the lower house or chief executive) for objectivity, unintended consequences and compatibility with the society's constitution. There would be an elected chief executive (as city mayors are elected now).

It would make sense if this structure was replicated at a local, regional, national, supranational and global level with each level attending only to that which it was uniquely competent to address. The emphasis would be on 'bottom-up' rather than 'top-down' decision-making so as to give political structures legitimacy. As the overriding objective would be on problem solving, one would expect a diversity of approaches which would increase the chance of successful outcomes (with the more successful approaches being replicated and the less successful ones being abandoned). Doubtless the pool of knowledge would grow and a cabal of professional practitioners take root.

Although it would take time, a polity would gradually become a dynamic whole with most people having a grasp of its mechanics and why structures existed. Incorporating this understanding into the educational system would be a crucial step, albeit one that would take time to bear its full fruit. At present almost everyone is separate from and largely ignorant of the social mechanics that govern their lives. This is unhealthy and overcoming it is what empowerment is all about.

Vested interests would be made explicit instead of being regarded as something murky and this would be to the good because every polity consists of a clutch of vested interests that must find a way to work together. The functions of government would be held to account by both houses instead of hiding behind the misguided notion that bureaucracies can only function successfully behind a cloak of anonymity like the Wizard of Oz. All this might sound radical but in reality it is not and to some degree or other it will come about because our present system is bust. The only question is how much pain will we choose to inflict upon ourselves before accepting that change is necessary.

31

The damned

RECENTLY I took a walk with my wife on the Warren Footpath. It runs southeast of St Margaret's along the Thames. I have no idea who Warren was, but I and countless others are grateful to her or to him. London is a magnificent city, the result of a trillion individual acts spanning centuries. Island communities are lucky in the main as they are less likely to have been trampled upon by invading armies, and London has been a beneficiary. Our plan was to cross over the river using the Richmond Bridge and have lunch at a favourite watering hole on the other side.

The day was perfect autumn: clear, crisp and with a sun that still had heat to give. We scuffed large brown leaves falling lazily from the two-hundred-year-old plane trees along the way. Apart from the occasional jogger puffing past, nothing rushed. Even the polers pushing their flat boards upstream appeared languid as the incoming tide was doing most of the work. Fathers - mothers having finally detached their charges - oversaw muffled little pedallers darting like adventurous ducklings. An elderly couple sat on a bench reading the Sunday paper. Perhaps their names would soon be on one of them: *Bill and Ann Cartwright loved this place.*

This was my England and these were my people. That is what I felt. But who was I and who were they? The passing accents were Polish, Indian, Spanish, not just English and my own forebears were Scots and Irish as well as American English and English English and some of my Anglo-Scots wife's ancestors were Italian and Portuguese. For 5,000 years or more, human families had walked along trails like this: mothers, fathers, grandparents, children, perhaps a lone hunter with spear and rabbit, all engaged in the business of living, all enjoying the autumn sun. Was there something in my DNA which recognized the moment making me feel comfortable and secure?

And then there was progress! The train that brought us on seamless steel rails drew its power from electricity generated by fired coal, nuclear fission and gas extracted from below the North Sea, distributed across a grid to every part of the country. We checked in and out of the service using a card that registered our location and account balance. My wife could talk on her mobile to our daughter, sons and grandchildren and check what someone somewhere thought was important breaking news. The food we would soon eat and wine we looked forward to drinking could have come from a farm in Scotland or vineyard in Australia.

Overhead an Airbus A380 was making its approach towards Heathrow which had finally been given permission to build a third runway after seventy years of political prevarication. Able to carry 800 people at 900 kilometers an hour over 8,000 miles, the machine consisted of 4 million parts produced by 1,500 companies from 30 countries around the globe. Ours was a connected world but also a disconnected one. That lovely autumn morning happened to be Remembrance Sunday, two days after November 11th the day in 1918 when the guns on the Western Front of World War I finally fell silent.

Unlike my wife, I have an uncomfortable relationship with Remembrance Day. The political folly of war makes my blood boil, but don't count me a pacifist. If anyone threatened my nearest and dearest I would want to grind them into the dirt and beyond, if that were possible. It is the pomp and circumstance that upsets me because it appears to throw a cloak of respectability around human savagery. Germany, France and Britain might have stopped their useless carnage on November 11th, 1918, but across the continent bestial revenge killings continued for another five years as groups struggled to assert their identity and project their power.

It is, I suppose, a mark of civilization that killing becomes a preserve of the state, otherwise tit-for-tat score-settling becomes the custom and anarchy the norm. In my school days, Tudor England was history's focus and Shakespeare English literature's. It intrigued us that roguish old Henry could cut off the head of his best friend on a point of religious principle, steal monastic lands, take over his minister Cardinal Thomas Wolsey's magnificent palace at Hampton Court (Wolsey himself managing to die of natural causes before falling foul of his monarch's suspicions) and dispatch two of his six wives to the executioner's block and still command our admiration as the man who created the English state (as well as lay the foundations of its navy). Under different circumstances Saddam Hussein might have been similarly regarded by Iraqi students 500 years hence. The bard of Avon would certainly have enjoyed writing about him.

An island Britain undoubtedly was, but the English and their Norman conquerors felt compelled to assert their primacy after the Romans left, to the chagrin of many Welsh and Scots as well as to the great vexation of the Irish who inhabited the island next door. But this only served to enhance London. Might was right. Or as Leo Tolstoy wrote in an 1897 essay: *Right is not the offspring of doctrine, but of power.*

And this is the thing. Our lust for power has caused us a great many problems and engendered a deep well of suffering. But before we self-flagellate, let us remind ourselves where that lust comes from. Chimpanzee colonies have been known to go to war with one another when geographic circumstance has resulted in their territories overlapping. The motivation is obvious. To survive requires territory. So survival requires that one's territory be defended. And it goes deeper. In many animal species the most powerful male (that is the one with the most exaggerated characteristics of its kind) gets to sire the most offspring. The logic here is that the best example of a species will be transmitted to the next generation.

Of course the flaw in this logic is obvious. If the environment of a species changes, becoming more wolf-like, tiger-like, whale-like or eagle-like may not enhance one's chances of survival. This is the evolutionary cul-de-sac: the progressive refinement of a design that has become redundant. The territorial logic suffers from the same flaw. If territory is finite, groups can slug it out until the strongest have eliminated enough of the weakest to bring numbers down to a level the territory can sustain. This is the logic of Thomas Malthus (1766-1834), the political economist who argued that, if food production increased, population would increase faster, eliminating any surplus and have to self-correct through war, famine and disease. He was skeptical about self-restraint, but not only has population growth in developed countries fallen, food production has increased.

In human society organizational smarts have handily beaten might, but the biological lust for power remains a potent and potentially destructive force both individually and collectively. Leo Tolstoy could not have been more wrong: right *is* the offspring of doctrine, *not* of power because power cannot be an end in itself. The biological lust for survival is blind, calling for more of the same regardless of circumstance: it does not adapt. Thanks to consciousness, however, human society has gradually learnt how to control this lust and ask what survival is for.

But as we walked and I observed those around me, especially the children, at peace with themselves, each other and the world, a deep anger welled up inside. How could we keep making the same mistake, again and again? How could we think it right to use violence in pursuit of our aims and in so doing consign our fellow beings to living hells? And then I remembered how I would feel and what I would do if my nearest and dearest were threatened. Did not these things all draw from the same well?

On that morning, two-and-a-half thousand miles away, the battle for control over Syria's ancient city of Aleppo was in full swing. Captured by Alexander the Great in 333BCE, the city had been part of the Roman Empire and Christian, briefly part of Persia before falling to the Muslims in 637CE and becoming part of the Ottoman Empire in 1516. Following the defeat of the Central Powers in World War I, the Ottoman Empire was broken up by the victors and France given control over Aleppo. But in 1925 the newly configured Syrian state fought to free itself from French control leaving Aleppo and Syria's capital, Damascus, to jockey for power. Decades of political instability followed: would Syria merge with Iraq or Egypt? Would this or that faction dominate? In 1970, Hafez al-Assad secured power with the help of business interests in Damascus and when his son, Bashar al-Assad assumed the presidency, following his father's death in 2000, factions in Aleppo saw their chance to topple the old regime and gain power.

Unsurprisingly, the Syrian authorities cracked down on dissent, prompting liberal governments in the West to offer support to the Aleppo rebels. This Western effort was a misguided attempt across the Middle East to stir up opposition to authoritarian regimes. Christened *The Arab Spring* by the Western media and described as a flowering of democracy, it saw some longtime rulers deposed but it also opened the door to Ba'ath Party fundamentalists (many from Iraq) anxious to carve out a new hard-line Muslim Caliphate across the region.

So while we walked in the autumn sunshine, mothers were losing sons, fathers their children, children their parents and families their homes in East Aleppo. Why? Because having destroyed the functioning state of Iraq, the West had set about destabilizing every other state in the region, creating a golden opportunity for competing groups and their paramilitaries to vie for power. Not only were our actions the height of folly, they were profoundly immoral. And here, with a slight reformulation, I have to side with Leo Tolstoy: right without might is wrong.

As armchair liberals in Washington and London tinkered with their Special Ops, propaganda channels and remote-controlled cruise missiles (in short anything they could get away with without committing their electorates to hard choices), they were consigning millions across the Middle East to the hellfires of damnation. The great Dutch painter Hieronymus Bosch (c1450-1516) knew a thing or two about the consequences of human conceit. Just take a look at his triptych, *The Garden of Earthly Delights*.

The revolutionary who places the attainment of his so-obviously right ideas ahead of the lives of the innocent is only slightly less bad than the bystander with no skin in the game who urges him on. The ascent out of hell requires order and yes, some orderings are markedly better than others and yes too: order, like might, is not an end in itself. But until we understand order and how to adapt it we should tread carefully. The exercise of power or might most certainly has its place, but that place is in defending our nearest and dearest from environmental disruption, be the cause of that disruption human or natural. Before anything else, we should seek to put our own houses in order – continuously. If we do not, the damned of East Aleppo will be us.

32

Truth

IS there such a thing as truth? This may not be as strange a question as it sounds. When Spain was going through its troubles in the 1930s, the political right painted a picture of a world in which their country's glorious past was being traduced by republicans, Freemasons, closet Islamists, Jews and Communists. According to this story, what these groups had in common was an abiding hostility towards Spain's Roman Catholic underpinnings which lay at the heart of its great historical past.

The nascent republican government, which the right was gunning for, did want to break the power of the Catholic Church, was socialistic in its objectives, did draw support from large parts of the trade union movement and did have some anarchist as well as communist hangers-on. However, after Isabella I of Castile and Ferdinand II of Aragon finally drove the Muslims from the Iberian Peninsula in 1492 they promptly set about expelling any Jews unwilling to convert to Christianity, so there was hardly a Jewish or Muslim 'problem' in Spain. Nonetheless, the imagery remained strong.

As for Freemasons, their often deist views had never endeared them to the established Church and of course communists had shown their true colours in Russia. At the heart of the concerns of the political right was a deep suspicion of the democracy which had brought the republican government to power and with the failure of democracy in Russia and Germany one could hardly say that these concerns lacked foundation. On the other side of the political divide was a hazy feeling that the old order of Church, aristocracy and army no longer reflected the realities of urban industrial life. However, the reformer's disadvantage was that (as it had been in revolutionary France and Russia and had just proved to be for Germany's Weimar republic) the exact shape of the new order was still to be discovered.

The civil war which broke out in Spain was profoundly unpleasant, as such wars are, and as is always their outcome, naked power won (as it did in revolutionary France, Russia and Germany), obliterating the distinction between left and right save in respect of who ended up holding the whip hand. The only truth that remained was the age-old one that might was right. Had both left and right been more interested in solving the problems of Spain's evolving society than in peddling their respective poisons, a great deal of suffering would have been avoided. But unfortunately, human societies are not very attuned to problem-solving.

* * *

The reason for this is that truth is contextual. Even the scientific method, mankind's truth discovering innovation, is predicated upon the assumption that a truth postulated must be disprovable and so is always open to revision. And as for problem-solving, well one man's problem might be another man's advantage: context is everything.

When we ask what is the truth about this or that we generally mean what best describes it. Such descriptions are devoid of moral content. We speak rather highly about Ancient Greece and the Roman Empire even though both relied on slave labour. All those whom the Greeks and Romans enslaved might have held a different view. Marxist revolutionaries, like their French forerunners, were of the view that some must die so that their brave new world could be born, a view shared by Spain's traditionalists save that the sacrifices they demanded were so that the world they knew could be retained. In both cases it is reasonable to assume that most of those sacrificed were less-than-enthusiastic victims.

Scientific discovery is concerned with finding out how things work. Sometimes this is born out of curiosity, sometimes it is stimulated by a desire to turn knowledge to someone's advantage. How knowledge about the relationship between things should be used is not the concern of science. All this suggests that *truth* is a concept we should handle with care. Even in describing something we can project our own bias. The twentieth century was scared by scientific determinism: only the fittest survive became its mantra, or should survive became its subliminal message.

Was this the truth against which everything could be judged? Well let me end with a truth: nothing does survive. So if this is the context within which we exist, should we not concentrate on the quality of our lives today as it will impact on the quality of our children's lives tomorrow? Beyond bare description, truth is always about how we as individuals behave.

33

A brave new world

A L D O U S Huxley's 1932 novel, *Brave New World*, set in CE 2540 London, is about social conformity and the individual's struggle against it. At the time of writing this (December 2016) *Rogue One* has just come out, a continuation of George Lucas's *Star Wars* epic, not improved by the franchise's new owner, the Disney Corporation. Although light on story (in inverse proportion to its special effects) the film's theme, like that of *Brave New World*, is one of mankind's oldest storylines: the tension that exists between what an individual wills and society demands.

Margaret Thatcher's often quoted (and as often misquoted) comment in a 1987 interview that there was no such thing as society drove her (in her 1993 autobiography) to put the comment back into the context from which it had been regularly extracted:

> "they never quoted the rest. I went on to say: There are individual men and women, and there are families. And no government can do anything except through people, and people must look to themselves first. It's our duty to look after ourselves and then look after our neighbour. My meaning, clear at the time but subsequently distorted beyond recognition, was that society was

not an abstraction, separate from the men and women who composed it, but a living structure of individuals, families, neighbours and voluntary associations."

I believe Margaret Thatcher was both right and wrong: right in the sense that societies are dynamic, being made up of individuals each with a degree of independent action, but wrong in that, as functional structures, societies exert substantial pressure on those same individuals to conform.

This tension should not surprise us as it lies at the heart of the universal dynamic we are subject to and is the very essence of life. As such it should be understood and nurtured with reverence, not feared and used as an excuse for human violence. The most depressing thing about the Star Wars stories (and sadly they are far from alone in this) is how they project human conflict in time and space. If that really is the best we can offer the future it will be good riddance if we end up destroying ourselves.

* * *

The theme running through these essays has been essentially this: for reasons we do not know and are unlikely ever to know because they are unknowable, the universe we are part of has been evolving for the last 14 billion years in a particular way. From an infinitely dense state in which time, space and energy were compressed there has been an unfolding, sometimes rapid, at other times slow, out of which dynamic energy-laden structures have formed, characterized by variable loose-tight relationships with one another.

A progression has been evident in that types of structure have served as platforms for the evolution of new types (such as from gases to stars to planets to galaxies), with consciousness (as an ability to act with intent) evolving out of biological structures (structures sensitive to their environment with short life cycles but with an ability to replicate and mutate). The interdependence of the biological world has entailed structures feeding off one another symbiotically (essentially energy-transfer mechanisms) such that a diverse array of entities populates the biosphere here on earth. Within each phase of this progression, the structures that could form have formed.

The sensitivity of a simple organism to its environment when combined with an increasing degree of individual locomotion in more complex organisms has mutated into awareness in animals and, in one of these, into an ability to imagine how alternative actions might give rise to alternative outcomes. Choosing between imagined outcomes poses two problems. The first is, because of its loose-tight properties, our universe is not deterministic. We can postulate a range of possible outcomes and even the most likely ones given what we know, but the creative nature of the universe (arising out of the interaction between its variable and loosely aligned structures) precludes absolute foreknowledge. We can calculate when something as seemingly permanent as our sun will die, for example, but not how biological life (nor more especially conscious life) will react to that eventuality.

The second problem arises out of the fact that all biological structures have evolved survival strategies based upon their prior experience. So while an imagined conscious choice might suggest we do this, our biological instinctive choice might suggest we do that. Collections of individuals acting as wholes (as societies) have developed elaborate ways of overriding or redirecting individual instinct. The soldier is cajoled into fighting for the greater good of his clan (or, in the heat of battle, for his fellow fighters). The instinct for species survival has mutated into intra-species competition. The instinct to counter a threat to oneself or to one's nearest and dearest has been suppressed in favour of giving society a monopoly over the assessment of culpability and the application of punishment, all in the interests of preserving social order.

Instincts are emotionally driven which is why all states (and those who aspire to control them) deploy propaganda (images designed to evoke deep emotional instincts and the actions they invoke). The basis of advertising is both informative (here is something you might find useful) and stimulative (here is something you must have because it will sate your latent desire for food, for beautification, for inclusion, etc.). These two problems combined – uncertainty and the conscious management of our biological drivers (our instincts) - have conspired to create a high degree of competition between groups of humans in the way we organize and exploit the environment.

The upshot has been twofold: we have become extraordinarily successful numerically while inflicting almost unimaginable suffering on one another along the way and we have turned the environment to our advantage so completely and in such an open-ended fashion that quantitative objectives threaten to run ahead of qualitative ones. In short we have turbo-charged our biological drivers while our conscious intent has barely moved off the chocks.

* * *

When some of the weary voyagers disembarked from the Mayflower onto Cape Cod in November 1620 in the hope of finding a suitable site, there was much anxiety. Not only had they failed to reach the spot for which they had a patent to settle, but a skirmish with local tribesmen persuaded them to move on, although not before some corn seed had been stolen from an Indian burial ground which would later be used to plant a life-saving crop for the coming season. In December the Mayflower sailed along the coast to a better anchorage which the settlers named Plymouth in honour of the English harbour they had left behind.

Like many with a drop of New England ancestry I owe mine to Priscilla Mullins, a young woman who lost her parents and brother during that first harsh winter in the New World. During the following year, aged only nineteen or twenty, she married another young Mayflower passenger, John Alden. They would go on to have ten children. I often try to imagine what these settlers must have gone through. Puritan by conviction, they had set out to build their *city on a hill* free from what they saw as the corruption of seventeenth century Europe. What would they have made of twenty-first century New York?

Human diversity has parallelled its biological counterpart, populating the cerebral structures we have built with customs, laws, institutions and buildings, none of them so much planned as being the outcrops of opportunity and personal desire, a consequence of the tension between individual will and functional order. While biological evolution has slipped into stable arrangements for long periods of time (until some external change has knocked the supports from under them), human arrangements have risen and fallen rapidly in comparison thanks to competition between them.

Just as a species introduced into an area without predators will multiply, so humans with the advantage of consciousness (the ability to imagine outcomes and act with intent) have exploded in numbers and effect. If we are to avoid running into a brick wall of our own making we are going to have to improve the way consciousness and the cerebral structures we build in support of it works. At various points in these essays suggestions have been made as to how we might go about this. Here, in this last essay, I simply want to outline the altered conception of ourselves which we will need to adopt if we are to take consciousness forward successfully.

* * *

First, however, some general rules of thumb. The fact that consciousness has enabled us to imagine outcomes and act with intent does not mean that there is a utopian final destination awaiting us. We live in the present, not the future. Peddlers of utopias have done a great deal of harm. Next I would say that we need to consider far more carefully than we do the architecture of the societies we are part of. To say, as the British prime minister did, that society is not an abstraction was only partly correct. Although every society's structural relationships are eminently real, we do abstract from them a general notion of what society is because societies are too complex to do otherwise.

These stories, as I call them, serve to legitimize the disposition of power (and the actions that power facilitates) in the minds of a society's individual members. Consequently these abstractions are immensely important because they reveal a society's morality. Fascism and communism took hold against a background of social failure and disintegration. When a society's architecture fails, people's biological drivers kick in and their raw survival instinct calls forth abstractions to serve it. Europe's 1914-18 war and its long aftermath (still playing out in the Middle East today) was a consequence of colossal social failure. The abstraction at the end of the 19th century was that of the nation state and empire, whereas industrialization and urbanization were crying out for a revised architecture and a new story.

At any given point in time, the social arrangements we have constructed to sustain ourselves are backward looking as they are in biological structures. So when altered circumstances (such as a crop failure, an unsuccessful war, the consequences of technological innovation or internal mismanagement or some combination of difficulties) cause individuals to start seeing things differently (to question the prevailing order and the story that sustains it) they come up against pressures to conform (a structure's natural tendency to preserve itself). This is a two-edged sword. Not only are these individuals dependent on the structure they are challenging but none of them really knows what structure to put in its place. This is why I suggested we need to build a continually updated and wholly transparent model of how we think our social systems work, showing all the interrelationships, so that we do not throw the baby, or even the bath, out with the bathwater.

This gives rise to my third rule of thumb: because what exists is real and what is imagined is not, incremental change is likely to be more effective (and do less damage) than revolution. Out of this comes a fourth rule of thumb. If a hundred tremors are better than a single earthquake, we need to build systems that are sensitive to individual concerns. To this end I proposed a more direct link between people and government. This was to be achieved by replacing party political representatives with legislators chosen to represent electors' specific vested interests and by having a polity's CEO elected directly on the basis of competence, not party.

Because our universe is only partly predictable, a fifth rule of thumb suggests itself. It is best we do not place all our eggs into a single basket so that, even though a few things will need to be decided at a global level, a number of large, broadly self-contained regional groupings makes sense (in *A Paper* [2011] I suggested eight). Even within these, however, a degree of redundancy and diversity will aid the discovery process (of arrangements that seem to meet people's needs) and protect against any failure knocking out entire systems. The great strength of individual consciousness is that it aids adaptation, but only if the ability to adapt is built into the system.

* * *

There remains, of course, the elephant in the room, so large that it is easy not to see. In enabling Man to imagine outcomes and formulate the relationships necessary to achieve them (and even, as a result of his curiosity, to work out relationships and then imagine the outcomes these facilitate) this evolutionary innovation has propelled Homo sapiens beyond the purely biological. But to what end? As stimulus-seeking organisms we look out for what pleases us and try to avoid what does not. We have even learnt to forego the former and embrace the latter in the hope of something better, if not for ourselves at least for those who follow us.

However, in much of the developed world today, there seems to be a growing sense of unease caused, as far as one can tell, by a feeling that for a great many people prospects are not improving. And although material conditions are looking up for most in the developing world, the pace of change is causing great stresses and strains. Underlying all of this is a pervasive worry that the world's political systems are inadequate, greatly aggravated by a form of mass communication which is little more than sensational gossip. With our systems in seeming disarray, the calls for *the certainties of strong leadership* are rising. While global elites gather at venues like Jackson Hole to preen and pimp like the blinkered aristocrats of the ancien régime, mankind's biological drivers are coming to the fore.

What has gone wrong? In a word, *truth*: we have lost sight of it. The elephant in the room is morality which we have come to regard as an outmoded concept in our modern world. And this is in spite of the fact that my generation was weaned on protest; protest against what we saw as the hypocrisy of our parents' generation. And we are still protesting: protesting against the war in Syria, Russia's incursion into the Ukraine, the effect of the fossil fuel industry on the earth's climate, the plight of refugees, the failings of global capitalism and much more – it is a long list. But I fear we have come to confuse self-righteousness with effectiveness.

So long as we are protesting about something we assume we are doing enough even though beneath our feet and on our watch all is not well. We have allowed poverty and racial prejudice to persist. We have fought unjust wars which have caused great suffering. We have neglected general education and allowed our prisons to fill. We have passed laws without bothering to analyze their effect, addressed the symptoms of problems rather than their cause and run up debts in the idle belief that an open cheque book could right all wrongs.

Certainly too much and too little can be made of morality. To debate endlessly about what is right and what is wrong does not make someone a moral person or the society which allows them to do so a moral society. If consciousness means, as I have stated, acting with intent it must run in parallel to the social systems we build that do much of our collective thinking for us. These systems are central to our survival, but if we do not question their impact on every individual they touch, we are no more than unconscious machines.

Consciousness gives us the means to assess the effect of the systems we build on our fellow individuals and it is through this interaction that our systems overall can be made to adapt. Was Edward Snowden (who leaked into the public domain large amounts of classified surveillance data gathered by and on behalf of the US government on its own citizens without their knowledge) a traitor or a moral being? The fact that whistleblowers generally fare badly (look no further than how Émile Zola was pilloried for exposing the disgraceful behaviour of the French establishment in the Dreyfus affair) is because systems, by their nature, must defend themselves whether their impact on individuals is good or bad. Only gradually are we coming to understand the importance of engineering arrangements able to monitor (<u>and remedy</u> where necessary) the impact of our existing social structures.

A free press is one such arrangement (and was the one Edward Snowden chose to use) but it is a mighty blunt instrument. Political oversight is another but can get bogged down in the mud of party political wrangling. Judicial oversight does offer an opportunity to weigh up issues against a polity's laws and constitution, but must be strong enough to withstand political interference and can only address a limited number of issues. If we are to build a brave new world, what is needed are not only improved institutions but a change of culture.

* * *

If consciousness is to develop and our structures are to evolve, individuals have to be more engaged than they are and this needs to be a bottom-up process, starting in our communities and schools. Community Councils are a good place to begin but they should be non-partisan, mandated to address problems raised by members of their community and empowered to do something about them. Their structure should feed naturally into regional, national and supranational bodies, so that an individual familiar with one will be familiar with the rest. Conceptually, the pyramid structure should be seen differently with power flowing upwards, not downwards. In many ways this is simply an extrapolation of the way in which Protestantism upended the hierarchy of the Catholic Church, giving communities control over religious practice and the administration of their church.

To such suggestions there is always the claim made that no polity can be organized in such a way. And certainly it limits the ability of a top-down leader to direct a polity's resources in this or that direction. But as there is no matter of concern to a leader (other than those of personal interest) which does not also concern the members of a community embraced within that leader's power structure, such a restriction hardly seems unreasonable. Paying more than lip service to empowerment requires such a reorientation.

Another criticism of such an approach is that the members of a local community can hardly be expected to possess the competence necessary to assess the weighty issues which those at the pinnacle of top-down hierarchies must wrestle with every day. However, mankind's long history of miscalculation surely puts paid to that. In addition, by building all of this into the schools system (i.e. by teaching the young how their societies actually work) the quality of debate and decision-making at a local level will improve.

Of course, as now, there will be many types of organization

that cut across these tiered decision hubs (local, regional, national and supranational), not least those which apply the law. And there will be situations where some communities lean one way on an issue and other communities lean another, making necessary a protocol for determining when collective action should be permitted to override a minority position. But there is nothing novel in that.

As a new political disposition, the European Union has had to grapple with many of these issues and if that union fails it will be because decision-making authority was not vested in communities but in political and bureaucratic elites. During the construction of the United States of America there were battles royal over what powers should remain with the states and which should be ceded to the federal government. With hindsight it is clear that too much power has been allowed to accumulate at the centre. It is almost inconceivable that some of the wars fought would have been had decisions not rested with organizations whose primary purpose was to wage them.

If these changes are implemented, will humanity march into sun-filled uplands free from worry and strife? Certainly not! The evolution of our collective consciousness is a journey, not a destination. But as each of us is increasingly empowered, the richer and more rewarding that journey will be.

END